11/15

THE ROAD HEADED WEST

A 6,000-MILE CYCLING ODYSSEY THROUGH NORTH AMERICA

LEON McCARRON

A HERMAN GRAF BOOK
SKYHORSE PUBLISHING

Skyhorse Publishing books may be purchased in bulk at special discounts for sales promotion, corporate gifts, fund-raising, or educational purposes. Special editions can also be created to specifications. For details, contact the Special Sales Department, Skyhorse Publishing, 307 West 36th Street, 11th Floor, New York, NY 10018 or info@skyhorsepublishing.com.

Skyhorse® and Skyhorse Publishing® are registered trademarks of Skyhorse Publishing, Inc.®, a Delaware corporation.

Visit our website at www.skyhorsepublishing.com.

10 9 8 7 6 5 4 3 2 1

Library of Congress Cataloging-in-Publication Data is available on file.

Cover design by Summersdale Publishers
Cover photo credit by Leon McCarron

Map and illustrations by Diana Heaney

Permission to use excerpts from Travels With Charley by John Steinbeck, published by Penguin, copyright © 2001, has been sought.

Print ISBN: 978-1-63220-644-2
Ebook ISBN: 978-1-63220-812-5

Printed in the United States of America

To Mum, for always wholeheartedly encouraging and supporting my adventures in life, even when they seem remarkably silly.

To Grandpa Jack, for teaching me how to appreciate the outdoors, and for showing me what it means to be a true gentleman. I think you would have enjoyed this journey.

CONTENTS

AUTHOR'S NOTE

The following story has been written using a mixture of memories, journal entries, photographs and video footage. On occasion I have seen fit to change the names of people and places to provide anonymity. From time to time I have transposed an event from one geographical location to another to help with the narrative flow, and sometimes I have moved a character in time and space to do the same job. I have even, once or twice, combined the attributes of two or more people that I met, in the hope that the created composite character does justice to each of the original individual personalities and helps portray their impact on me, and my story, as clearly as possible.

There are two incidents in this book that I feel are of a particularly sensitive nature, and for these events I have muddied the waters of detail even further.

I hope you will forgive these liberties. There may also be a few downright mistakes in my recollections, and for those too I apologise. For better or worse, however, this is my story of spending a summer cycling across America, told as well and as accurately as I can tell it.

PROLOGUE

It seemed a terrible shame to meet my end in Iowa; I couldn't imagine anywhere more disappointing to die. If I were a betting man I'd have reckoned on the most dangerous thing in this state being sheer boredom. Corn, beans, corn, beans… a cow… corn, beans… the scenery hadn't changed for weeks and I was slowly dissolving into stimulation-deprived madness. The only other feature even remotely worthy of note was the headwinds, but even these were more nuisance than hazard. My current predicament, then – attempting to escape through cornfields from a gun-toting alcohol-soaked rancher – was not something I expected.

I squeezed the bike through a small gap left by the partially closed garage door and jumped on. Standing on the pedals my feet automatically began to pump rhythmically; by now an action as natural as breathing. Dirt and gravel groaned underneath the tyres and my luggage bumped along behind in counterpoint. I wasn't even midway on this journey across the USA by bicycle, and it seemed terribly unfair that such a (seemingly) harmless invitation to stay with a rancher could have gone so wrong. But wrong it had gone, drastically so – a steady decline in civility had reached its lowest ebb when alcohol and madness were poorly mixed and I had been led to an outhouse full of guns. One was pointed at my head. Seconds after that I'd panicked and pushed the owner of the gun into a shed, closing the heavy lock as he tumbled inside.

I was riding away now as hard as I could, the trailer that trundled along after the bike serving as a constant reminder of just how slow and vulnerable I was. Light had long since faded from the day but the moon picked out features here and there, hinting at a bigger world beyond my narrow vision. To my left and right flat cornfields extended for miles, broken only occasionally by a small clump of trees assembled around each homestead.

Looking over my shoulder, there appeared in the distance behind the inevitable headlights of a large truck, beams bouncing wildly. It was still a way away, but I knew already the details – a grey Dodge Viper; inside a bald man with a goatee driving, peering into the darkness through eyes infused with a crate of Bud Light. He would be carrying at least one firearm, and until recently he had been lying on the floor of the shed into which I pushed him.

Ahead was the only possible route to freedom yet ironically, ridiculously, this direction promised something perhaps even more dangerous than a drunken rancher with a rifle disorder. Up ahead, stretching from dirt floor to brooding sky was a violently rotating tornado, the best part of half a mile wide. A deathly silence surrounded it. Like the crashing of a huge wave or the collapsing of a skyscraper, the movement seemed to happen in slow motion and I could only tell its true vigour by the way it decimated the landscape. The whole scene was ludicrous, like a Hollywood B-movie.

I thought briefly of how one day I might tell people about this and few would believe me. A group of trees swayed, snapped and were swallowed like twigs. Next a small lean-to for livestock crumbled, and this too was sucked up in a heap of corrugated iron and bricks. I was sure I saw sheep bleating their way into the abyss. A similar fate (with only slightly less bleating) was promised to me if I kept going, now just a mile away.

This was not what I had expected when I set out to cycle across America. In fact, I had actively hoped to avoid anything even remotely similar to this. I was a kid, barely twenty-three years old, off in search of adventure. Well, here it was, served American style – big, brash, balls-out. As well as being afraid, a large part of me was annoyed – my journey to this point had been full of the most wonderful people I could have hoped to meet, all going out of their way to be kind and hospitable. It seemed unfair that one boozed-up idiot could ruin that.

Despite it all, even despite the intense fear, there was an odd, hard-to-pin-down buzz about the scenario.

In a strange sense, I was feeling more alive than ever.

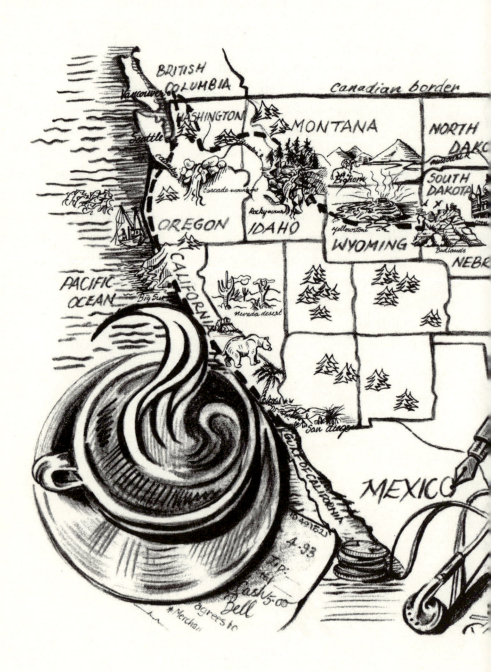

PART ONE – BEGINNINGS

Afoot and lighthearted I take to the open road,
Healthy, free, the world before me,
The long brown path before me leading
me wherever I choose.
Walt Whitman

CHAPTER 1

THE LEAVING OF IT ALL

I had stayed in New York too long, and gotten far too comfortable. My six months as a resident passed in a flash; warm, sunny evenings were first replaced by snow swirling along the wide corridor-like avenues of the Lower East Side. Winter fell like a brick, and life was cold and raw, but this was a good place to feel the wind blow through you. When finally the frost left, it was slower than how it arrived, but steadily warmth and life crept back into the world. There was a brutal energy here in New York City, and I'd been drawn into it.

My internship programme at a documentary production company came to an end on the first day of spring, and with that my honeymoon period was over. I'd only come here in the first place so that I could leave – six months working and then off to cycle across the country, I'd cheerfully told everyone. It wasn't quite as simple as that – there was much in the city that attempted to shackle me permanently. Coffee houses, bars where everyone sits on stools by the counter, bookshops full of Kerouac and Ginsberg wannabes. Live music everywhere at all times, cheap opera tickets, free shows on Broadway. Life moved at a million miles an hour and no one seemed to sleep, least of all me. There was so much to do here, many lifetimes' worth – how could I even hope to scratch the surface in half a year? When winter finally retreated north and my departure became imminent, I found myself immersed in the joys of Big City life – the idea of pedalling for thousands of miles all alone seemed to lose its appeal. How much easier it is to dream than to act, I thought.

I pressed on with plans anyway, set a date for departure and told my room-mate I was moving out. He found a replacement; with that, I really did have to go. On my last night I went to a concert in Tribeca, drank too much Irish whiskey in a swanky wine bar (for fortitude) and didn't come back until 4 a.m. – I felt great, and ready for anything.

A few short hours later I awoke feeling awful – ready for nothing, good for nothing. Whiskey is a great cure for many things, but only ever temporarily. It was Sunday morning, the best time for a would-be cross-country cyclist to slip through a busy city unnoticed, and the following day someone would move into my bedroom. Regardless of how sore my head was, I had to get out, and from there I might as well keep going.

For many years I'd read stories of great journeys across the North American continent – Lewis and Clark, Steinbeck, Kerouac. All started east and struck out west, hoping to discover themselves as much as anything else. These adventures were the spark that lit my own fire of wanderlust, the writings fanning the flame. Now I was finally setting off on my own humble quest – a far cry from the heroes of old, but about as noble as I was likely to manage.

For quick-access inspiration on the road, I had scrawled a passage of Walt Whitman's 'Song of the Open Road' onto a piece of paper that was now wedged into the bar-bag of my bicycle:

Henceforth I ask not good-fortune, I myself am good-fortune. Henceforth I whimper no more, postpone no more.

I myself am good-fortune. That seemed like a good line to focus on. I manoeuvred my heavily loaded bike into the lift and took it down to the lobby – a 6-foot-square cubicle of cheap blue tiles that opened out to the stairwell and front door. Next I brought down my trailer, full of the belongings that would constitute my life for the next few months. A mandolin case and a plastic bag full of books were strapped haphazardly to the top, emphasising just how overpacked and underprepared I was.

I checked over the apartment once more for anything left behind. In my angst at leaving, everything seemed tinged with melancholic memories. The open-plan living room with spongy sofas where I'd taken many a comfortable nap in lieu of a proper night's sleep; a balcony behind sliding doors on which I'd drunk beers and watched the sun set over Queens; my windowless box room, so small that I'd had to position a sofa bed diagonally in order to lie down. All were now void of anything belonging to me. A chapter in my life about to finish. I left the keys on the table, scribbled a note for my room-mate Chase and went down the lift for the very last time.

CHAPTER 2

MELANCHOLY

'B*llocks!'

I looked through the glass door at my bike and trailer. It takes a very special type of fool to lock their bicycle inside a building for which they no longer have any keys. I was that special type of fool. It might have been comical, had I not been on the verge of tears. I would not get very far if I kept up this standard of 'adventuring'.

'Explorers don't cry,' I reminded myself, not sure if this was true or not.

I went next door to call Miguel, the building superintendent. His wife was unimpressed at being woken up so early on a Sunday and despite my apologies she berated me through the buzzer while Miguel got dressed. Thirty minutes later he arrived in a white vest and shorts, much the worse for wear. 'Heavy night?' I asked by way of conversation. The look on his face said he'd have smacked me on the nose if only he had the energy. Bike and trailer were released and Miguel stared hard, but he was either too tired or just not *quite* interested enough to ask any questions, so he left me with a nod and went back to his angry wife.

Hitching up my shorts I stepped over the crossbar, perched onto the hard leather seat and took those first few, tentative pedal strokes. Millions more would follow; months of spinning my legs in seemingly aimless and endless circles, circles that in the end would take me further than I ever thought possible.

A couple of days earlier I'd cycled from my apartment to the beach at Coney Island and back inland again. If I made it across the country to the Pacific Ocean on the west coast I wanted to be able to justifiably claim to have ridden the entire cross-continental distance from the Atlantic. Reasons of posterity, I guess – a guy in a bike shop told me that's what everyone else did and I didn't want to feel left out.

I merged into the bike lane outside my old apartment, legs heavy with whiskey and fear, and thought how enjoyable that ride to Coney Island had been. It had taken me just a few hours and all I had to concern myself with was making sure I got back home in time to meet some friends. Now, from here on in, I had no plans – no friends to meet, no deadlines, no certainty nor guarantees. This unknown quantity, which had at one time seemed liberating, now put me ill at ease.

I freewheeled off down the broad Brooklyn avenues, away from all that I knew. I passed Hasidic Jewish synagogues, lively with a bustling sea of black hats, then through the tall and tightly packed apartment blocks of the Bed-Stuy projects – high-rise, low-income council estates that seemed to be thought of by other Brooklyn residents as a location synonymous with gangs and crime. Impressionable as I was I'd stayed clear of the area for the most part, except for once when I walked out to look at the humble and bland building where my room-mate told me Jay-Z grew up. The road bent now towards the river and I slowed from time to time to watch groups of elderly Russian men with carved stony faces and grey flat caps playing backgammon under the shade of broad oak trees.

I turned off Bedford Avenue and wheeled up onto the Williamsburg Bridge. There's a smell on the Williamsburg Bridge that I'll always recall – stale and sharp, maybe like mothballs on a houseboat. A large metal gate barred my way with an enormous and irrefutable 'Closed' sign. I shook a little, and reversed back down to roll along the river until the next crossing point. Already my senses and nerves were on edge, and on some level I was waiting for my bike to break down and fall apart. At least then I would have something concrete to worry about.

As it was, the bike groaned under the load but struggled on. Every ten yards I would glance over my shoulder to check the progress of the trailer; mandolin bouncing along on top merrily, held rather unconvincingly in place by two bungee cords. My bum cheeks ached already and I shifted position constantly to ease them. By the time I arrived at the Brooklyn Bridge I had ridden all of three miles (1/1,000 of the straight-line distance to the west coast, I noted) and I was exhausted.

CHAPTER 3

NEW YORK BLUES

On the ramp I finally heard the sound I had been expecting all along – a loud impatient scraping, accompanied by a heavy drag on the bike. I'd snapped the frame, I was sure of it. I knew it was too heavy, and all for a bloody mandolin and some books! But no, not yet. The hitch for the trailer had just slipped and was trailing on the tarmac. I readjusted and tightened it and everything was back in working order. No reprieve.

Tourists and joggers were beginning to crowd the Brooklyn Bridge. A streak of sunlight broke through the cloud and bathed the East River in golden morning glow. Steel struts vibrated with a soft pulse, the impact of a thousand footsteps, deflecting the light northwards. Across the water Manhattan was slowly waking. There are few greater views of the man-made world than those from the Brooklyn side of the bridge. The Empire State and Chrysler buildings reach always a little higher than those around, though the effect is of a whole rather than any separate structures. The horizon is firmly blocked off by this vertical urban sprawl, but there is too much beauty in the scene to complain.

Steering clumsily between pedestrians, I admired for a final time the detail in the view – the reflective silver windows of Pace University, ladders crawling up the red-brick village apartments, and the ever-changing, glinting face of the skyscrapers.

A smart navy corvette slowed as it passed me on Delancey Street, and I looked around to see a middle-aged brunette with a cheeky grin flicking up her middle finger. We made eye contact briefly, and she sped off. I wondered if she was annoyed at my trailer – a two-wheeled flatbed model – taking up too much of the road. It will be great to get out of the city, I thought.

I hit the West Side greenway – a multi-use path that runs north to south along the side of Manhattan Island – and rode along it towards the George Washington Bridge. There I would temporarily cross out of New York State, and begin my journey through New Jersey. That, I reckoned, would be where this adventure really began.

The river rolled relentlessly past on my left and by now the city was teeming with weekend activity – rollerblading, bicycling, couples venturing out for a romantic stroll. It was this vibrancy that I loved so much about New York.

I stopped at a grubby bench halfway along the greenway and dug out a jar of peanut butter. This would be my major sustenance over the next few months. Life can be so simple – no gourmet meals necessary any more. I plunged an expensive plastic 'camping' spoon into the jar and it snapped almost immediately. Carefully I used a penknife instead, tilting my head back and scooping chunks into my mouth.

A haggard-looking man of maybe forty years loped past, then turned back. His hair was matted underneath a peaked train-driver's cap, his clothes stained with the rigours of living rough. A grimy hewn animal-feed sack was thrown over his back and he clutched onto it with both hands. His eyes were wild.

'Spare a dollar, son?' he whispered.

'No, sorry pal.'

He looked long at my bike and then at me.

'You sure you don't got anything?'

'You can have a sandwich, if you like,' I offered.

The man took a seat on the bench beside me and I handed him a cheese and olive sandwich, regretting having made such a middle-class lunch. We sat in silence for a few minutes.

'You can cross this here country 'hundred times, and see it different every time,' he started. 'Just take my advice: don't get yourself caught up with guns, girls or government. That's the unholy trinity. Avoid them, you'll do just fine.'

Further north, the man's warning words still ringing in my ears, the George Washington Bridge soon loomed large over me – a hunk of silver steel spanning the Hudson and dominating all around. Traffic rolled back and forth on two levels, and a small trail switchbacked up the hillside from the greenway to allow pedestrian access.

A handsome young couple, hipsters to the core with skinny jeans and hair that blended into their hats, stopped me to ask what I was doing. They jotted down the phone number of a friend who lived in Michigan. 'Call him up if you get the chance, he'd just love to get you some food and a place to stay.'

I thanked them and started the climb up and onto the bridge. There was no going back from here.

CHAPTER 4

WANDERLUST

At university, I had learned that academia was not for me. During stints in employment, I found that offices only succeeded in making my feet so itchy that it's incredible I didn't scratch them off completely.

It was the idea of a job, however – a real one with a decent wage and important, responsible duties – that I felt obligated to move towards. From a young age I had been told that I should study hard, be sensible, and eventually get the fabled 'good job'. Everyone seemed to understand that phrase, 'a good job', to be shorthand for a comfortable and happy life. A sensible life. And that was that.

A month after I graduated from university with a degree in Film Studies, I was offered my first 'real' job – to become, on a temporary basis, a Cinema Manager. My role was ensuring that screenings went smoothly and all the other employees turned up for work. It was a fine job, I suppose, but not what I'd hoped for. There was nothing about it that got me excited, nothing that made me feel alive.

There was so very little to do, yet I was obliged to be present for a large part of each day. Ninety-five per cent of that time was spent in my office with the door closed, poring over maps of the world in a clandestine manner. Maps facilitate dreams better than anything else; I can tangibly feel the separation from reality, the point at which the suppressed adventurer within us bursts forth and cascades wildly across continents. Maps were my escape from the humdrum mundanity of what was becoming my life. Internally I held a violent desire to one day explore the world for real.

I told myself to stop complaining about a lack of fulfilment, and instead to be thankful I had work at all. Many of my peers from university, through no fault of their own, had not only struggled to enter their chosen field but had roundly failed to acquire any sort of job at all. So poor was the market that when a position opened up in the local supermarket, 650 people applied to become a 'Till Operator'. Of those despairing souls, 460 had undergraduate degrees, 135 held Masters, and fourteen were in possession of a doctorate. For all of us, to graduate in the summer of 2008 was to be released kicking, screaming and thoroughly unprepared into a global recession.

Once, on an evening jog along the rain-spattered cobblestones of Canterbury's side streets, I dodged in and out of shelter beneath awnings, watching the bowed evening light pierce through sky behind the cathedral. This was a beautiful city, I thought, but there were very few jobs here. There were equally few jobs in all the other beautiful cities, too. With a degree in Film Studies I was bottom of the heap. I was left with two options. I could keep hunting for a job – lower my expectations and content myself with working at something that didn't proffer anything useful in any sense but which would keep me adequately fed, sheltered and entertained –

or I could cut and run, and see this situation as opportunity rather than obstacle.

I felt woefully incompetent to be considering real-world activities. The idea of settling down for (potentially) the rest of my life into a career just because it was the only thing available in an economic downturn seemed disastrous for everyone involved. Challenges, Experiences, Happiness. This is what I sought, I decided. I was young and naïve and enthusiastic. A friend told me that he thought, above all, I ached for a lifestyle that would require me to actively participate in my own existence – to strive, to seek, to find, and not to yield. Someone else called it wanderlust.

CHAPTER 5

THE PLAN

The recession, it turned out, had done me a favour. An 'Adventure' was what was required to drag me out of my rut. 'Where' didn't matter hugely, nor 'How'. 'When' was the important factor – it had to be now.

In my penultimate year of high school, when I could still barely tie my own laces, I had cycled across some of western Europe and discovered that bicycles were wonderfully forgiving to a clueless novice. The beauty is in the simplicity: you gather some belongings, find a trusty (or cheap) steed, and go. There are some minor maintenance issues to learn about, but those can absolutely be acquired en route to enlightenment – in fact, it's positively more fun that way. Bicycles are slow enough to force interaction with the world around and ensure that each sight, sound and smell will find its way to the correct orifice whether you like it or not.

It's no lie, though, to say they can also be beasts of pure speed. Once fit enough, a state which takes at most a couple of weeks of pedalling, just about anyone can happily ride a hundred miles in a day. This is at the very least a morale booster, at best a lifesaver. There are few landscapes in the world that will not become altered over the course of one hundred miles. The same is true for cultures. It comes down to this: if a journey becomes tiresome or daunting, then you can pedal breathlessly for ten hours to find yourself free from the tedium and uncertainty which had been a plague that very same morning. Finally, crucially, bicycles insist upon a reduced and minimalist lifestyle. Even the most overloaded bike is considerably more liberated than an average bedroom. It never occurred to me to travel by any other method for my Big Adventure.

* * *

I had moved to New York to take up an internship partly because I had a vague notion of trying to self-film my bicycle adventure, but mostly because it was a good excuse to live in New York. I remember clearly a day in primary school, I must've been about seven years old, when Seamus Hunter came into class with a New York Yankees cap on back to front and no one knew what to do. We just weren't used to that sort of thing in rural Northern Ireland. Since then I'd had the city on a pedestal and waited for an opportunity to go – it's funny the things that stick with us from childhood. More recently I had heard Bob Dylan say it was 'a city like a web too intricate to understand, and I wasn't going to try'. Anything that flummoxed Bob was worth seeing.

I looked at a wall-poster map of the United States of America and realised that the country I thought I knew about only really existed in New York, Washington DC and Los Angeles. The coasts. Here's the thing: it is about three thousand miles from New York to LA but, with the exception of Chicago, very little information about what lies in between makes it out into the wider world. Not my wider world, anyway. How could it be that something so big and powerful and seemingly well known could have so many secrets? What does an average American look like? Is there such a thing? What happens in that huge space in the middle of the country? One way to find out would be to bicycle there and see for myself.

I bought a bike and a travel map of the USA before I left Britain, both things that would have been more sensible to purchase once I got to New York. I quit my temporary job only to be offered a permanent one. I thanked them for the offer and told the boss I was going on an adventure. At home I counted my loot. In total I had around £4,000; more than enough to fly to America and cycle across it. What happened after that would be anyone's guess.

Finally I said goodbye to the people I loved – family, friends, girlfriend. This last farewell was, inevitably, the hardest. We'd been dating for two years and had graduated from the casual and carefree nature of a university relationship to a relatively mature and loving couple. Unfortunately the idea of sitting on a bike saddle for eight hours a day and sleeping in a hedge every night for an indefinite period of time did not appeal to Clare. My heart broke to leave her, but I was certain I'd have more regrets if I stayed. With only vague mentions of when I might be back I left her and flew to New York, alone. Our chosen paths in life were, for now at least, not compatible.

CHAPTER 6

BRIDGE TO THE OTHER SIDE

Once across the George Washington Bridge and officially out of New York City, I found myself swept helplessly into the nonsense of the New Jersey Township system. I'm not sure who it was that designed these roads, but they were surely drunk or having a laugh. Equally at fault was whoever drew the map I was following. I suppose one gets what one deserves for buying the cheapest map in a crumby gas station ('Only $3, with free laminated pullout!'), but I still feel that the very purpose of a map is to correctly show a road's location, name and destination. This map did all three, I suppose, but just mixed up the details.

For two hours I rode in circles, occasionally finding myself at something recognisable, lamentably because I had already passed that way. By luck or judgement I eventually drifted back on course and returned to the Empire State – the state of New York – which arcs around New Jersey in a large loop. Boundaries were such that state-hopping would become a frequent activity over the coming days and weeks. As long as I headed north-west, however, the city of New York would fall further behind my rear wheel, and slowly become but a distant memory.

Passing through Suffern, a tiny town I only noticed because it had a sign, a cop on a Harley pulled me over, lights flashing. His bike glistened with a sheen that only true love could produce.

'Where you headed to?' he asked, face mostly hidden behind Aviators and moustache.

'Sloatsburg, sir.'

'Well, it's only five miles up ahead. Where's home?'

'New York City. I guess it was, anyway, until today.'

'You're not from there though – I've heard enough New York accents to know that. Where's your *real* home?' he asked, chuckling and taking his glasses off.

'I'm from Ireland originally. So I suppose that's home. Or maybe England, that's where I was most recently...' I trailed off.

'Sounds like you don't really know! Maybe you'll find out on this bike ride of yours. I hope so. My home is right here in Suffern, and I wouldn't want to be away from it for more'n a few days.'

'I like the sound of that,' I said. I was slightly envious of his contentment. He'd never see as much of the world as I would because he had no desire to. All the challenges, rewards, hopes and dreams he could imagine existed within the borders of Suffern – a town of just a couple of thousand people. It struck me that it was the prevalence of this very mindset that led me to leave Northern Ireland in the first place – it had seemed in my experience there that a narrow experience of the world could so often lead to a narrow mindset when it came to issues of tolerance and understanding. Now I wasn't so sure – even just a few hours into my ride I could sense the emotional impact of the journey, and its effect on my beliefs, previously held certainties. I've heard it said travel only teaches you how much you don't know. Perhaps you *can* exist in the same place and learn everything you need. Freya Stark talks about the two types of explorer – the physical and the mental. She tells the parable of an old Chinese man who, after years of wandering for thousands of miles all over his vast country, eventually finds he can go further in his mind while pacing around his back garden. As usual I was drastically overthinking the situation, but nevertheless there was something comforting about how happy this cop seemed in his own skin and town. For him, the world really was a small place, and one which to all intents and purposes ended at the county line.

'Enjoy New York State,' said the cop. 'It's a fine place wherever you're from. Here's ten bucks… that's just from me. Keep it in your wallet and maybe someday it'll help you when you really need it. Ride safe to Sloatsburg.'

He shooed me away when I tried to thank him, then kicked the Harley into life and roared off, waving over his shoulder. I started moving too, though much slower, and soon the town of Sloatsburg appeared over the brow of a hill and promised a warm bed for the night. Friends of friends lived here, my only contacts between New York and San Francisco, and I was welcomed in without delay. My first day on the road was over. Greater challenges would lie ahead but for now this would do just fine. I ate more food than the rest of the family combined and then lay by the fire. Instantly I was asleep, dreaming of roads past, roads future and everything in between.

CHAPTER 7

THE EMPIRE STATE

As it turns out, you can never really know what's essential for a journey until afterwards, for it is impossible to predict what obstacles will lay strewn along the way. I had made the anticipated mistake of packing too much, and now with a minor mountain range ahead it seemed wise to cull unnecessary items – a process that would continue until the final days of my trip. I purged myself of excess clothes (leaving me with two T-shirts, one hooded top, one pair of shorts and a set of waterproofs), all but two books and, with an air of inevitability, the mandolin. I hadn't even had a chance to play it but with a heavy heart (and a lighter bike) I entrusted it to the garage of my hosts.

I called Day Two a 'rest day' and spent most of it in bed eating sandwiches and reading diary excerpts of Meriwether Lewis and William Clark. Lewis and Clark, explorers in the nineteenth century when exploring was a wild and dangerous business, were charged by President Jefferson to find a route across the country as far as the Pacific Ocean, and help claim the western lands before colonial European powers could do so. On the eve of departure, from the frontier of St Louis, Missouri, Lewis wrote:

We were now about to penetrate a country at least two thousand miles in width, on which the foot of civilized man had never trod. The good or evil it had in store for us was for experiment yet to determine, and these little vessels [we are travelling with] contained every article by which we were to expect to subsist or defend ourselves. However, as the state of mind in which we are, generally gives the colouring to events, when the imagination is suffered to wander into futurity, the picture which now presented itself to me was a most pleasing one. Entertaining as I do the most confident hope of succeeding in a voyage which had formed a darling project of mine for the last ten years, I could but esteem this moment of my departure as among the most happy of my life.

Our purposes, processes and predicted journeys were a world apart, yet I felt a sense of shared desire leap off the page. In Lewis's words were the spirit of adventure, the need to explore. I heard him loud and clear: in this too-short life we have, the lure of a quest is too enticing not to launch oneself into it fully and enthusiastically.

There were hints of other motives, too. Whether it was for a new place to call home, or perhaps a way to delay ever having to settle for that very concept, I didn't know. The notion of home was very much present in my head as every pedal stroke took me farther from it. America had by now been explored and settled for hundreds of years (and lived in peacefully for thousands before that) – but not by me. I wanted to come from the coast to the hills to the lakes to the plains to the deserts to the mountains and on to the coast once more. I wanted to see it for myself.

* * *

Back on the road I followed Old County Road 17 past Harriman State Park, a vast area of wilderness and a haven for weekend hikers. In all my time in New York City I never knew that just fifty miles north from Times Square was such wild and remote countryside. Rain began to fall and another fear, that of getting wet and cold and not knowing what to do, was debunked – my waterproof clothes worked as one might expect them too, and even when the rain soaked through to skin I could happily dry out quickly in the warmth of a roadside diner. The afternoon took me through Monroe, Chester, Goshen, Middletown – tiny nondescript New York towns that passed in the blink of an eye.

At the top of a small hill I stopped to catch my breath and a Lycra-clad, cropped-haired waif of a man pulled in on his sleek racing bike.

'Everyone, I mean EVERYONE goes the other way – start in California and head east. Go from here and you'll be fighting headwinds the whole goddamn way!' he blustered when I told him my plans.

'But I really want to see the country going the other way. Besides, I'm here now. Maybe I've got to earn that Californian coastline,' I said.

'Screw that,' he argued, 'you'll be miserable the whole way. You probably won't even break twenty miles an hour on some days!' A little chortle escaped his throat with this notion.

'That doesn't bother me – I'm not in any rush.'

'But do you want to cycle, or do you want to spend your whole time going so slowly that you have to see every godforsaken sh*thole in this country?'

Well, that pretty much summed it up. I did want to see every godforsaken sh*thole, very much so. Sure, I'd rather that the cost didn't involve headwinds, plus the scorn of the cycling community, but overall they were a small price to pay.

West already felt like my natural course. This was a continent orientated in one direction for the explorer. My fellow cyclist clipped back into his pedals and flew off with the wind, arse in the air as he powered back towards the city. I was glad I met him, just so I never had to do it again.

CHAPTER 8

MON-TAH-SELL-OH

Old County Road 17 twisted, turned and spun me around, spitting me out after a few days into downtown Monticello. This was for sure the most unpleasant place I had seen yet in the entire USA (which must put it high in the running for most unpleasant place worldwide). Dark clouds overhead set a tone and small ugly blocks of buildings scowled out at the road. Garbage bags had piled up on the roadside and brick walls grew in ill-advised places. Nothing looked like any care had been taken over it. Even the trees were ugly.

The entire main street had been dug up for repair, and there were no half-measures – the powers that be had lifted an entire mile of blacktop clean off the ground. Small, sad, crushed piles of tarmac sat at regular intervals on the sidewalk, like spectators of a losing football team.

Unlike most of the small towns I'd so far passed through, like friendly Suffern and Sloatsburg, no one here smiled or came to say 'hi'. I hadn't previously met a single unwelcoming person on the road, yet now absolutely everyone in Monticello seemed as if they'd just been on the receiving end of some very bad news. I counted ten pedestrians who staggered past me looking straight down at the floor. It was impossible to tell what age anyone was, as all I ever saw was an occasional eye appearing from beneath a hood and piercing straight through me. No one spoke, even as I trundled past with my circus-like bike get-up. This was a miserable place.

The main street was the only way out and, as the ungraded, makeshift road was guaranteed to shred my tyres, I went on foot along the sidewalk. The stores on either side were shut, save for a single bagel shop. It had a big red sign, and all the letters were missing except two Ps and a U. I don't know why I went in.

Inside were two smear-stained metal tables, six collapsible chairs in the upright position (plus two that were permanently buckled) and an extraordinarily greasy counter. Nothing else and no one was to be seen. Behind the counter an opaque curtain draped over a doorway to some unseen horrors behind.

'Hello?' I tried. 'Hello? I'd like to buy a bagel, please.'

A slow moaning arose from somewhere behind the curtain. It was definitely human, but not a very normal human. Moaning is pretty rare, these days. Certainly in public. A local dialect perhaps? I'd already been told off on the road for asking for 'Monty-chel-lo'. ('You mean Mon-tah-sell-oh? You'll never get there if you can't say it right.')

The moaning continued and after five minutes I gave up. I like to think that I am an adventurous person, curious about most things, but there are some that are best left alone.

Outside I found a small man rubbing his leg against my bicycle. I didn't even bother asking. I wheeled away and he shouted something incomprehensible, and when I looked back he skulked away into the bagel shop. Ten minutes later I was back on the pedals and riding as fast as I could the hell away from Monticello. So far I'd enjoyed the uniformity of the eastern towns – safe, predictable and all with a common line in shops and diners. This was the first exception. It was horrible, yes, but as I rode off I did feel a flicker of gladness that I had at least seen some diversity. How boring the trip would be if all settlements and people were carbon copies of the same thing! Luckily, as I was to find out, this trip would eventually show me more variations on America than I ever thought possible.

CHAPTER 9

A MAN'S BEST FRIEND

I was slow and cumbersome when riding, still unused to the rigours of this new life. The bike, however, was doing just fine, and this encouraged me greatly. A few days before leaving I'd asked around among friends if anyone had an idea what I should call her, and, amongst the silly and downright odd suggestions (Billy, Bikey, Jeremiah, Susie-Q, even Mary-Kate and the trailer as Ashley), one had jumped out as promising. 'Lola' was offered up in reference to the Kinks song, ostensibly about a man's encounter with a possible transsexual in a bar. The inference was that although the bike was female, she was not the most *feminine*. It was meant as a joke, but I liked it anyway. 'Lola' stuck.

She was designed by Dutch masters, as all good bikes are, then shipped to Lancing, West Sussex, where I went to get acquainted. For a few hours we were both measured and tweaked. She gleamed black and towered over other bikes in the shop. Angular, sleek, she made all the other bikes looks like kiddie cycles. Her cross to bear was that she was a heavyweight – unloaded already near 20 kilograms due to her construction out of 'chromoly', a strengthened steel compound (my ignorance of such issues was betrayed in the bike shop when I was offered chromoly and replied, 'No thanks, I've heard steel is best.').

I was instantly confident that she would not break. I chose simple features – flat pedals, a basic Shimano gearing system and straight handlebars with a perpendicular grip on each side. My bicycle knowledge was pitiful and I had been nervous collecting her from the store, in case I would be asked to distinguish between a top tube, a derailleur, a crank or some other bit that makes the wheels go round.

My final addition was thick tyres that I hoped would deal with gravel tracks, and I fitted an extra couple of water-bottle holders. The racks to hold my panniers were already bolted on, along with mudguards, kickstands and a bell (I later replaced the standard bell with one that had a novelty compass on top). My pannier bags were black, waterproof, equally robust.

These four bags and the bicycle were the constant background against which everything else in my life would change and develop.

* * *

I was now in the area of New York State known colloquially as the 'Catskills', after the small mountain range of the same name that dominates the landscape. For six months in the city a friend had sworn blind that the term had something to do with a juggling, fire-breathing feline, but I could see now he was a liar or a moron.

A dramatic escarpment out of the Hudson River Valley announces these hills have begun and they run for roughly a hundred miles to the north and west, undulating with a gentle, consistent lilt. I was certainly in a different world from the city. Narrow roads banked by dense hedges wound through arable farmland, often dropping to one of the many rivers that permeate the area. This scenery was to characterise my first full week in the saddle.

Hills, wind and rain meant that I was often positively exhausted and ravenous. Often I could not tell which affliction it was that I was struck down with at a particular point in time. The best remedy was to lie down by the roadside spooning peanut butter into my mouth in the hope of curing all ills simultaneously.

On those virgin evenings while the sun was in freefall, drawn irresistibly towards the western horizon, I found myself pedalling along the banks of the Delaware. One of the nineteen great waterways of America, the Delaware here flows with an air of understated majesty, hemmed in by tall broad conifers. Smooth gravel banks and islands of brown soil rise from the depths, amongst and around which its eastward progress meanders.

The lower Delaware, out towards the coast, is home to impressive ports and industry but here it has a much more humble and peaceful demeanour. Its major job is to separate the states of New York and Philadelphia, which it does with aplomb. I crossed back and forth on unsteady single-track bridges of rusted steel girders, risking occasional glances at the water bubbling far below.

By night I ambled through tunnels of overhanging tree branches until I saw a clear spot by the river's edge. I knew better than to camp too near a river in the wet season, especially one with such obviously fluid banks as this, yet being alone did wild things to my brain and common sense abandoned me along with the sun. I began to hear unspeakable terrors lurking in the undergrowth nearer the road and decided more than once that I would take my chances with the river. Better the devil you know.

On my first night of wild camping it took three times as long as it should have to pitch my tent (at least according to the impressively swift duration claimed by the attached instruction leaflet). Eventually it was up, my bags unloaded and Lola resting calmly alongside. All my panniers went inside the tent for notions relating to security and a guy rope was tied around the bike. I reasoned that any would-be thief trying to silently make off with my bicycle would inadvertently pull at my entire tent and wake me up. Quite what would happen then was a mystery that I would have to wait to uncover. Dinner was a rather unceremonious affair of bread, biscuits and peanut butter; my camping stove lay unused at the bottom of a pannier, the fuel bottle empty. A job for another day.

***

Evenings spent alone in nature have a way of being darker and more silent than anywhere else on earth. At some point I realised that before leaving New York I had never in my life been camping by myself – all previous forays into the wilds had come complete with brave companions to fend off monsters.

By surviving alone in a tent I wasn't going to win any medals, but I'd be one step closer to defining myself, to myself. The fact that I slept at all was a miracle; perhaps I just passed out from pure angst.

CHAPTER 10

AN IRISHMAN ABROAD

Those early days were marked by a rapid and exciting increase in fitness and cycling ability. It's not natural to sit with back hunched and legs spinning endlessly, squeezing butt cheeks over a wafer-thin strip of leather. In fact, apart from studding the leather with nails and broken glass, I can barely think of anything less comfortable. It was a pleasant surprise, then, to learn that it is a position that becomes sustainable with time. My body found the sweet spots into which to contort itself, and the relentless pedalling slowly dropped into the subconscious level of action. I was adapting to this new life physically; the first stage in my development as a cyclist.

Sweating my way north-west, I would spend hours dreaming of the next place where I could buy a cold drink and refuel with snacks. In rural New York State, old-fashioned General Stores were my ideal companions. As towns first began to sprout up across the New Continent in the mid to late nineteenth century, General Stores were among the first establishments to be constructed, forming the central hub of each new neighbourhood. They were a place where the townsfolk could gather, and they epitomised everything about that flourishing American spirit – community, survival, self-sufficiency, business, routine.

Nowadays a few still hold a position of prominence in small settlements and are easy to spot: wood-panelled exterior buoyed by neo-Greek columns holding up a first-floor balcony, giving what was inevitably always a humble store an air of grandeur. To me these were something distinctly and beautifully American, and amidst the new global order of Walmarts and Costcos they harked back to a vanishing time when each country in the developed world was unique.

I visited all the stores that I could as I moved across the country, and in the heat of the midday sun I'd often take a break and sit on the wooden porch sipping cheap juice or coffee and idly kicking pebbles. My favourite was in the town of Lookout, where I lazed for three hours watching a scruffy dog chase its tail in an empty parking lot. Every so often the owner would come out and say 'Get you some more joe, son?' and then refill my cup and toddle back inside.

A few folk came by to pick up this and that, and tipped their caps or nodded heads. Life was so slow I could almost see the grass grow.

Buoyed by these regular supply stops, I followed the old highway further into the vast New York hinterland with its cracked blacktop and overgrown hedgerow. A woman in a car pulled over to ask me where I was headed, and gave me the phone number of a friend just north of Shipton. 'Just around the corner!' she promised. Two hours later I came around the 'corner', which was in fact a large series of hills designed to weary the brave cyclist.

These rural towns were becoming familiar. Almost all would be set up in the same way – a 'main street' stretching a few hundred yards, bookended by four-way crossroads on each side. America was built from the East Coast inwards – it seemed like by the time they got this far on the frontier they knew what they were doing and would just replicate the township system all the way across.

Shipton's only difference was that it boasted an Irish bar, one that dominated the street in an obnoxious way with oversized flags hanging out into the road. It's widely supposed that Irish bars can be found in remote and ridiculous places all over the world. Upstate New York shouldn't have been a surprising location, but still it drew me in – it was the first I'd seen since I took to the pedals.

I had a couple of bucks of my daily budget left (five dollars a day, I hoped) and decided to bank on a free dinner tonight from some kindly soul – perhaps the friend of the woman who didn't know the difference between a corner and a hill.

'McCormack's' looked from the street to be a turn-of-the-century-built homestead: old style exterior, wooden panels running horizontal across the front and set back from the road by a porch. The street itself was deserted save for the air of tranquility that roams these towns in the early afternoon. Inside, a long bar faced a row of one-armed bandit machines. A back room was dominated by a pool table and two slumped figures in the shadowy periphery, every bit as much a part of the furniture as the neon lights that gave the place a seedy strip-club atmosphere.

'Get you a beer?' A shadow grew a face as it emerged behind the countertop.

'Please. Bud Light.' The stuff tasted like carbonated toilet water, but I wanted to try to fit in.

'What brings you here?' asked the face.

Towns like this always know an outsider. Granted I was not the most inconspicuous – my ripped, stained T-shirt and tattered shoes yelled 'foreigner!' if not also 'vagabond!' – but I'd have been rumbled no matter how covert I was. Townsfolk know by a process of elimination: it's not necessarily that there is anything about you, or me, that is so discernibly different, it's the key fact that the locals have not seen you before. In these towns everyone knows everyone, and that's only a slight exaggeration. Personal business is there to be shared, like it or not.

A small and solid man with receding hair, a booming laugh and a firm manner was my bartender for the day. Being on the right side of him felt like a good place to be. I told him how I got there and he had to take his hat off to understand.

'You're kiddin' me... you're kiddin' me! Babydoll, c'mon out here and see this!' A fifty-year-old woman dressed like a twenty-year-old slid out of the murk and into the arms of her man. 'This here... is an Irishman!' I could've sworn she stifled a gasp, and the two drunks in the back room awoke at the news.

'I'm Dane, Dane McCormack. I own this here place – best bar in town!'

'Only bar in town,' added Babydoll. They both chuckled. It was a well-practised routine.

'I've been running this place for thirty years, and my father before that, and we ain't NEVER had a real Irishman inside!'

'No sir, not even one,' chipped in Babydoll.

'What do you make of that?'

'That's quite something!' I thanked myself for brightening their day. 'Glad I stopped by.'

'We are too, that's for damn sure! Babydoll, get him another beer, it's on us!'

The afternoon played out in similar manner with a rotating cast of locals. A Shipton resident would enter, have their gosh-darn socks blown off by the news of a real Irishman being in the Irish pub and then they would make their offering to the provider of such fine entertainment – me.

Three hours later I was five beers deep, without any food to soak it up. I attempted to sneak off to my bike to devour a few quick snacks but a large gentleman in a too-small-by-far polka-dot shirt caught me red-handed and led me back to the bar. 'Get this skinny sonova b*tch one of them big pizzas, Tuff. We'll get some fat on you before you leave Shipton!' He delivered this last comment like a punchline and everyone laughed raucously, including me. I'd cycled fifty miles and had five beers – I'd have laughed at a brick wall.

When the food arrived I surreptitiously picked off the meat and fed it to a portly dog that darted around between drinkers' legs. A 12-inch pizza's worth of meat later and he lay heavily in the corner panting slightly. *Please Lord, I haven't killed him.* I was a pretty heretical traveller here – a vegetarian in a meat-eater's land. I'd been brought up as one and had never suffered without eating meat, so never saw the point in starting. I was never much of a foodie, I suppose – food was fuel. Better if it tastes good, but no big deal if it looks and smells like dog food, so long as it does the job.

By 9 p.m. I was so deep in alcohol that even my teeth hurt. I played my role well and as the whiskey arrived my accent got stronger with each drop. Before long I was telling wild stories about fairies in the homeland and promising to say 'hi' to everyone's ancestors when I got home. Just enough sense was retained to wheel Lola around the back and set up camp. I made a drunken phone call to the number I'd been given by the passing car on the way into town, explaining why I couldn't come and stay. Evidently they hadn't been expecting me in the first place and were very confused. Apologising profusely, I offered to take back some greetings to Ireland to make up for it.

Sleep in my little tent came easily, but I was regularly disrupted by punters from the bar coming to ask me some important questions that could only be answered by an authentic Irishman. The tent would shake and a foot might gently kick me awake. 'Do people in Ireland have normal jobs, like American jobs?' or 'What whiskey does the Pope drink?' or 'Did you ever see that thing on leprechauns on Discovery? It said they were nine feet tall and ate children.'

CHAPTER 11

MONSTERS

My hangover came with ferocity, straight out of the seventh circle of Hell. It took three hours of drinking water and moaning into the wind before I could even see where I was riding. As clarity slowly made a descent I noticed that my T-shirt was covered in people's names. Not those of anyone I'd met, though, but of their relatives in Ireland. Everyone at the bar had been very keen that I speak of them when I got back home.

I would discover this again and again as I made my way across America – a deep yearning for a sense of belonging, tinged with a hint of desperation. No one was American, it seemed, not really. They were half Irish, a quarter Italian, a quarter German. An eighth Dutch maybe. Some would even list in sixteenths. I wondered if a few hundred years was not long enough to forge a permanent identity, or if there was another reason for clinging onto such lineage.

In Binghampton, not far north of Shipton, I met an old war veteran touring the country in an RV (Recreational Vehicle). I would come to know these things pretty well out west but here they were still a novelty. A small house on wheels, I would learn of their popularity with the retired community of the US, many of whom tour the country for half the year chasing the sun.

Ex-Army Officer Christopher Hilcrest ('Name's Hilcrest, Christopher Hilcrest. Pleasure to make your acquaintance') had caught shrapnel in his right leg in Vietnam and moved around with it sticking out stiff as a board. He was in constant pain, he said, but couldn't give a damn because it gave him something to think about. Plus, he was seeing the country he loved.

'If I stayed at home more'n two weeks in a row I'd blow my head off. Clean off, son. Boring goddamn place, home.' He toured around thematically – this year was civil war sites. He shook my hand firmly, pressed five dollars in it and told me to enjoy myself, show due respect to the country, and then go back to the UK and get a good job. It took him five full minutes to haul his wretched body back into the driver's seat, and he drove off with a salute and a pump of the horn.

Approaching my two-week anniversary on the road, the land started to open out a little; the peaks not quite so high nor the troughs low. Passing through Cortland, I was granted for the first time a perspective of the land and a decent view of the world that lay ahead. The road to Syracuse was flatter than anything I'd seen since leaving New York City. I wondered how long it would be before the cities of Cortland and Syracuse, currently twenty or thirty miles apart, gradually become one. All over the country industry and populations were growing, here in the east more than anywhere, and these current city boundaries would inevitably expand to engulf outlying villages and towns.

For now, though, there was still some beautiful wild countryside, stretching out golden under the spring sun. I could count myself in the number that saw America as it was in 2010, and perhaps in fifty years I would tell unbelievable-sounding tales of open green space that is incomprehensible to a new generation. I have certainly heard enough people older than me talk about how great things were in 'their' day. I wondered how many years it would be before I began stories with 'Back in my day...'. I hoped that cycling across America would at least make a good story.

* * *

Blake, a friend with whom I shared many good times in New York City, worked for a large entertainment company and called to say he was in Syracuse on business over the very same weekend that I'd be passing through. He pulled some strings so I could sleep on the sofa in his hotel room, and that night promised me a quintessential American experience. He would not be drawn further on details.

As directed, I arrived at the city fairgrounds around 7 p.m. The place was just outside of town – a bunch of fields cordoned off with a huge perimeter fence around the outside. The street to the entrance was lined with a procession of empty beer cans, the harbinger of most mass evening gatherings. A kid cried on her daddy's shoulders and two hunched figures smoked cigarettes inside a ticket booth.

Through the gateway was a crowd of thirteen thousand very excited country folk, crammed onto rows of seats in a run-down grandstand looking out over a dirt track. I could tell from a quick glance around that this was not a wealthy audience – slightly tattered clothes matched the beaten-up trucks I'd seen in the car park. It didn't matter one jot to me.

Almost everyone, I was pleased to note, seemed to be smiling, at each other, at me, and most of all at the action out in front.

On the far side, amongst some ramshackle makeshift garages, the Monster Trucks were being prepared. Rarely have I seen such a ridiculous sight: vehicles the size of small buildings were lined up neatly, bright neon paint jobs screaming out their team colours – Spiderman, Grave Digger, Back Draft, Black Stallion. I had no idea that my friend Blake worked for a company that organised this kind of thing.

Men scampered around doing this and that to the machines and occasionally an engine would rev, sending the crowd wild. The most ludicrous thing of all was that in order to move these trucks from the garages to the track, the oversized Monster wheels had to be removed and replaced with regular car tyres – the result was the mechanical equivalent of a T-Rex's front arms.

I took a seat in the middle of a row; on one side was a man wearing a string vest and a mullet, and on the other an entire family wearing string vests and mullets. At first I was concerned about sitting between them, assuming that the mulleted man to my left must belong to the mulleted family on my right. When I asked if I should move, I was met with looks of incredulity – 'No sir, we ain't together!' It took me a while but I soon realised that, in fact, almost *everyone* was wearing string vests and mullets. I rolled my T-shirt sleeves up to the shoulder bone to try to fit in.

The three hours that followed were mayhem. A booming voice announced various races that, to my untrained eye, all seemed the same. Big trucks would start at one end of the track, bash over a few mounds of dirt and flaming car wrecks, then bounce their way down to the end. The crowd yelled mercilessly for one of the vehicles to flip, but alas none consented on this night.

A half-time break was marked with some impressive motorbike stunts mostly involving accelerating up a ramp and over a large amount of things on fire. 'More fire!' screamed the man beside me as if his very life depended on it. I spent the majority of the show stifling small chortles and viewing the whole thing in a silently superior manner. Thus it was a real surprise to me that when the announcer told us the evening's entertainment was nearly finished, I felt deeply disappointed.

Beyond the frenzy and madness, it was seriously good fun. Let's be straight – a Monster Truck Rally would not be my first choice of recreation. Watching some of the huge families stuffing themselves with hot dogs and pouring beer down their throats made me feel a little sad, too. Yet the whole event was a spectacular display of ostentatious, unapologetic American flamboyance – the good and the bad (and the ugly).

One member of the mulleted family on my row bought everyone around them beers (including me) just because he was having a good time. A small huddle formed to help an elderly man up the concrete steps. 'The greatest thing you can learn,' another man told me after very little by way of introduction, 'is that nobody is any better than anyone else. Some might think they are, but they're not. You, me, the President, that guy driving the truck – really, we're all the same.' Despite his awful mullet, he had a very good point.

Afterwards I went to meet Blake once he had finished working. He was in the pits (literally, not metaphorically), where everyone who was involved in the show had gathered together to eat fried chicken and debrief on the day. Blake said no one would mind if I joined them there so we sat amongst

PR teams, truck drivers, engineers and ticket sellers, watching them all share that same camaraderie that anyone in the business of travelling will know well. The whole concept of giant hunks of metal with supercharged engines bashing into things is mad, but equally wonderful in the absurdity. Only in America, I thought. What a country.

CHAPTER 12

FRIENDS AND MILES

Leaving the Monsters of Syracuse behind, I struck due west on my bike once more into arable farming land, then dipped down to the northern shores of the Finger Lakes. These elongated bodies of water have made the region well known as a tourist destination for city folk looking to find a little natural beauty, and also as a home for one of the best wine regions in the eastern US.

The heat burst forth around midday, and I bathed in Lake Skaneateles just south of the town with the same name. Here and there lanes diverged from the main road and ended at the gates of a house on the lake with a private jetty. I had to work hard to find a non-privately owned yet relatively concealed place, and upon doing so took the opportunity to dive in completely nude. To the south an endless point of blue ripped through a land of green. A cool wind swept over the water and drove me back onto my bike rather sooner than I'd have liked.

By now I was navigating using multiple methods. A map of the entire eastern USA, donated by a passing driver, gave me a rough idea of where I might be. I could see the major freeways on it and used my compass (and the sun which rose at my back and set at my nose) to orientate myself with their direction. This was as much as I was willing to acknowledge the existence of those vast motorways; I hoped never to see the freeways in person if I could help it. Their place was on the map along with other things that were of little interest to me.

The university (and party) town of Ithaca lay just a day's ride south and, if accounts were to be believed, I'd have had a great time there. But I didn't have a great time, because I didn't go. I didn't go for the same reason that I didn't visit the state capital, Albany, or ride through the Adirondack Mountains: because I simply couldn't go everywhere.

My journey was a challenge to myself, to see what I was made of. Along the way I would see plenty of America whichever route I took. This, I hoped, could be achieved happily by visiting an arbitrary selection of locations across the country. If I want to know about Ithaca or Albany, I can probably get a fairly decent idea of what I'd find there by reading a book or Googling them, or visiting in a car. But what if I want to know where the best place is to swim naked in Lake Skaneateles, and if I am brave enough to attempt it knowing that cars may drive past and see me in full glory mode? There are some things one must discover in person.

My other method of navigation was to keep faith in asking people. Sure, directions were skewed and distances off by some margin, but in a much more general sense local people had a good idea of where might be of interest. As it happened, I wasn't too bothered whether their suggestions were good or not. Their recommendations gave me a purpose and a destination and, as long as I was generally headed west, then that was good enough for me.

* * *

Passing through Montezuma Wildlife Refuge I was disappointed to see only a dead dog, which didn't fulfil either the Wild or the Life part. A pretty ride through bright fields further on brought me to the banks of the Seneca River, and beyond, the town of Seneca Falls. I pedalled slowly alongside the water distracted by the glittering reflection of the low sun easing its way to rest. By a statue of three women I paused for a break and was approached by an elderly lady weighed down by her bonnet. We nodded at each other, I said 'hello', and then she came out with it.

'Well, we're famous for two things here – women's rights, and *It's a Wonderful Life*. Which are you more interested in?'

Was this a test? I could only assume that these two things were in fact associated with the town, but I wasn't sure what the stakes were regarding my decision. She was small and frail, though her handbag looked rather dense and could've done some damage if swung towards my head. Women's rights was probably something I should know about, I conceded inwardly. And *It's a Wonderful Life*, presumably the Frank Capra movie, was indeed very enjoyable. I wasn't particularly interested in either just at that moment, if truth be told; I was too hungry to seek out cultural enrichment. Yet here I was, faced with an ominous question from a tiny old lady.

'Eh… women's rights?'

'Great!' she replied. She steadied herself against the railing and let rip.

'Well, in 1848, July nineteenth to be exact, a group of New York women organised a meeting right here in Seneca Falls…'. She spoke at a hundred miles an hour and I lost track almost immediately. I tried very hard to look as if I was concentrating, nodding and laughing occasionally, but really I was dying inside. I was hungry and I wanted to sit down.

Minutes passed, and she showed no sign of slowing. I pieced together that a group of women had gathered at a convention where they proposed equality for women. The event was revolutionary in that sense, and is now cited as where and when women's rights in America began. That, in itself, was quite interesting. Couldn't this kindly-but-relentless old lady have just summarised it? I thought. I tuned back in to find she was now quoting, seemingly verbatim, the address delivered by Elizabeth Cady Stanton on that fateful day…

Secondly, if we consider her as a citizen, as a member of a great nation, she must have the same rights as all other members, according to the fundamental principles of our government…

I gave up, and tried to count ducks on the water instead. Inevitably I ran out of ducks before she ran out of words. I berated myself for choosing women's rights. *Is this what Elizabeth Stanton was fighting for? Damn her!* (I later found out that the link between Seneca Falls and the Frank Capra movie is that many people assume the town was the basis for the fictional Bedford Falls in the film. That too, was a rubbish story, although at least quite a short one.)

Finally the history of women's rights, or whatever topic she had moved onto, came to an end and I mumbled a thank you. The elderly lady nodded, levered herself off the railing and ambled away in the direction from whence she came. I couldn't make head nor tail of it – who she was or why she came to speak to me – but she'd wasted enough of my time with her goodwill and history lessons and I set off furiously west.

I followed the Seneca River for a couple of miles. The town never quite managed to disappear – just as it had nearly faded away into fields and open space, neighbouring Waterloo began its own slow development from suburb to downtown. Here was another pretty town, named, although I'm not sure why, after its Belgian counterpart where Napoleon was famously defeated.

I pedalled past quaint buildings from the early 1800s – a two-storey red-brick house sporting Doric columns out front; a Presbyterian church with soaring spires and large rose window; a terracotta Queen-Anne-style library. These buildings to me felt so uniquely American, although of course the styles were borrowed from much older European architecture. There is an essence though, perhaps ethereal, that makes them feel so distinct out here. Perhaps it is the trimmings – the US mailbox out front, the large sidewalks, the perfect manner in which the lawn is kept. I couldn't quite put my finger on what it was but it pleased me immensely. I was so enamoured, in fact, that I didn't mind when an elderly gent offered to show me the William H. Burton House ('Home of Memorial Day!').

'Memorial Day, there's a lot of history around here, eh?' I said.

'Oh yes, we got a lot of industry here too – pianos, organs, wooden goods, wagons, plenty of that sorta thing.'

'So, eh, what about women's rights, eh? 1848, wasn't it?' I asked, eager to show off my knowledge. God knows I'd earned it the hard way.

'Nope,' he said.

'Oh, but I thought…'

'You'll have to go back to Seneca Falls if you want to hear about that sorta thing. Now, this here is the Memorial Day museum…'

The Memorial Day Museum was, I admit, presumably interesting to some, but again the true relevance passed me by. What was important was that the festival was now celebrated on 30 May, and in the USA is typically seen as a harbinger of summer. A couple of times on the road I'd been told that a certain gravel track, path or even local store wouldn't be open until after Memorial Day. Now the date wasn't far off – just a few short weeks. After a winter in New York colder than any I'd known before, I was ready for the high sun and the long days. A summer riding my bicycle across America – what a thing to do.

* * *

When 'at home' in England, and by that I mean the location where I slept and kept my belongings, most days blended into one. One day in a job I didn't enjoy morphed very much into the next. Every night in the same soft bed. Comfortably numb. For two years I lived in the same room in Canterbury and I can recall just a small handful of memories from within its walls. There were good times, of course, but the predictability was stifling. I felt like there was so much more to know and see and do. Now, on the road, each day took on a unique story arc etching itself into my grey matter.

The nights too would stay with me for many years to come; each in a different place, the result of whatever fortune or misfortune befell me in the twilight hours of the day. 'Home' now was a concept split in two. My family home was, and always would be, a place that I held dear. The combination of people I loved and formative steps taken in life there assured that. But other places that I had lived – Canterbury, London, New York – these were now just places where once I laid my head. The second strand of home to me at this point was centred around Lola, my tent, and the ever-changeable face of the road.

I spent a night near the town of Phelps with a family who saw me trundling along Route 96 at sunset and insisted I come to stay. Mary kept calling me a 'daredevil' while her son Rob, a keen cyclist, made sure I had everything I could possibly want after a long day's ride. They were sweet and I was amused to be seen as such a wild thing. I'd entered into this journey having read Ernest Shackleton and Robert Falcon Scott; Thesiger and Hillary and Cousteau. I'd devoured travel literature from all eras. I'd also read of contemporary adventurers who'd crossed continents by bicycle and had pedalled through some of the most extreme places on earth. I certainly did not see myself as a daredevil for my amble across the USA.

Relativity, though, is key. Mary had never read of Ernest Shackleton or Wilfred Thesiger. Even if I'd told her about them, their journeys were too big to contemplate. Here in front of her, however, was someone who was interacting with her stable, safe, unchanging world, and screwing around with it by pedalling a bicycle over unheard-of distances. Doing extraordinary things to the ordinary environment. When I told her I slept in a tent in a field she just about flipped out with excitement. Later she asked me what I deemed to be the most extreme thing I'd done. 'I guess that's quite easy to answer. Stepping out my front door in New York and knowing I couldn't, and wouldn't, come back.'

CHAPTER 13

SUSIE FROM THE SOLOMON ISLANDS

Near the end of my second week of cycling I reached Lima, a small and unremarkable tree-lined town in northern New York. New York, I was discovering, is a vast and sprawling state that takes up a huge portion of the north-eastern USA. It is bordered by five other states and boasts around twenty million inhabitants, nearly half of whom live in New York City. This makes it the third most populous state in the USA. Like most foreigners to the Eastern Seaboard (and even many Americans from further west), I had no idea that you could travel over four hundred miles north-east from Manhattan, all the way to the border with Canada, and still be in the Empire State.

With that much space and so many people, it shouldn't have seemed unusual to me, then, that I made a friend. It was the manner that surprised me most of all, I suppose, as it began virtually. Through an online blog that I'd begun to write about my trip, I'd been encouraged by a couple of readers to take a foray into the world of specialist cycling forums. Most seemed full of bike geeks talking about gear ratios and bearing-size preferences, but there were a couple that I could understand.

Through one of these, my blog had come to the attention of an Australian girl called Susie and we exchanged a few emails. In one of those curious coincidences that travel bestows, she was just a few miles south of me in New York State. She was also riding a bicycle.

I arrived at our arranged meeting point a little late and found her sitting under a tree, writing in a home-made journal. Blond dreadlocks hung over her eyes as she stared at the pages in concentration. Her skin betrayed many years of rich exposure to the sun and on her left arm was tied a faded length of coloured string. A seasoned traveller. She looked also like she'd walked straight out of a 1960s flower-power commune. When she glanced up her eyes radiated warmth and enthusiasm and she greeted me with a firm hug.

Susie had been born on the archipelago of the Solomon Islands, raised in Australia. After college in Melbourne she had set off on a series of adventures: pedalling across Europe on a single-speed bicycle, working on boats in the Mediterranean, sailing across the Atlantic. It was this latest journey that had brought her to the eastern coast of the USA, and she soon found her way to New York City to look for inspiration. That came in the form of Cody, a vintage Raleigh touring bike that she fell in love with in a bike co-op. A few hundred dollars later and Susie and Cody were on the road, headed, vaguely, for San Francisco.

We rode due west in tandem, cresting endless hills with abandon during the day and spending the nights in some of the small but regular state parks that bordered the road. Little pockets of government-funded countryside – step through the gate and into an ancient woodland. I loved them as an antidote to the road. It struck me as sad, though, that nature was now so controlled. These were all that was left of the real backcountry – organised wilderness.

At Darien Lake we left our bikes by the treeline and found respite from the heat of the day by paddling along Ellicott Creek. It was only a couple of feet deep, with water so clear you could see the timeless rocks lined up below.

I couldn't have been more impressed with Susie's attitude and approach to bike touring. She carried barely a quarter of what I housed on my bicycle and saw little need for anything else. Riding with her I found my insecurities and mental wanderings disappeared, shooed away by her utter enthusiasm for the life we had chosen.

'You haven't been in a car in how long?' I exclaimed.

'Well, I'm not totally sure, but probably about a year. There's just no need. And it would be silly if I went around telling everyone to use bicycles and sailboats and then took a ride in a car every time I was stuck. I used to hitchhike quite a bit... and I will do again, I don't have a problem with that. But I just feel like most people don't think about what they're doing to the world. How many cars pass us on this road with just one person inside? It's not like I'm judging... but I feel like it's a super-important issue that not enough people are thinking about. I love this world, and I don't have any intention of helping to destroy it, y'know?'

Susie told me of Issac, a character she referred to as her 'lover'. ('I don't like boyfriend, that sounds childish. Partner sounds like a business thing. We're in love, so he's my lover. It makes perfect sense!') He was into his fourth year of pedalling around the world, eschewing motorised transport of any sort; including ocean crossings that was quite an undertaking. They had fallen in love in Europe before he set off and now didn't know when they'd next be reunited – neither would fly to see the other as it went against everything they believed in. She said they'd meet up somewhere before too long, when it was right and they'd both gotten there under their own steam. He was currently in North Africa and they spoke very infrequently, relying only on emails back and forth to keep each other close.

I thought, inevitably, now of my own 'lover' (I couldn't quite get comfortable with the term; I was too British for such abandon) left behind in England. Clare and I had been together for two years before I left. I was in love, at least I had thought so – it was a new emotion for me. It felt like what I thought love might be though – Clare was a beautiful, smiling, talented girl who made me happy with everything she did. Yet it still wasn't enough to help me shake the desire to head off on this journey, and for that I carried a great deal of guilt. I felt pulled violently in two very opposing directions.

Clare was training to be a teacher, a life now so entirely different from mine that I struggled to reconcile my feelings. There was such love there, but at a distance of five thousand miles it was very hard to feel it burning and alive. There was a lot more road to travel before we would see each other again, if we were to see each other again. It briefly occurred to me I hadn't yet dealt particularly well with the loneliness of travelling solo, and that perhaps I was learning something about happiness being 'only real when shared', to borrow the words of Christopher McCandless.

I'd survived the first weeks on my own, sure, but I had hardly thrived. Now that I had Susie for company I was noticeably cheerier and could feel a spike in my confidence. There's a lot to be said for facing challenges alone, for only then do we truly know what we are capable of, but to share joys and fears, hopes and disappointments with someone else – that seemed now to be a remarkably special thing. I was torn between feeling the need to push ever onwards on my own in a kind of rite of passage, or trial, and on the flip side listening to my intuition which said that I operated better with some companionship. Too much of this thinking led inevitably to a dull ache for the life and girl I left behind, so I reverted to my previous state of denial, pushed Clare from my mind once more, and rode on.

CHAPTER 14

THE FALLS

Susie and I pedalled into the city of Buffalo, New York, groggy after a poor night's sleep under rainy skies. Grey clouds streaked overhead as we sat on a verge in the suburbs eating a breakfast of granola and milk powder. I'd given up on porridge, as no matter how hard I tried, it always stuck to the bottom of the pan.

Ahead the city proper began. Here was a place that had really been hit hard by the financial recession – coming in from the east the road was atrocious, cracked every which way, sporting potholes big enough to swallow a man whole. Building facades hinted at a better time but now lay derelict, graffiti their only companion. For a few blocks it seemed we saw no one at all. Apocalyptic decay lay thick all around.

Towards the centre was some sign of life again, and I followed my nose to the house of my host. I'd found Freddy via the 'Couchsurfing' website – the latest tentacle of the Internet age to take hold of my journey. Couchsurfing is an online social network where people post a profile offering information on themselves and, crucially, whether or not they have anywhere to put up travellers passing through for a night or two. Susie had extensive experience, she knew all the tricks, but I was pretty new to the concept.

Freddy, a jolly, round fellow, worked as a flight attendant for a national airline and when he wasn't flying around the country he lived here in the most enormous house with more rooms than I could count. 'Recession's screwed up a lot of things, but there are some benefits for those of us still here. Rent is about as cheap as anywhere in the country.' Too right – for this mansion he was paying about half of what I leaked away for a windowless box in New York City.

He was keen to show me his town. My first impressions of decay were accurate, the place reeked of it, but there was still a certain charm to Buffalo. Like a phoenix rising from the ashes, the community had worked hard on the upkeep of some splendid parks and the centre shone brightly with a buzz of activity.

'See that building over there?' asked Freddy. I looked to my right as we drove north. A dark stoned fortress stood in the distance, ringed in behind a grey stone wall. Turrets and crenellations graced the top. Wooden boards filled every window.

'That was the basis for Arkham Asylum in the Batman stories. Know where Gotham City is based on?' he continued. It seemed like a loaded question, but I answered in good faith.

'New York City?'

'Nope! That's what everyone thinks. It was actually right here: Buffalo. And that building right there is one of the reasons why.'

I spent three days in Gotham City. Freddy was flying to LA for work, but happily left me with his keys. I was surprised at how trusting he was but Susie told me that many couchsurfing hosts took this relaxed approach. That seemed like a nice community to be part of. I hoped no one took advantage of it.

Susie and I wandered the streets looking for cheap coffee shops and second-hand bookstores and made plans for onward travel. We were both planning to cross the border into Canada and it seemed to make sense to keep riding together.

Her endlessly positive attitude helped me to avoid slipping too far inside my own psyche as I'd begun to do during the first weeks of my ride. More than that I was just enjoying the regular dialogue with a friend. Fleeting exchanges left me feeling empty after a while and although Lola was great, a steel (or rather, chromoly) bicycle only has so much conversational ability.

* * *

We wound north-west out of the sprawl. The border point we were headed for, right by the colossal Niagara Falls, is arguably the most spectacular of all the crossings in the five thousand plus miles that separate the USA and Canada. Both Susie and I were excited to see the falls but I couldn't shake a feeling of discomfort over visas and passports.

My American visa was now just a few days from its expiry date. I'd applied for a six-month extension before I left New York and rather casually assumed that this would definitely be granted. In Buffalo I had called up my old room-mate in Brooklyn to see if anything had arrived for me. Chase told me that yes, a letter from the US government had arrived, but he'd forgotten to call me. He couldn't open it for me at that moment as he'd got drunk and locked himself out on the balcony. He promised to phone me with details of the contents once he got back inside. When I rang back later that night he was on an overnight bus to New Orleans and had forgotten again.

Eventually Marie, my other old room-mate, was able to open the letter and give me a tracking code. I punched it in on the immigration website and... hey presto! I had been accepted for an additional six months. At the time I was hugely relieved, so much so that I promptly forgot all about it. Now, as I pedalled towards the border, I began to worry about the small details. I'd been instructed to tear off part of my original visa to post with my application for an extension, and its replacement was in an envelope in Brooklyn. This didn't seem like a big deal to me, but I wasn't sure the US immigration department would see it like that.

The road to the falls was suitably miserable. When we finally arrived the whole area felt like the world's biggest car park. Pushing through endless busloads of tourists I was surprised to somewhat suddenly find myself face to face with a small metal fence and, beyond, a three-hundred-metre drop. Standing by the precipice I could see ahead the Horseshoe Falls, and below and to my right the air was thick with a permanent mist from the cascade of the American and Bridal Veil Falls further along.

'Niagara Falls' is the collective name given to these mighty waterfalls, of which Horseshoe is the largest of the three and the most powerful in North America. The Horseshoe Falls belong to Canada (the small, permanently soggy and uninhabited 'Goat Island' which lies on the river below marks the international boundary), while the American and Bridal Veil Falls sit on the US side.

'Make sure you head over and see it from Canada as well, it'll blow your mind!'

I was being addressed by a large man with an even larger wife, who were wearing matching polo shirts and leaning their considerable combined weight on the fence beside me. An image of the fence giving way and the poor fellow flying headfirst into the heart of the falls flashed through my mind. That would definitely be a good way to go.

'It's pretty impressive from here too... I've never seen any waterfalls this big before,' I answered.

'Oh this is nothing, they're even bigger from over there! A hundred thousand cubic feet of water per second, can you believe that?'

I was pretty sure that the falls weren't actually any bigger when seen from the Canadian side, as that would be against the laws of physics, but I could see this man's heart was in the right place. I'd been warned that there was a competitive nature between the twin cities of Niagara as to which claimed the better vistas and the general consensus seemed to agree with my new friend that Canada had the edge.

Susie and I proceeded along the walkway, revelling in the damp mist from the falls as the sun took residence directly above us. I loved how open people had been so far on the ride. Perhaps it was due in part to my travelling on a bicycle and the vulnerability that is associated with that, but it was true that all along my journey to Niagara locals and (American) tourists alike had stopped to take the time to chat to me. Often they wanted to expound views on whatever their chosen topic of conversation was, but I liked that. In the UK it's rare that people will talk to strangers on the whole. It's even more unlikely that they will air a strong opinion about something, usually out of misguided reservation. I fall into this category far too easily. It was a breath of fresh air to have people approach me and tell me unequivocally how they felt about something without a care in the world what I might think of their opinions. I knew there could be a downside to this philosophy too, but so far I'd stayed clear of anyone racist, xenophobic or with otherwise questionable ethics.

The border post was suitably grey and imposing and instantly sucked the beauty from the nearby falls. We left our bikes outside and walked in grubby clothes through the numerous scanners and other machinery that is used to distinguish between acceptable and unacceptable human beings. An extremely unpleasant man asked me a lot of questions about what I was doing and didn't seem to listen to any of the answers. He told me that my internship was illegal and that Susie and I were lucky to have arrived at this border crossing; bicycles weren't allowed at any of the others. I told him we came here for that very reason, but he'd already started his next line of questioning. My visa was invalid, he said, without the piece of paper that had been mailed to Brooklyn, and the list of accusations continued for at least ten minutes before finally he stamped me out of the country and turned his back, question marks still hanging over the multiple apparent indiscretions.

Susie and I left quickly and walked our bikes to the Canadian border, where we were quickly and efficiently issued a thirty-day visa and no questions were asked. I calmly pushed my bike out of the office and down the road until I was out of sight.

'YES!'

I still had to get back into the USA in a few weeks but that was a bridge I could cross then. A new country lay ahead; one so similar to America, yet with enough nuanced differences to make it feel a universe away. The midday heat abated slightly and Susie and I stood by a smooth, quiet minor road which we were told would wind its way along the Niagara River all the way to the banks of Lake Ontario. I jumped back onto Lola and we rode north, with me cathartically releasing pent-up stress through each pedal stroke. I left my fears and worries with the hard-ass at the US border post and readied myself for Canada.

CHAPTER 15

O CANADA

The province of Ontario is the most populous in all of Canada. The southern part, which Susie and I now entered, is dominated by Lake Ontario, one of the five 'Great Lakes'. Pedalling west along its southern shore I felt for all the world as though I were looking upon an ocean. The water lapped at a shingle beach and the horizon was an ethereal blur of lake and sky blues mixing together, as if skillfully blended in an artist's pallet.

Susie wanted to stop for a swim so we left our bikes under a tulip tree and ambled onto the shore. The pebbles were smooth and slimy underfoot, and on closer inspection were covered in thick black sludge. The nearer the water we got the worse it was, and now from just a few feet away I saw that the gentle waves which glistened so beautifully as they broke in rows under the afternoon sun were, in fact, the colour of sewage water. It was like opening a classy box of chocolates to find inside only slugs and mud.

I now looked along the shoreline and realised why there was no one else coming to the water. It was disgusting. For once there wasn't a local resident close by to fill in the gaps in my knowledge, but I could have a pretty decent guess on my own. The cities of Hamilton, Burlington and Toronto all sit on the banks of Lake Ontario, not far from where I was standing. It seemed clear that industry run-off was to blame for the pollution here; I would later be told that the area around Hamilton Harbour was the dirtiest in the whole body of water, boasting floating needles and condoms to supplement the chemicals, and the only reason the entire thing wasn't a complete cesspool was because it is just such an enormously vast lake (the fourteenth largest in the world), which helps disperse the bacteria. Nevertheless, the fact that this is the source of most of southern Ontario's drinking water is a little disconcerting.

On the road to Hamilton we were waved down by a passing cyclist, who had sped past on his unloaded mountain bike before pausing to catch our attention. Jonathan was a college student, not long out of high school, and much to my delight also an amateur magician. He had spent the previous summer touring around Europe in a beaten-up car with some pals performing street magic for holiday funds.

'I'd love to do what you guys are doing. How long did it take you to train for this?'

'We didn't,' Susie answered definitively. 'At least, not specifically. You get fit as you go. All you need to train is your mindset – get yourself a positive and open attitude, and you're good to go.'

'Do you think it would be possible to carry a bunch of props and tricks and stuff on the back, or would that be too heavy?'

'Have you *seen* how much crap Leon has on there?' Susie laughed. 'You can pretty much carry anything you want on a bicycle. And doing a bicycle-powered magic tour would be bloomin' cool.'

Jonathan was beaming from ear to ear by the time we reached his junction at a quiet spot just south of the suburbs. One of the great privileges of bicycle touring, I was learning, was becoming an automatic inspiration for anyone else who felt the tug of wanderlust constantly at their sleeve. I looked like a complete amateur, with my overloaded bicycle and trailer and inadequate clothes. And Susie was a *girl* (ironic that people would assume her the bigger liability because of gender, when in fact she was a much more competent adventurer than I was). Between us we were an unlikely pair, which was even more encouraging to those who harboured hopes of future travel and escape. Jonathan, I could tell, had just had an idea planted in his head and would spend many pleasant hours dreaming it into fruition.

As a gift to us, he provided entertainment while we ate our lunch of peanut butter sandwiches. With no props to speak of he still managed to pull off some quite impressive tricks, the best of which was balancing the mountain bike on his forehead, and later his chin. It wasn't magic, but then neither is hiding cards up your sleeve or stuffing rabbits down your trousers. When Susie and I set off again, I thought about what it would be like to impress people with magic tricks when I passed by on my bicycle. My only trick to speak of was a rather impressive dismount over the handlebars once in a while, but unfortunately I could never predict when that was going to happen.

CHAPTER 16

DOWN IN THE DUMPS

My time in Ontario was characterised by enjoyable riding, easy conversation and an unexpected pining for Northern Ireland. The landscape in rural parts of the province reminded me more than anywhere I'd seen so far of my family home. Undulating fields of wine-bottle green rolled out in every direction and herds of cattle looked up between mouthfuls of grass as we pedalled past. I was sure they mooed in a Northern Irish accent.

The people we met seemed, for the most part, to live a simple and fulfilled lifestyle in the outdoors. At gas stations farmers would come and chat with us in a casual, colloquial manner. They seemed more unassuming than their American counterparts; perhaps a little shyer, less opinionated.

'The countryside is full of good people,' I'd been told about the Canadian country folk (albeit by a Canadian). Simple, honest men and women living good and working hard. They said similar things about the folks in Northern Ireland, and it was this that I now dwelt upon.

The oddity of all this was that I had never before felt a real affinity to or longing for the land of my birth. It was beautiful, I appreciated that, but when I was seventeen I'd been only too glad to get out as quickly as possible. Since then I'd only ever gone back for short visits and never wanted any more. Now I romanticised every little thing – the accents, the conventions of conversation. (How are ye? Lovely/Miserable wee day, isn't it? And how's your brother/mother/father/child/dog? Right ye are then, I'll be off. Keep 'er lit!)

Perhaps most of all, I missed the sense of *fitting in* without having to try. All I had to do when I was there was amp up the regional accent a bit and I felt right at home. It was symptomatic, I supposed, of the hard work of pedalling, the stresses of the road and the constant, fleeting interactions when travelling long distances by bicycle. Had I really wanted to get to know a community and its people anywhere along my route, I could always have stopped for a week or more. The lure of the road, however, was always too strong; more powerful by far than my brief bouts of homesickness. Equally, I quite enjoyed wallowing for a bit – allowing temporary misery to take hold so that I could rise out of it again in full glory with a renewed lust for my adventure.

* * *

In our efforts to get across the province, Susie and I first went north through the major cities on the banks of the lake before we cut west. Hamilton was dire – a dull and grey city with cracked streets – although full of pleasant people who waved as we passed. Toronto was another matter entirely. Approaching along the shoreline we were treated to a panoramic view of the skyline, dominated by the CN Tower with a host of smaller buildings nestled around forming a platform to the sky. On the day we arrived the city was bathed in a glorious afternoon light, and we cycled slowly under the shade of red oak trees. The great lake lapped onto a stony beach, combining with birdsong to give us a soundtrack. This seemed a heck of a place.

I couchsurfed again, this time with a filmmaker who immediately upon meeting me departed for a work trip to Ottawa. Before she left she handed me her keys. I could get used to this. ('Hi, lovely to meet you! I'm off, as it happens. Here's the keys – beers in the fridge, food in the cupboard. Have a nice time and don't set fire to anything!')

Susie stayed with some members of a cycling co-operative, and in the evening I met them in Koreatown for a ride around the city. Matt and Friel were both recent graduates, very active in the environmentally conscious scene in Toronto. They rode bikes everywhere to avoid using gasoline and oil, and their co-op organised food and shelter for groups of like-minded people. Susie was a kindred spirit and the three chatted enthusiastically about the woes of the world. I agreed, for the most part, but felt a little uninitiated in the ways of the uber-green. However, by riding a bicycle I was accepted and so I pedalled along behind, a fringe member of the club.

'I'm hungry, man,' shouted Friel as we sped through downtown.

'Yea me too – you guys want to get some food?' Matt asked. Susie and I nodded enthusiastically. I couldn't remember the last time food wasn't on the agenda. I hoped we wouldn't end up somewhere expensive.

We rode off the main drag and onto a small street that ran parallel. In stark contrast to the bright lights and traffic of the strip this was dimly lit, a few shadowy figures in the distance our only company. The main-street stores backed onto this access road and the air was thick with the stench of dumpsters.

Matt and Friel hopped off their bikes and walked over to the bins. Helping one another up they jumped on top and lifted the curved metal lid.

'Sweet man, check this out!' Matt lifted out a bunch of bananas, quickly followed by a crate of tomatoes.

'Dammit, I think we're too early for the sandwiches. Here's some couscous though.'

Susie jumped up to join them, and together they uncovered a mound of edible food from amongst the black trash bags.

'This is the dumpster diving I was telling you about!' squealed Susie in excitement. A few days previous she'd been waxing lyrical about how she found food in New York City by going through the trash of restaurants and supermarkets after they closed, and promised to show me sometime.

'They throw out anything that says it's past its expiry date.'

'Or anything that's just left over when they close up,' added Matt.

'Do you guys do this every night?' I asked.

'Mostly, yea,' answered Friel. 'It's a good way to save money, but more'n that it's our way of trying to reduce the wastefulness of this city. We try to gather as much as we can and take it back to the co-op. Sometimes we load it onto our bikes and hand stuff out to homeless folk around town.'

'What do the cops think of all this?' I asked. Susie had told me that in New York they had to be watchful for the police who were under orders to break up any dumpster-diving activities.

'It depends,' said Friel. 'Basically, it's illegal, and there're a few hard-ass cops who will try'n bust us. We haven't been caught yet but they've chased us all over town. There're some others that turn a blind eye. I think they know what it's all about. Most folk who just walk past assume we're living on the street. Some are too scared to question us and some yell at us for making a mess. A few come to ask what we're up to. Generally they're pretty surprised at all the stuff we find in here. Anyone with a brain can see it's a huge waste – it's bad enough packing all this stuff in plastic in the first place, but then to just chuck it out to rot because no one has bought it... well, I think that's the criminal act, man, not what we're doing.'

We cycled to a park where we ate some packaged tabouleh and gorged on fruit. After, Susie and her hosts headed back to the co-operative headquarters and I pedalled home alone through Toronto. On the way I stopped at a supermarket and bought a $2 pre-packaged pizza, which I went home and put in the oven in the house that I was now in charge of. I had huge admiration for people like Matt and Friel and Susie. Their drive to change the world was inspiring. It was true too that I got a kick out of travelling by human power, but I also felt much more apathetic than them; I wasn't yet prepared to change my whole way of living. Hanging out with Susie made me feel a little guilty about this. But I was hungry, and tired, so I ate my pizza and chucked the plastic wrapping in the bin. Then I fell asleep in front of the TV, lights burning and heating running. I had a long way to go.

* * *

Susie and I rode out of Toronto together, both figuring that we were enjoying the company too much to separate just yet. I had many more lonesome miles ahead, best to keep company while I could.

West of Toronto was rural once again, and as rain settled in for the long haul we had days of damp cycling through farmland. Some nights we were invited in to stay at isolated homesteads along the back roads. The invite usually came with the promise of a warm dinner and we never refused. The rest of the time we pitched our tents under whatever cover we could find.

I slept more deeply in those first few weeks of cycling than ever before in my life. By this stage I had ridden somewhere in the region of eight or nine hundred miles. My body was beginning to get used to it and I no longer endured cramps in my thighs, or stiff hips in the morning. I'd learned the importance of keeping regularly hydrated, even when I didn't feel thirsty, and consequently I no longer suffered from headaches. My back knew now to mould to the ground upon which I lay each night and not to complain or be expectant of a springy mattress. My neck accepted that the only pillow available was a solitary spare T-shirt. The process was beginning to feel natural. The things we need to survive and thrive are extremely minimal.

There was a reasonable amount of unpleasantness, of course. Cold, wet nights and cold, wet mornings; hunkering over a camping stove boiling pasta while the wind whipped down my back. I remembered Susie telling Jonathan, the cycling magician, that cycle touring is 'about two-thirds miserable, and a third endurable. In that last third there's also a bit of enjoyment too!' This was just about bang on – much of each day was spent bored, or tired, or suffering from whichever of the elements seemed to be too extreme at that moment. Yet each evening I felt a deep-set contentment; a sense of achievement. The reward I craved was just the very act of being a little further down the road in a spot I'd never been.

Every day had a clear aim and a challenging but reachable goal. When I settled down at night under shelter and took a sip of Irish whiskey from my hip flask, I couldn't imagine anywhere I'd rather be or anything else I'd want to be doing.

The city of Sarnia was to be our final stopping point before Susie and I headed back into the USA, and from there I planned to stick to the American side of the border until I hit the west coast. This was the last I'd see of Canada for quite some time.

CHAPTER 17

THE SEAT BY THE DOOR

A pretty port city, Sarnia sits at the southernmost tip of the mammoth Lake Huron. Riding through the downtown area we passed by the waterfront where folks busied themselves walking or jogging along the towpath, and 'salties' (one of the types of Great Lake freighters) idled in the deep water offshore. There was nothing special about the place, except that it was clean, the streets wide and everything seemed to be at a happy slant going up or down a hill.

As with the previous international border at Niagara, this one too was signalled by a bridge. On the Canadian side we were stamped out merrily ('Have a good time, now, I sure hope you enjoyed Ontario!') and told to wait by the roadside for a truck that would transport us over the river. A cheery female immigration official informed us that 'it's a freeway bridge, see, and bicycles aren't allowed on it at all. I'm sorry, but that's how it is, you'll have to take this ride.'

I was slightly disappointed to be forced into motorised transport, placing a blemish on my hitherto unbroken line of cycling, but I wasn't pedantic enough to argue fruitlessly over a 200-metre stretch in a truck. The truck arrived, our bikes loaded on, and we were deposited by the US border station. As our ride drove back to Canada, so began one of the most frustrating experiences of my life to date.

It started out OK, Susie going first to the desk and answering the questions in a polite and calm way. She'd been anxious as her visa only had a month left to run and, with no proof of onward travel out of the country (because she had no idea what she would be doing next), there was a chance they might suspect her of planning to disappear permanently, *sans* visa, into the world of illegal immigrant workers. But she smiled sweetly and fluttered her eyelids and was stamped into the USA after just a few moments. One of the (many) benefits of being pretty and blonde and female.

I was next and from the get-go it was clear that Rankin, my Border Official for the day, didn't like me. He was late twenties, early thirties at most, with a cropped GI Joe haircut and a hard angular face. A pair of slightly-too-narrow spectacles were jammed onto his nose, and he fiddled with them regularly as if annoyed that they were there. He took my passport without saying a word and I began to wish I'd changed into my slightly less smelly (and less stained) T-shirt. I smiled sweetly and fluttered my eyelids.

'Where's your I-94 form?'

'I sent it off to get an extension, which was granted, but I don't have the new...'

He cut me off. 'It should be here. This isn't valid without an I-94.'

'I realise that, but I had to send it off to apply for an extension...'

He interrupted again. 'You shouldn't have touched it. And you can't apply for extensions to this type of visa. Were you working illegally in the USA before you went to Canada?'

'What? No! I was doing an internship in New York, eh... for six months. But it was unpaid, it wasn't work. I cleared that with, erm... the people on the phone. And they said it was fine. And then I wanted to get this extension...'

'It's illegal to undertake an internship on a B2 tourist visa. You're in violation of the terms of your stay. And you've tampered with government property. There's no way you're going anywhere. Take a seat by the door over there and someone will come and talk to you.' He paused. 'And don't try to leave.'

I sat down in a daze. Susie had stood quietly in the background but now came to sit beside me. 'I don't understand!' I told her. 'Everything's in order. If this guy would just listen to me for a second...'

'Don't get frustrated. It'll make them suspect you more. You know it's all in order, right? So just wait it out. Keep calm.'

That was good advice. I suggested that she should go sit outside with her bike in case they changed their mind about letting her through so easily. Once she had gone, I tried to formulate my spiel so that it was clear and concise.

'Were you two hitchhiking?' Rankin was back.

'What? With a bike like that... are you kidding?' I thought of my overloaded bike – bulging panniers overflowing front and rear, clunky trailer hanging off the back – and tried to imagine the fiasco that it would cause if I tried loading it into someone's car. Hitching a ride with Lola would have been an extremely involved and near-impossible task. 'No, we're not hitchhiking... we're riding bicycles!' *Calm. Reserved.*

'Guy out front says you came in a truck. It's illegal to hitchhike here. We'll have to report that.'

It was clear to me now that this man was a complete jackass.

'We got a ride across the bridge because bikes aren't allowed on it. But it was all above board – Canada organised the truck. The driver works for them. Call over to their side and they'll tell you.'

'That's not what we heard. Guy out front says you arrived in an unmarked truck. Nothing to do with Canada.' He went back into the office and I was alone once more.

Over the next three hours Rankin paid regular visits to inform me of new and terrible things that I'd done, all of which were illegal. Some friends joined him and together four officials berated me. I was moved to an interview room; a windowless silver cell where I sat on one side of a wooden desk opposite three new clean-cut border employees. It was explained at the outset that I shouldn't speak until asked a direct question. It was just like being back at school, except that when I *was* asked a direct question here, I was interrupted before I could answer fully. *All jolly frustrating*, I thought, trying to keep spirits high. Eventually I was moved back to the main office. A further three hours passed without visitors and I was beginning to wonder if they'd forgotten about me. The doors were locked and I was getting very hungry and thirsty.

Finally Rankin reappeared. Before I could ask him for some water he said: 'We're enquiring now as to whether Canada will allow you to re-enter. Otherwise we'll begin the process for deportation to Ireland.'

Deportation. I couldn't quite believe this was happening. Having ridden my luck so far on this journey it now seemed I'd struck out and was going to be sent back to Ireland, just a few short weeks into my 'Big Adventure'. It was all too much. I felt a deep sickening feeling boring its way through me, like a foot pressing down on my ribs.

I also had a pounding headache from the dehydration; I'd pedalled twenty miles that morning under an early-summer sun and now hadn't drunk anything in nearly seven hours. I desperately needed to use the toilet. I considered urinating in the flowerpot in the corner of the room, but accepted that that probably wouldn't help Irish-American relationships here.

Ten minutes later, Rankin returned again and this time he had a very impressive-looking man at his shoulder; tall as a ten-storey building, broad and with a large amount of extra items attached to his perfectly turned-out uniform. Combined with his peaked hat, it was clear that he was of a higher rank than anyone I'd met so far.

'Tell me a story,' was all he said. So I did. I told him how I'd applied for an extension, and how I hadn't been able to put the new slip in my passport because the letter was in Brooklyn, and that I was terribly sorry for that but that I had the tracking code right there in my pocket and if they wouldn't mind logging onto the US Immigration website then I could show them the proof.

He took my slip of paper with the tracking code and went into the back office. Rankin and I stood and stared at each other with mutual disdain. Less than five minutes later The Boss came back out.

'This is all in order. You should've made sure to get that letter forwarded on to you.'

'I know. I'm sorry,' I replied.

'We can print you off a new I-60 form here, same as the one that was in that letter. It'll cost six dollars.'

I gave him six bucks and he pasted the new form, about the size of a business card, into my passport. He stamped it and into the 'Expiry' box wrote a date exactly six months away.

'Have a good journey.'

He walked back into the office, but Rankin remained, staring at me all the way out the door. I was through with him now. I found Susie under a tree a little way down the road, asleep on her camping mat. When she woke we hugged and whooped. 'But… how?' she asked.

'I dunno,' I said, 'but right now I don't care. Let's get the hell away from here as quickly as possible!'

Eight hours after arriving at US Border Control we got on our bikes and pedalled off into Michigan, the fourth US state of my journey. I'd come through the closest shave yet, and from a source I hadn't expected to cause problems anywhere near this serious. Almost everything I'd stressed out about so far had turned out fine, and occasionally those things I assumed would be fine caused varying degrees of stress. The lesson, Susie said, was to try not to worry about anything and just enjoy the ride. That seemed good to me.

CHAPTER 18

THE GREAT LAKES STATE

It's a shame the extent to which I quickly developed a hatred for Michigan, considering how much I like saying the name. Port Huron, on the US side of the border, was a ghost town, spectres of a better time hanging over the derelict buildings. The areas of it that I saw were nothing short of a ghetto – cracked and unpaved roads, run-down semi-collapsed housing and a dearth of people anywhere to be seen on the street.

This absence of pedestrians was more than made up for by the number of cars. Twice Susie and I found ourselves inadvertently directed onto an expressway, then upon our attempted escape from town we hit rush-hour traffic. An extremely large lady squeezed into a regular-sized car yelled at me to get on the 'sidewalk'. In the UK we call it the pavement, of course, but the American terminology means it should be even clearer to all involved that this particular allocated section of paved ground is a place at the side of the road for people to *walk* on. *SideWALK, it's not for bicycles, you moron!* I thought all this quietly while trying to avoid getting run over. It felt like every single passing driver was beeping a horn or yelling obscenities. There was no hard shoulder to speak of and even the sidewalk ran out. Susie and I were remaining uninjured by the grace of God alone.

'F*ck off back to your f*cking hippy commune and stop f*cking up my drive home!'

Our accuser was now a very attractive woman of middle age in a red SUV. Her face was nothing short of angelic but she had a voice that could've curdled milk. In Ireland we call it a goul (pronounced 'gow-uul') when someone shouts and their voice drops a couple of octaves to take on demonic overtones and makes everyone around panic (even the innocent). This lady was a pro at gouling. She revved past me and shouted something else that I couldn't hear over the revs of her engine. Naturally I flicked her the V and thought nothing more of it.

Five minutes later at a backed-up junction Susie and I pedalled past all of the cars that had just overtaken us. Our fiendish friend in her red gas-guzzler was there and quite apoplectic with rage that we had overtaken. When the lights changed she gunned past me, then slowed and drove diagonally in front of my path. I had to break hard and steer into the verge. My front wheel bounced over it and the bike crumpled in a heap behind. I had been moving slow enough to jump off before I was dumped off, and quickly I dragged Lola behind me so that none of the cars following would run her over. A dainty hand thrust out the window of the SUV, pretty middle finger extended, and the beast was gone. Lola was fine and so was I, physically, but inside I was burning up.

On a steep residential street a large dog bounded out of a driveway and chased me uphill. Susie, lighter and faster as always, watched from the top of the road, tears of laughter running down her cheeks as I trundled towards her. My legs burned as I tried to power my behemoth of a bike up the gradient and win the race. 'Piss off, you furry b*stard!' I shouted in fury. Shouting at animals is not one of my regular pastimes but I learned now it could be extremely cathartic.

Outside the city limits conditions weren't much better. For the next few days Susie and I had to contend with more bad roads and insolent drivers. 'Everyone here is a dick!' shouted Susie as we rode in single file along a busy narrow through-road. I couldn't disagree. Even the animals were assholes.

By the third day in Michigan, morale was at an all-time low. We tried to find alternative routes but ended up taking a 15-mile detour down a gravel path that ended in the field of an angry farmer. ('You go ride on your own darn field, freeloaders!') Was there no one pleasant in this damned state? Perhaps anyone with a hint of personable civility is banished at a young age (to Canada, perhaps?) and everyone else is trained in the way of just becoming utterly contemptible.

Susie and I complained to each other as we rode, and I longed for the ease and hospitality so prevalent in Ontario and New York State. A positive of the Michigan debacle was that it helped reveal to me just how pleasant and accommodating the rest of the country had been. And, as always, there was also the ever-calming act of pedalling to lift our spirits. Whenever we found ourselves on even a short stretch of open with no angry drivers or man-sized potholes, I could feel my blood pressure lowering and the Zen state of cycling taking over. There is something about the slowly spinning legs and smooth glide of riding a bike that is ultimately relaxing and it provided great solace to know that, with just a little luck, this experience might always be around the next corner.

Right at this moment, unfortunately, that 'next corner' seemed to be taking an age to reach, and there was no light relief in sight. I bought a $5 bottle of Canadian whisky at a gas station and we found a patch of grass at the edge of a state park. I had to work hard to remember that I was drinking to unwind, not to forget. Neither of us had the energy to cook so we ate fruit and canned beans, cold, and went to our respective tents in silence. This was mostly rubbish, I concluded. I wasn't having fun any more, not even a retrospective type of fun. It was just hard, miserable riding, and for the first time I felt in danger. Annoying people were just that – annoying – but the traffic was becoming a real issue. I didn't come out here to get run over by a pissed-off woman in a rush to get home, or a trucker who was so busy trying to make it clean across the country in seventy-two hours that he couldn't be bothered to slow down to pass a cyclist. Sleep that night was one of uncomfortable thoughts of failure and self-doubt, and images of what I might look like post-encounter with a truck.

The next morning morale took a further hit, and this time right where it hurt – breakfast. I am a fan of all food but breakfast is my *raison d'être*. Whereas some people can wake and begin their day without a second thought of what they might eat, I actively jump out of bed excited about my first meal. Here in eastern Michigan I climbed out of my tent to find the perishable contents on my pannier bags strewn around the ground. Fruit decimated, bread packaging ripped apart. Breakfast cereal completely gone, save for a few crumbs pressed into the mud.

'Susie… raccoons!' Susie popped her head out, sighed, and went back inside her tent. That was a sensible approach. Meanwhile I stormed around looking for the perpetrators, which were of course now long gone back into the woods with full bellies. 'I swear, if I find one, I'm gonna kick it, Susie!' I shouted. She mumbled something back reminding me I was an animal lover, and that we should've put the food in a bag and suspended it off a tree branch with a rope.

'I don't care! These are greedy little vermin. I'm gonna find one, and I'm gonna kick it right into the forest!'

After a while I calmed down, and luckily (for me as much as anyone) I didn't come across any of the raccoon population. It was a stupid mistake born out of exhaustion and frustration. I had known there were raccoons around. I'd seen them on previous nights. Big ugly buggers with eyes of purest evil, but this was their place much more than it was mine. And Susie was right – we should've put our food in a secure bag, looped a rope through the handle and flung it over a branch high up in a tree. Ostensibly a technique for keeping bears away from your campsite, Susie and I had discovered that thus far in New York and Michigan it was a great way to stop raccoons eating your breakfast. Could've, would've, should've.

We rode west with empty bellies. Behind us was Lake Erie, and to the north Lake Huron, which we had already seen in Canada. Ahead on the far side of the state was Lake Michigan. I rode with every ounce of energy I had in order to get there quickly, and move the hell out of this place.

* * *

To our south now was Detroit, infamously hard-hit by the economic downturn and poster-city of the global recession. In the middle of the twentieth century, Detroit put itself and Michigan on the national and international map as the home of the automobile industry. As the base of Ford, it became synonymous with the manufacturing of small cars, and business boomed. Things didn't stay strong; gasoline crises in the 1970s hit the industry hard and consumers began looking east to Asia for their vehicles. Since then Detroit, and subsequently Michigan, has been in freefall. The population is down over 50 per cent since 1950, and thousands of homes and buildings in the city now lie derelict. There is some talk of a renaissance but things seem bad.

I wanted to see Detroit for myself, but couldn't bring myself to detour south and prolong my time in the state any longer than necessary. Instead Susie and I rode into the city of Flint, a smaller but equally ravished seat of the car manufacturing industry. I knew it only as the home of General Motors; a once-mighty car giant now valiantly fighting to keep its head above water.

The outskirts were not promising. Derelict facilities, which I assumed were once associated with General Motors, littered the landscape. Some pretty Victorian houses sat back in amongst the detritus but mostly the road was lined with poorly cared-for tenements. The depopulation and urban decay here can't have been far off that of Detroit itself.

On our approach to the main drag of Saginaw Street, Susie and I stopped at a roadside store. A man of Hispanic origin in a white sleeveless vest and back-to-front cap approached with a swagger. He had a gold chain around his neck and a scar on his shoulder. His left hand swayed as he walked and his right was down his trousers. This guy had walked straight out of the Oxford Book of American Stereotypes. Removing his hand from his crotch he extended it first to me by way of greeting and then to Susie. We shook it grudgingly, and he asked where we were going.

'Across the country? Damn! Why the hell did you come though Michigan?'

I didn't have an answer.

'You're not gonna stay here in Flint are you? This place is crazy, man. Right here, this is the Number One Most Violent City in the USA.' Then he added, with more than a little hint of pride, 'as voted by *Forbes* magazine.'

'What does that mean?' I asked. 'Is it really that bad?'

'Hell, yes! We got over thirty homicides so far this year, and we ain't even hit summer yet. They reckon it'll double at least. Knife crime here is crazy, everyone's got one.'

'Do you have one?' I asked, instantly regretting it.

'Yea… I'd rather not, but you just got to here. It's an issue of self-defence. Our nickname here is "Knife City, USA"! Welcome to Knife City, guys – make it through without getting robbed or stabbed and you're doing good!' He found his own joke rather funnier than we did and laughed with a high-pitched squeal.

'It can't be that bad... surely. I mean, not for people like us passing through anyway.'

'No man, maybe you're right. But you gotta know one thing about cities like this. There's places you just don't go. Like Northside, Fifth Ward... even Eastside proper where I live is rough. You just can't be riding your bicycle through there. I'm not even kidding, you won't last.'

'So where should we go?'

'The hell out of Knife City!' He squealed with laughter again. Then he gave us both a can of Pepsi from his bag, shook our hands and went back to lean against the wall.

Susie and I looked at each other. I could see my own fears reflected in her eyes. We both wanted to believe that we'd be fine just riding through this city but equally we knew that we were out of our depth. It seemed the only thing we could do was ride straight out the other side as fast as possible and hope for the best.

Just then, in one of those wonderful serendipitous incidents that happen when you are at your most vulnerable and uncertain, a car pulled up alongside us. Three young guys got out; two went into the store and the other leant by the car. He was shy, but curious enough to ask us what we were doing. An English major at the local college, he and his friends had moved from upstate Michigan to study. He asked where we were going and we told him we had no idea. It was getting on for five o'clock and we were running short of daylight. While we chatted he squinted at us, as if the sun was directly in his eyes. We moved around, but he kept squinting. I hoped that he'd be able to help us out and that the squint wasn't a physical manifestation of some psychotic tendency – aside from that I liked him, and his body language relaxed gradually the longer we talked. He was clearly naturally reserved, and speaking to strangers seemed out of character. I would find out in time that being on a bicycle made me seem extremely approachable to all sorts of folk on this journey – it was a great icebreaker, and gave off an air of vulnerability that put people at ease.

'Well, if you guys wanted, you could probably stay at our house. I'd have to ask my room-mates, and my mum 'cuz she owns the place, but it's probably cool.'

Susie and I glanced at each other. 'OK,' I said.

Five minutes later we were tailing his maroon sedan through the streets, keeping one eye out for any shady characters. His house was just north of downtown, in River Village. It seemed pleasant enough and when we pulled into the drive he told us it was a 'mixed-income area', but pretty safe. His end of the street was mostly well-kept bungalows with wooden facades and tall trees separating them from neighbours.

We took a tour of the city in his car. He told us many of the same facts that we'd heard back at the gas station. Driving through the 'dangerous' districts, it was hard to really tell how bad things were. Sure, everything looked run-down, and hooded figures gathered on street corners. Eyes turned to watch us drive past. But it didn't seem any worse than other cities I'd pedalled through – Syracuse, Buffalo, even Hamilton and Toronto in Canada.

I didn't have a great basis for knowledge, and it was definitely a city that was suffering, but it also seemed that residents we'd met sought identity from its image as a dangerous place. These students moved in very different social circles from the guy at the gas station but both told us the same story and both with a degree of pride. We all seek identity, and I suppose we take it where we can find it, even if that means boasting that you live in the most dangerous city in America. The next morning Susie and I left early and rode out through the suburbs with few problems other than a buffeting wind from the north-west.

* * *

The landscape had by now taken on flatness as a primary feature. Little interrupted the uniformity save an odd tree or herd of livestock. It felt like the beginning of what people refer to as the Midwest – the point at which one is certainly no longer in the east, but not quite in the centre of the country. Travelling by bicycle is slow enough that transformations in landscape and culture happen so gradually it is easy to miss them, until one day you find yourself in a different world from that which you last took notice of. Perhaps the Midwest started when we crossed the international border, but coming out of Flint accentuated the change and I soon settled into this new domain.

The only way to characterise it was to recognise that it lacked anything that could be deemed memorable. It was the geographical equivalent of instant coffee; harmless enough at first but eventually leaving a heavy hollow feeling and a growing realisation that actually, it's pretty rubbish.

Each night Susie and I arrived in a place that looked very much like the one which we had left that very same morning. But the headwinds had relented and the road surface improved. The camping was easy and the going, overall, was good. Out of sight to our south passed Ann Arbor, a popular college town, and Lansing, the state capital. While things bustled busily in those cities we trundled our way obliviously onwards along straight, wide highways.

The weather now was gaining an element of uniformity on a par with the scenery. The maps suggested I'd covered nearly a thousand miles, and it felt like summer was not all that far away; cool mornings quickly burned off by a searing sun that grew at our backs and bubbled away in a mostly cloudless sky right until its departure on the western horizon. I could've lined up my front wheel with the sunset and been sure to hit the Pacific Ocean before too long.

During a lunchtime siesta, while Susie dozed in the shade of a box elder, I walked across the road to one of the many roadside diners that were strung out along these state highways. A biker in black leather had just stepped out of 'Bertha's Home Diner' and came over to speak to me. Grand Rapids was the next major city that I would encounter in Michigan and I asked directions, as much for something to say as anything else. He told me to just keep on the same road, then asked where I was from.

'Ireland? Well, listen here, son. You tell your brothers back there that things have been set in motion here. The New World Order is arriving, my friend! And when it does, we'll all unite – you and me as brothers. So go spread the word!'

He clapped me on the back, and put on his helmet. Before he rode away I noticed a fading sticker on his visor that read 'Having children is like getting pecked to death by a duck'. I walked back to Susie smiling to myself at what an odd and unpleasant (although undeniably friendly) character he was. Encounters like this often cheered me up – there's nothing like a nutcase to break up an otherwise routine day.

Susie was still asleep, so I sat down by my bike and stared off at the vanishing point on the road ahead. *Maybe I'm ready to ride alone again*, I thought. It wasn't necessarily that I was hoping for more biker interactions (or invites to other male-only New World Orders), but I had noticed that Susie and I were treated differently as a pair. Some people thought us a couple ('lovers') and were less inclined to go out of their way to come and talk to us. Others, usually older men, took a particular shine to Susie and bought us ice-lollies and offered lifts. Usually they were somewhat reluctant to shower me with gifts as well but felt obliged to, in order to keep Susie's favour. It didn't bother me – I certainly got more presents that I would have otherwise – but slowly it was dawning on me that this chapter had a very finite lifespan.

These had been fun new experiences but I was ready again to be lonely and vulnerable and to take ownership once more of my own decisions. I wondered how I would have reacted alone to my problems at the international border or the worry of passing through Flint. Riding in a pair takes the edge off feelings of fear, regardless of whether or not the danger is lessened any. It had been comforting, and Susie's company a delight, but I now needed to face what lay ahead solo.

That afternoon as we cycled through yet another stimulus-free part of Michigan, we talked about where we might split up. Not long after Grand Rapids we'd reach Lake Michigan. I'd hoped to handrail the shoreline south through Gary, Indiana, and into Chicago, Illinois (doing a large U shape around the water before leaving it behind and heading west once more), but Susie had mentioned that there was a ferry across the lake. I liked the idea of seeing a bit more of Lake Michigan, even if it was from a passenger boat (confident that, being a large body of water the size of a small European country, it would not share any of its namesake state's torrent of assholes and bad roads).

That would drop us straight into Milwaukee, Wisconsin and save the hassle of riding through days and days of industrial suburbs; from what I could tell the whole southern tip of the lake was one extended metropolis. We agreed to split on the western side of the lake – a day's ride from the port we would arrive in Madison, where Susie would stay for a couple of weeks with the family of her bicycle lover. I'd keep going to the Mississippi River, alone, and then onwards into the heartland of the United States of America. We had less than a week of cycling together before we would pass out of each other's stories as quickly as our paths had joined – the fleeting, criss-crossing intensity of friendships on the road.

CHAPTER 19

HANDSOME JACK

The state of Michigan had turned from Hell into Purgatory; we were relatively content now that we were unlikely to get killed by traffic or knives and instead pedalled through a *Groundhog Day*-esque time warp. On one occasion I even began to dream of the heady days when I'd had the excitement of being shouted at and run off the road. The only proof of progress was noticing that Susie and I were infinitesimally further west on my *Michelin Road Map of the United States of America*. From Purgatory, however, we were about to be delivered directly into Heaven.

Jack Larsen found us sat by the roadside eating peanut butter. He must have been at least sixty, with a red face and bushy grey moustache. He moved with an energy and sprightliness belying his years and hopped from foot to foot as he spoke to us. There was something very 'Mr Toad' about him, though a much friendlier version.

'Come see my town, come see Fowler!' he implored us upon hearing our story. 'Listen, I'll show you what it means to live and breathe America. Come and stay with me and Milly and we'll show you the town. Please.' He was so sincere and earnest that we couldn't say no; it was only just gone 3 p.m. but it had been a while since we slept inside and I couldn't help but like Jack straight away.

We followed his silver Corvette for a couple of miles off the road and into the town of Fowler, 'Population 1,206' according to the sign. It seemed that Jack knew every single one of those people by name. Passers-by waved at him and many stopped to shout a greeting in through his window. Down a cul-de-sac not far from the main street was his house and immediately we were ushered in for pizza and ice cream. Jack spoke and listened breathlessly. Susie told him about sailing across the Atlantic.

'You sailed across the ocean in a boat with no engine! Geez, aren't you just something! I'd sure as hell have sh*t myself at the first sign of a storm! And now you're riding across America… well, that's just so neat. I'm so happy I met you two.'

And so it continued. He took us for a walk to the town. Kids from the local school were filtering back to their homes and all ran to Jack to give him a high-five. 'Handsome Jack, Handsome Jack!' they shouted to him. He grinned and produced sweets from his pockets for all. When we finally made it back to his house he handed us each a beer and sat down. 'Jack,' I asked, 'what do you do?' We'd been so busy seeing this and that, yet I still knew relatively little about the enigma of Jack Larsen.

'I worked for General Motors, for fifty years. That's where my heart is and always will be. I loved that place, and hell, if it didn't love me back. I did marketing for 'em, but it was a family, y'know? When I had a heart attack three years ago, needed triple bypass, and the managing director of General Motors called in to see me every single day for a week.'

'How is it there now?'

'Well sh*t Leon, it's hard work. Lot of layoffs, lot of broken promises. But it's still a good place. Everyone started looking to Japan to get their automobiles and there was a lot of back-stabbing. But I think people're coming back now. There's jobs again and they know how to compete with the Asian market. I did a lot of my work down in Lansing and that place is booming. There's enough folks like me who will stick by GM whatever, and it's up to us to drag it back up.'

He leant back in his chair and took a long swig of beer. 'It's a family, that's what it is. A ninety-billion-dollar family.' He had a wry smile on his face, and with that got up to refresh our drinks. Susie rolled her eyes and grinned. I knew she was bored with this particular conversation. I smiled back but in my head I was still processing what Jack had said.

The story of General Motors had previously interested me only in passing, yet now I was intrigued. This is the way to learn about the world, I thought – first-hand. Before meeting Jack Larsen, if I'd heard someone talk about the American automobile industry it would have passed through my head almost instantaneously. Now it meant something; on a human level I could see how it mattered and what effect was felt from its rise and fall. Empathy and connection are stalwarts of understanding.

The evening finished with Jack's son, Peter, arriving to play some piano for us. He did the classics – Billy Joel, Elton John. Jack had a few more drinks and before long he was up dancing. The next morning he took us to an ATM and withdrew $100, which he pressed into my hand. He cried and told us he felt like the luckiest man in the world for having met us. As we cycled away he stood on the sidewalk sobbing until we were completely out of sight. It was a touching scene, albeit a slightly elongated and awkward one on a straight road with a flat horizon.

My faith in Michigan, and in the power of people to look out for one another, had been restored by Jack Larsen and his cast of Fowler townsfolk. This was one of the things I'd hoped to find in the USA – the real-life, middle-class small town that I'd seen in the movies. Bill Bryson says in his first book that he spent a long time hunting around for the perfect little town from *It's a Wonderful Life* – he never did discover it, but then I guess he didn't pass by this way. Maybe Fowler was too homogenous, or one-sided politically; most probably it was flawed in a number of ways, but the spirit of the population there was insurmountable. Meeting Jack left me with a smile on my face for days.

* * *

Susie and I passed through Grand Rapids, a pleasant if unremarkable place. We were temporarily waylaid by an old dreadlocked artist who rode a rainbow-coloured bike and ushered us to follow him home. We did, and found it was filled with psychedelic artwork. Once we saw the handmade 'Hello Kitty' alarm clock that morphed at the bottom from a kitty to a snake, we left him to it and rode on.

Susie and I paid thirty dollars apiece to board the ferry at Muskegon. It was a vast sum, equal to everything we'd spent in the previous week, but we figured it a good way to use Jack's gift to us. Lola sat deep in the belly of the boat, unrequired for this stretch. It was odd to suddenly be moving westwards without having to power myself. Now I was a spectator, watching rather than pedalling as I edged still slowly across the surface. The boat struck out into the void and soon there was nothing but water and sky. The afternoon sun dropped to separate the two at the edge of the world and we glided effortlessly towards Milwaukee in the space beyond the horizon.

PART TWO – THE MIDDLE

*The sins of the Midwest: flatness, emptiness,
a necessary acceptance of the familiar.*
Stewart O'Nan

CHAPTER 20

THE BADGER STATE

Nestled on the western shore of Lake Michigan, Milwaukee is the most populous city in Wisconsin. The state is famous as the dairy-production capital of America, so I'd heard, but in Milwaukee it's the breweries that have given it notoriety – since the nineteenth century Miller, Pabst, Schlitz and Blatz have kept the city firmly at the forefront of the USA beer culture. Cheese and pints seemed a fine way to be welcomed into a state.

Susie and I made our way from the ferry to the Hoan Bridge, a tied-arch bridge in downtown, and together negotiated our way out of the city. We had directions to the Glacial Drumlin State Trail; a converted railway line, it was a combination of paved and gravel sections and provided almost total escape from the road. Intensely green hedgerows grew tall on either side of the trail, mostly eliminating any view of the outside world. Life was lit directly from above, the spotlight of the sun casting eerie shadows on the uneven surface. When occasionally a gateway or other footpath broke through these barriers, we saw rolling fields stretching out to the south, the vivid hues of impending summer colouring the scene. A constant companion was the calming gurgle of a fast-flowing creek running parallel to the north, its torrent already buoyed with rainfall from upstream. Progress was slow but I quieted my frustration by taking regular dips in this creek and the many lakes that bordered the path. In the distance storm clouds rolled past, hinting at future encounters.

We reached Madison in good spirits and paused on the edge of the city to say goodbye. Susie was going to meet, for the first time, the mother of the man she called her soulmate and lover. She was nervous but determined to make a good impression and so had (bravely) decided to stay indefinitely to get to know Issac's hometown. We hugged and agreed to keep in touch with the vague possibility of meeting up somewhere further west. Susie pedalled off. There was no way for either of us to know it now, but two years later she would again be pedalling a bike through Madison to see Issac's mum, but this time it would be as relatives – mother-in-law and daughter-in-law.

I was very sorry to leave Susie behind and spent a few hours pedalling myself into a slump. She had been a hell of a motivational influence – full of integrity and strong will. I would miss her self-confidence and passion for the causes close to her heart. But I needed to be alone once more; the things I sought most from this journey – the stuff of personal development and character shaping – I would not find in the permanent company of others. Ahead of me was the Midwest, the real Midwest of corn and beans and straight roads and farmers with necks red from the sun, and I was determined to launch myself into its belly without a hint of holding back.

On this journey I longed to roam unchained from the shackles of regular rhythm, yet in reality I was mostly swapping the routine of a 'normal' life in a normal job with that of riding a bike every day. My riding patterns even held standard office hours of nine to five. I found I also spent many hours poring over maps and calculating distances, despite my claims of being free and unrestricted in where I went or when.

Under the surface, I suppose, some part of me demanded that I remain in control, refusing to let go completely and rallying against the liberties of the open road. This internal battle raged all the way across the country. I could be content, upon waking, to not know what road I would start out on that day. And I made my peace with the fact that I didn't know what would happen when I reached the Pacific coast. The ocean was enough of a long-term goal to provide the requisite motivation, and whatever followed would become its own, new challenge. But in the medium term I struggled without structure and couldn't help but organise the country into sections to 'tick off'.

Reaching the Canadian border had been one. Now with the Midwest ahead of me, I resolved to power my way across until I sat at the base of the Rocky Mountains. That would be the second section complete. The next stage of crossing to meet the sea could be dealt with then. For now I could while away free hours by idly calculating the distances between towns on all possible roads around me. The irony was not lost on me; only through structure could I find my freedom.

* * *

Not far out of Madison I picked up the Wisconsin River; a tumbling, meandering torrent of deep blue that would lead me all the way to the great Mississippi. I was now as fit as a flea and found it of no consequence to pedal ten hours a day. Alone, I pushed to see just how well adapted my body had become. My daily distances increased to seventy, eighty, sometimes ninety miles. The landscape around had lost the flatness of Michigan and now crumpled together to form small rolling hills in all directions. I stayed as close to the river as possible to minimise climbs and descents, and spent the nights under birch trees with a view over the river valley.

Now was beginning the summer season of storm fronts which, although milder here than further west, still have a power that demands respect. Large black clouds rolled in with the wind picking up brutal speed. I would watch as they gradually came to fill my horizon, then at the last minute dive for cover. The first time I encountered a large weather system I thought that perhaps I could out-cycle it. Some hikers I passed told me a storm was coming in, so I pedalled hard and tried not to look back. Nature, somewhat speedier than I was on my loaded bicycle, played with me like a kid picking wings off a bug, and soon I was nailed by horrendous winds that threatened to blow me clean into the now tumultuous river. On that occasion I wheeled Lola through a gap in the hedge and both of us snuck into a large, red and (thankfully) empty cow barn, praying we didn't get busted by an angry farmer. I fell asleep until it passed and woke to find a goat licking my toes.

From then on I would meet a storm almost daily. Sometimes barns were well placed to provide a hideout, but more usually I would push Lola into the ditch by the roadside and climb in after her. Lying there watching the hail crash diagonally into the trees about me I felt as safe and warm as if I was inside my very own four-walled house. Increasingly I was learning to let weather and circumstance dictate my otherwise pragmatically planned days. I would wake early, eat quickly and cycle until the sun rose at my back. From there on in I would aim to ride hard when the road was quiet and straight. When it got hot and the river meandered within striking distance I would dive in for a cool dip. My water bottles were filled here as well and iodine drops killed any bacteria.

Gas stations and small towns were always tempting to hang around in but I found that I could inadvertently lose two or three hours sitting in the shade talking to some or other farmer about how many cattle he had. This was, early on, interesting to me for the novelty value and social interaction, but before long the conversations grew skull-meltingly boring. (Well, I used to have sixty. No, seventy! And a horse. Of course that wasn't for milking, har har har. Then the horse died, and I got another. And then I thought, I don't even know if I want another horse! So I swapped it for some more cattle. That made seventy-five, or maybe eighty...)

For the most part I'd limit myself to one gas-station stop per day, where I'd buy coffee for a dollar and sit around on the step draining my polystyrene cup. When it came to coffee I had no interest in flavour, origin or style – the only words that mattered to me were 'Free refills'. I could rarely afford much else but I enjoyed just sitting and watching life go by nonetheless. These were the Midwestern equivalent of General Stores, the hub of small backwater communities. Sit at a Wisconsin gas station for a couple of hours, and you'll meet just about everyone in town. Sit there any longer and you'll meet all their relatives who've driven in from all over the countryside especially to see this guy sitting on the stoop all day.

Typically the rest of the time was spent firmly inside my own head. Cycling was by now an automated function, as was traffic avoidance, waving to cars, and even navigation.

My mind was free to wander between pressing concerns such as hunger or thirst, to more substantial questions such as how many miles it might be to the next state, or the west coast, or how far it would be possible to cycle in a day. At times I pondered the great questions of life too – why do Americans lose the 'u' at the end of 'our' words like favour and saviour? How much peanut butter would it take to kill a man? Do cows get bored?

Often though, I just seemed to exist. My mind worked away on something or other in the background but I (the rest of me) seemed largely separated from this; unconscious in my own body. At night I'd wonder where the day went and what happened, struggling to recall anything since first light. Within this unusual state I found a sense of contentment I had not known before. I strive for more than just mere existence, sure, but being happy just to *be* is surely a good start. The soul-searching would take shape in time. At last I seemed to be kicking some of the self-doubt. Who knew if I could make it out to the Pacific but I'd come this far and, in some ways, that was further than I'd expected.

* * *

Prairie du Chien, the name a legacy of the city's establishment by French voyageurs in the seventeenth century, was to be the site of my farewell to the state. I followed the Wisconsin River to its confluence with the Mississippi and caught my first sight of this great river; here the flow was braided with large rich-green islands in the middle. It was less brown that I'd imagined, and I thought how odd it is that we know seemingly timeless and inarguable little facts about the world from childhood (such as the Mississippi being brown from carrying so much sediment) yet mostly we'll never see the subject to verify it, or enjoy it.

A long two-lane bridge crossed the flow and with traffic squeezing past I had no way of stopping to admire the view. Through gaps in the struts I caught glimpses of water tumbling past below. I'd heard it said that the Mississippi was the boundary for the eastern United States. I freewheeled down the ramp and onto a broad shoulder in Iowa – the heartland of America.

A few hundred miles south of here, in 1804, the expedition of Meriwether Lewis and William Clark had set off from St Louis, Missouri. They too were headed into the plains, knowing little of what lay ahead, yet still they set off into the unknown, seemingly fearless and brave, purportedly seeking a route to the Pacific yet clearly searching too for adventure. I re-read their diaries as I sat on the same banks of the river that they too would have seen. In their words was pause to remember that things for me could be a lot tougher – at the very least I would not have wild roaming bison to deal with, and fewer people hostile to my wanderings.

One extract caught me off guard – as they set off along the banks of the Mississippi, Clark rode alongside Lewis and told him:

This is an undertaking fraited [fraught] with many difficulties. But my friend I do assure you that no man lives with whom I would prefer to undertake such a trip as yourself.

CHAPTER 21

THE HAWKEYE STATE

Within ten miles of leaving the Mississippi behind, the undulations and irregularities of the landscape were gone. Iowa welcomed me in with a view ahead unencumbered by anything vertical from the natural world, save the odd tree here and there. An unfortunate detail was that although *mostly* flat, it was not *perfectly* flat; the road had an annoying roll to it that denied any uniformity to my rhythm. I was mildly perturbed; if I had to cycle through somewhere so unstimulating and simplistic, I at least wanted an easy ride.

Even more conspicuous, perhaps, than the barren prairieland was the wind; the fabled wind of the plains. For thousands of miles it rushes across the grasslands without mountain nor ocean nor lake to break its speeding journey. Like a snowball it gathers pace and power and gusts from the Rocky Mountains clean across to the Mississippi. From Montana in the west to Wisconsin in the east, and from the southern states of Oklahoma and Arkansas up to North Dakota and the Canadian border. And I was here to spin my little pedals straight into the face of its oncoming fury.

These central prairies have historically been the quiet, humble home of agricultural America. Unburdened by the stresses of the coasts, I expected life here to be altogether simpler. And in many ways, despite my initial doubts based on the lack of anything to look at (or to do; the tourist information booth by the Mississippi River had a rather limited selection of pamphlets which seemed to be mostly about cornfields, and the things one could do in a cornfield), it was actually quite pleasant to be in such an unassuming landscape on such a vast scale. If only it wasn't for the bloody wind.

My first night in Iowa was spent in a cornfield, and it was not to be my last in such a location. By the middle of the second day I had already forgotten that initial sense of pleasant unassuming-ness, and had sunk to a further level of hell than even Dante knew. Every mechanical revolution seemed futile; I stood on the pedals and pumped my legs for all they were worth. I put my head down and shut my eyes hoping to become more streamlined. I puffed and panted and sweated and grunted. After a few minutes of this I'd look up, only to see the road passing below my tyres at an agonisingly slow pace. Tumbleweed moved quicker. It was like trying to cycle into the rear engine of a jumbo jet just before take off; no matter how hard I pushed, the wind pushed back harder. By the roadside the corn stalks leant horizontally as if they knew it was not even worth fighting. If I stopped pedalling I actually began to go backwards.

* * *

During my breaks from the torture sessions of riding, I read through the promotional material I'd picked up. Iowa, I'd learned from the tourist office, took its name from the Ioway people, one of the tribes who called this land home before the Europeans decimated them in the name of exploration. Then the newly independent Americans bought it from the French (as part of the epic-scale Louisiana Purchase, which saw a million square acres, now fifteen US states and two Canadian provinces, swap hands), and from that point on it was firmly at the heart of the 'Corn Belt' – a term I'd heard used a number of times and which seemed to pretty accurately sum up the purpose and strengths of this region.

It seemed that Iowa suffered, as most Midwestern states did, from rural flight – people leaving behind their agricultural heritage in search of a new life in the burgeoning cities. On ground level, however, I found it hard to discern this. Every inch of land was planted with crops and although ranches were few and far between they still dotted the landscape, each managing huge sections of land around their homestead.

Agriculture, I was surprised to learn, while crucial to the economy both directly and indirectly, was in fact not the major sector. Not by a long shot, professed the 'History of Iowan economy!' pamphlet, with a very inappropriate use of an exclamation mark. Manufacturing is where the real money comes and goes, especially relating to food processing and machinery. I was now in the home of Heinz Beans, John Deere Tractors and Winnebago motorhomes. And John Wayne, apparently, although I'm not sure why he was included in the economy publication. Perhaps there was not enough material for an additional 'Sons of Iowa' pamphlet.

I found out too that Iowa was not necessarily the homogenous Republican hotbed I had expected. At least not the Republican part. My preconception was born of ignorance, assuming that the self-proclaimed enlightened peoples of coastal cities were a breed apart from single-minded nationalistic farmers in the centre. Although, historically, voters had leaned Republican, recently it had shifted to the Democrats, and Iowa is now a crucial swing state. Every four years, battling presidential candidates throw huge amounts of time and money into trying to convince the Iowan people that their particular party is the best way forward.

I had taken many of these various leaflets from the tourist centre, hoping to discover new and interesting facts about the state. Disappointingly, though, I was pointed to the largest Danish settlement in the country (Elk Horn), the only fire tower in the state (Yellow River Forest), and the fact that Cedar Rapids was home to the largest cereal company in the world (Quaker Oaks). This last fact was *almost* mildly interesting, but still not enough to stop me wishing I'd left the leaflets where they were and instead used my precious time to pour boiling oil down my shorts. Times were tough in the Midwest.

During a very depressing lunch break in the shelter of a ditch I looked once more at my map. I was twelve thumb-lengths from the next noticeable elevation; it was fair to conclude that the next sight of remotely possible interest was over seven hundred miles away. At my current speed that would take two weeks, and feel like two years. I was adrift in a great ocean of corn, floating helplessly at the mercy of the prevailing current.

Navigation, at least, was not to be a problem. I'd entered the grid system where a lack of topographical features means there is no point in having roads that twist and turn. Instead, they all run near-perfect north-south or east-west, creating huge squares and rectangles on the national map. Every so often the immensely long and straight roads have to turn at a right angle (north or south) for a few miles before turning back ninety degrees to their original course. This is to account for the curvature of the earth, which gives some idea of just how vast these plains are.

In between the main highways, smaller dirt and gravel roads run parallel, to and from ranches or other places where someone might need to go (although I cannot imagine where those places might be). I joined State Highway 9, a rather grand-sounding title for a rubbish road with cracked tarmac and an inconsistent gravel shoulder. Another arrow-straight highway ran across the state about thirty miles south of me, and below that the Interstate I-80, a freeway running all the way across the country from New Jersey to California.

Most traffic in Iowa was just passing through, I imagined (or, for their sake, I hoped), and thus took to this freeway. I thought of the thousands of people that would cross the state of Iowa in just a few hours. Those same people could cross the country in a few days, at most. And what would they see? The interior of their vehicle. The lanes of similar-looking cars with similar-looking people. A gas station once every few hours and the inside of a grotty motel. If they left the Atlantic Ocean on a Friday night they could be standing by the shores of the Pacific before the weekend was out. What a waste. A means to an end, perhaps, but such a vast and varied country deserves more. The people crossing it in a matter of days deserve more. Such thoughts comforted me; at least I was having some sort of experience rather than the absence of one altogether.

The busy freeway had the desirable impact of leaving my road, Highway 9, reasonably quiet. Two or three times a day I would pass a small town, each planned and constructed in almost exactly the same manner. From a distance, these settlements are heralded by an interruption of the smooth horizon; broadleaf trees growing in clumps, planted to act as a windbreak. Closer in, the water tower becomes visible, its bulbous top bearing the name of the town and sitting high above the rest of the buildings like a sailor on a mast. A few houses then announce the start of what we might call 'downtown'; usually individual homes with a good deal of space between each other. In a state like Iowa there is no need to be bunched together. They say you can tell a Midwesterner in a city store because he's the one standing alone in the spot furthest from anyone else.

Next comes a gas station or possibly two, each boasting an attached traditional American Diner serving eggs and home fries and coffee to hungry tuckers. Depending on size, there may be a John Deere garage nearby. These are not much more than fields full of tractors, but they are always filled with men in dungarees pointing at engines and scratching their necks. ('Seen this one Bill?' 'Yep.' 'Yep... me too. Hell of a tractor.') A church announces the start of the main street complete with small store, bar and, if the residents are lucky, a community centre and barber shop. Houses sit on smaller driveways in a mini-grid system radiating outwards. Then, as quickly as it begins, the town vanishes. And that is the excitement that Iowa provides to the long-distance cyclist.

On these quiet roads it was becoming regular now for cars and trucks to stop and ask what I was doing (perhaps as much out of pure boredom as any real curiosity). Drivers would pull up alongside and putt-putt-putt along at my pitiful speed shouting questions over the wind. 'Where ya headin'?' or 'Where'd ya come from?' Then: 'No, really, where'd ya come from? From NEW YORK CITY?' Other favourites were: 'Where ya gonna sleep?', 'On yer own, are ya?', and 'Want a ride?'

This last question was always the one that elicited the most emotion from me. On a good day I'd feel grateful for the offer and thank them for being such a generous and kind person, but tell them I was keen for the challenge of riding and that I'd see their fine country better in this way. On a bad day (most days in Iowa) I'd get incredibly annoyed at them for being so inconsiderate as to test my patience and resolve. It was all I could do not to throttle them on their thick necks through the wound-down window. 'Of course I want a bloody lift, you moron. Do you think this is FUN?' I wanted to shout. 'I'd strip naked and dance a polka on Capitol Hill for a lift but I can't take one because I'm too goddamn stubborn for my own good!'

Whether or not I ever actually said this I'm not sure, but they clearly got the point and usually drove on quickly. It was true: I was starting to dream of accepting a ride from a passing truck. It'd be so easy – chuck Lola and the trailer in the back, hop in the front, down a few cold ones with my carefree driver, stop for some eggs and before we could say 'Hey, isn't that cornfield beautiful?' we'd be out the other side and much less likely to die a slow and painful death of monotony-induced heart failure.

The problem was that to do so, to take a ride, was to go against everything I had set out to do. Accepting, to save the misery of a few hundred miles, would have most certainly felt like cheating. The only rules were those that were self-imposed, of course, but if I was the only person I had to answer to then it was surely even more important to keep my integrity. Maybe if I was still utterly depressed once I reached the West Coast states – maybe that would be the time to think about a little hitchhiking. But for now any forward movement other than bicycle tyre to cracked tarmac would be forbidden. Besides, a little misery never did anyone any harm. *Good for the constitution*, I remember being told at primary school when I was ill. If I could cycle across Iowa on my own without going mad or jumping in a truck, then maybe I'd be a little closer to realising my potential. And if I did go mad or jump in a truck, then I would at least know my limits.

All of this pent-up frustration was wonderful fodder for daydreaming and a couple more days took me longitudinally level with the state capital Des Moines, sixty miles to the south. More relevantly I found myself resting by the excellently named Pilot Knob State Park. In Estherville, beyond, I found minor fame by the entrance to Walmart.

I had taken to hanging around outside grocery stores when I felt there might be a decent crowd, hoping that my bedraggled appearance might induce older and more susceptible shoppers to engage in conversation and ultimately buy me some snacks. This time, however, I was approached by a middle-aged lady with cropped hair and glasses worn at a friendly tilt. She was a reporter for the local newspaper and told me to wait while she fetched her notepad. In return for answering some questions, I was rewarded with a sandwich. I left and pedalled through the other side of town only to then be apprehended by a sharply dressed man with grey hair (looking like the sort of US Republican who appears on British television once in a while talking about why guns actually *save* lives rather than cost them) and an accompanying cameraman. They worked for Iowa Television and wanted to quiz me on what I thought of the state.

'It's, eh... wonderfully flat,' I managed. They nodded and smiled, encouraging me to keep going, but I was all out of compliments.

'The people are friendly,' I added finally. A truly memorable piece of local TV history. I was slightly annoyed when the crew wrapped it up and drove off abruptly, leaving me with neither gift nor reward; I'd been quietly angling for the offer of a bed for the night. I pedalled off regretting saying that bit about how friendly the people were.

CHAPTER 22

BETWEEN A ROCK AND A HARD PLACE

I was now faced with a dilemma. More than anything I needed a break from the bike and from the experience of cycling in Iowa. I was reluctant to subject myself to a tent-bound rest day in a cornfield though, and couldn't afford a motel. And I was still at least a week from anyone that I could couchsurf with. I refused to accept rides, and I passed through towns so infrequently that I was unlikely to be able to charm anyone into giving me a place to stay for a whole day. I needed some excitement in my life.

By the time I rode into Boulder Rapids I had already dodged two weather fronts that cascaded wildly across my path. The first I watched from inside a bright-red barn filled with farm machinery, and for the second I took shelter in the lee of a John Deere tractor which lay empty just a few yards into the corn. In Boulder Rapids' solitary pub I was bought a pint by the girl behind the bar and asked the by-now standard questions.

A TV blared away in the corner, also a standard feature of these rural bars. Normally no one paid much attention to it, but now lots of hairy, heavyset men began to gather in front of the screen mounted high up in the corner above the poker machines. I was more interested in watching the watchers than listening to the news. They were an interesting bunch. All looked like they made a living from the land – stained clothes, calloused hands and wind-burned faces told me that much. They muttered amongst themselves and pointed at the screen.

'Well, at least we're not this feller on his bi-cycle!' one voice said above the general chatter, and the others all laughed. The girl from the bar turned around. 'We got us a tornado warning.' I asked what that meant. 'What it *means*, darlin', is that there's a tornado nearby that's made landfall. We've been on Tornado Watch all day. Tornado Watch is when conditions is favourable. Very favourable, seems in this case – it's touched down about ten miles away.'

I couldn't believe it. Tornados? Surely I wouldn't get to see a tornado. The idea that they were dangerous didn't occur to me at all, I was far too excited about seeing one up close.

'You can't be out on a bicycle in this, son,' said a burly bald man with a goatee hiding his extra chins.

'I have to, I… I need to keep moving.'

'Not today,' he said, with an air of finality. 'We don't have a motel here in town, though.'

'Oh,' I said, relieved. I'd be spared the awkwardness of explaining that I didn't have enough money for accommodation. 'I guess I'll pedal onto the next place that does.'

'No way, bro. Too dangerous. Why don't you come stay with me?'

'Eh… do you live here in town?' I asked.

'Just about four miles out, on a ranch. We can dump your bike in the back of the truck and I'll drive you there, and tomorrow morning I'll drop you back here.'

I was quite easily convinced. Before I could tell him this, however, he had taken out his driving licence.

'Look, see here, Michael John Peterson. See? Nothing weird, I just want to help you out. I ain't no... no, *homosexual*, or nothing like that.'

I doubted that information would be on his Iowa driving licence, even if he was. ('Your driver today will be Michael. He's gay, but don't worry, he won't try anything funny!')

'OK, sure. Thanks, Michael.' We shook hands and ordered more pints.

An hour later and the first tornado had petered out, but another had touched down just west of it. Michael and I went to his truck and put Lola in the back. He told me to wait by the vehicle while he went to the store. Five minutes later he arrived back with a twenty-four-pack of Bud Light beer. 'Could be a long night!' he laughed.

As we drove he cracked open a can of Bud for him, then one for me. The radio blared out some horrendous Country and Western and Michael told me stories of things he'd done in his truck with his girlfriend, some whilst driving. He was about forty years old, give or take, and had a cherub-like quality to his face. He carried a hefty paunch but his squat frame was solid from years of manual labour. 'I got two hundred acres here. Mostly corn, but we got a few beans out by the main road. When it's time to harvest, my buddies all come down and we have a few days of gatherin' and partyin'. It's tough work, bro, but I love it.'

We drove down dirt tracks away from the town to the south, and twenty minutes later pulled into the driveway of a large house surrounded by small sheds; the only homestead in sight. Within an hour Michael was six beers deep and, like a cat proudly bringing dead-animal offerings to its owners, he had shown me both his tractor and his quad bike. Next up was his horse, and I worried that it wouldn't be so happy to be paraded around for a guest while he tried to make it do a wheelie.

The horse's fate was delayed when a truck full of teenagers rattled past at full tilt and skidded to a halt just beyond the gate. They reversed back. 'Been out in the corn,' answered the biggest one matter-of-factly with a voice like a dull blade when Michael asked them where they'd been. There was a brief moment of mutual machismo, but once it was established that the boys had been careering through someone else's valuable crop, not Michael's, parity was restored and he gave them all beers for the road. 'Don't say anything to your folks, ye hear?' They promised not to and drove off.

To say that Michael and I differed on our opinions regarding drink-driving would be putting it mildly. I'd been brought up to abhor the idea, while he seemed to think it part and parcel of living in the sticks in Iowa. 'Driving out here is just boring without a beer, y'know? And there's no one around anyhow. We know how to drive after a few drinks, and the cops don't really mind. We've all been caught a time or two, but usually just given a fine which is their way of saying, "Don't get caught next time." It's not like in the cities, it's not doing any harm on these here dirt roads to weave around a bit!'

I'd begun to hide my still-full beer cans under the parked truck when Michael wasn't looking. Three cans had left me light-headed and I hadn't eaten in hours. Sitting, drinking, and looking out over the corn. Our pattern was only broken by a second Dodge Viper truck bouncing into the drive with a small, angry-looking man behind the wheel.

'Hey Leon!' shouted Michael. 'Meet my buddy Paul. He drives truck cross-country.' 'Driving truck' was a phrase I enjoyed, meaning, in British parlance, that the purveyor was a long-distance lorry driver. Unfortunately it seemed I wouldn't have a chance to tell Paul about my thoughts on American semantics, as it was instantly clear he didn't want me around. He ignored my greeting and outstretched hand and went back to his Dodge to fetch another forty-eight cans of Bud Light and a large bottle of Jack Daniels. And it went rapidly downhill from there.

Michael and Paul talked and laughed and I sat beside them feeling increasingly uncomfortable. They knocked back can after can. A small battery-operated radio sat beside our lawn chairs reporting the movement of the tornado between crackles. There was news of tornadic damage just six miles away. Here the sky was relatively calm, but black clouds to the south looked ominous. At some point after darkness fell, my two Iowan companions disappeared into the house. Michael returned after a while and said, 'Don't worry about Paul. He doesn't meet many strangers. He's just a bit... shy.'

Later I went to find the bathroom and met Paul coming through the kitchen. We stopped for an awkward moment. He was short, much shorter than me with the effect that I towered over him. His face was lined by years of squinting into the sun, and a black sleeveless 'Harley Davidson' vest was pulled tight over his stocky frame. His upper arms were both covered with tattoos that I couldn't make out and on his left forearm red flames danced towards the elbow. We looked at each other and he placed a meaty hand on my shoulder. When he spoke it was slow and methodical. 'I don't like you. You don't belong here. You've taken advantage of the kindness of my friend. I don't like that. Right here, this is America. And it's for Americans. We don't need no British here. We got enough problems with the blacks, the Mexicans – you name it. We like America to be pure. And that means you're not welcome.'

I made to talk but he squeezed my shoulder, silencing me. 'Problem is, you're Michael's guest. He's easily offended, so now you're here, you gotta stay. But I'll be watching.' His hand left my shoulder and Paul walked out of the room.

I wanted to fly; to just hop on my bicycle and take my chances in the storm. But what would Paul do? The beer had dulled my senses and I struggled to focus. I needed to get away, but I couldn't settle on a plan. So, eventually, I just went back outside and sat down.

After a little while Michael threw up all over himself. He went inside to clean up and I was left alone once more with Paul. Thirty minutes passed – the clock on the little radio read 9 p.m. Paul started on the Jack Daniels and we didn't speak. Then, without warning, he stood up and took me by the elbow, lifting me to a standing position. 'I want to show you something.'

He frogmarched me around the side of the house, wobbling slightly with the vast quantities of alcohol consumed. We passed the quad bike that Michael had shown off to me earlier – those seemed innocent times now. A brick shed, in need of a paint job, stood alone on the grass facing inwards. Paul stopped by the door.

'Open it up.'

I lifted the latch, and swung the door open. Inside was pitch black.

'Go inside.'

'Eh, no. Thanks,' I said. Best to show British politeness even in these most severe of circumstances, I thought.

Paul reached inside without taking his eyes off me and felt for a light switch. A strip of fluorescent halogen came to life on the second attempt. Three walls of the shed were lined with every sort of gun imaginable. Pistols hung from single hooks, rifles supported by small shelves. A shotgun rested on the ground, nozzle pointed to the roof. Paul moved one foot over the threshold and reached for a smallish pistol that was closest to us.

All the while I stood there, watching and doing nothing. He looked blinkingly at the gun, and then placed the cold metal tip against my forehead. He was silent. I felt nothing. This was a new experience for me, and with nothing even remotely similar to relate it to I just stared back.

He was struggling to focus – his eyelids flickered, and he blinked frantically. Somewhere deep down my internal panic mode became engaged, and responsibility for the outcome was passed over to instinct. I suppose this happened almost instantaneously, although it was hard to tell as time had lost all meaning or relevance. The decisions I made after that weren't based on thorough reasoning – I just acted in the way that my body told me to, much like when riding a bicycle. Paul was perched off balance, swaying like a cornstalk in the wind; I pulled my left arm away from his grasp and simultaneously used my right hand to bat the gun away. This knocked him off balance more and the gun fell from his hand onto the concrete path. I kicked hard at his right leg and put everything I had into a firm two-handed push at his chest. He crumpled, toppling over backwards. Flicking the light off I pushed the door to, closed the latch and kicked the gun into the darkness beyond the shed.

I was alone in the gloom with a madman locked in a room full of guns just feet away.

This is new.

My legs struggled for speed, but carried me safely to Lola and we pelted away down the dirt track. It was a good five minutes before I saw the tornado. The last warning on the radio said there had been a touchdown to the north, but that it didn't look like it was headed this way. I guess that had changed. This beast took up the entire horizon and looked like something from another world. It tapered to a fine point at the bottom and the blurring rotations reminded me of a potter patiently sculpting a vase on their wheel. For the second time that night I was experiencing something so utterly new I could find no relatable event in my psyche.

Looking back towards the house, I could see now the headlights of a truck bouncing along, headed in my direction. I imagined that Michael and Paul together would've worked themselves into a drunken fury, loaded the truck with every single gun they owned, and set out to cause ultimate devastation. I pictured grenades and rocket launchers; Paul with warpaint on his face running through cornfields with livestock exploding behind him.

Twice the world went deadly calm, then wind began to howl again. I didn't know why or how this was happening, and the uncertainty unnerved me further. They say it's silent and peaceful in the eye of a storm, while chaos holds court all around. I was quite sure I never made it into the eye – I wasn't close enough – but perhaps the moments of unnatural calm were related to the rapidly moving storm front. It felt for all the world like each silence would be followed by something awful.

The chasing headlights were bearing down on me, closer now than the weather system, yet I still couldn't quite fathom that this might be the end of it all. I wouldn't make it much further along the track before the truck reached me. On the right was a steep ditch of maybe 10 feet – too deep to safely jump into with a bike. The left bank sloped down in a kinder gradient then disappeared into corn.

The corn! That was my only choice now. I jumped off Lola and pushed her down into the thicket. With each crouched step away from the road the crops became denser, growing to 5 feet and higher. Rough stalks rubbed at my bare legs and the air was thick with powdery pollens. Half running, half walking and wholly ridiculous, I used Lola as a battering ram to move forward. Eventually I could handle the pressure no more and collapsed to the ground. Everything was still, save the occasional howl of wind that passed above my forest of corn, and the menacingly gentle hum of a Dodge Viper engine somewhere in the darkness. Rocks and gravel crunched agonisingly under wheels.

I could see nothing through the corn; it was too thick. Suddenly a light pierced through the black, only to be blocked by stalks just feet in front of me. It darted away again then came arcing back. *A flashlight.* The beam did a couple more passes but I was out of range. Seconds felt like days and I couldn't allow myself to breathe. A lifetime passed, maybe more. Men were born and men died, and mountains fell into the sea.

Reality came back into focus with the first crack of gravel under rubber as the truck began to move again, and it was like being taken off death row just before being led to the chair. Slowly the unseen truck moved on, crawling down the track at walking pace. They knew what they were looking for, those boys with their guns, they just didn't know where exactly I left the road. I prayed that they wouldn't get out and come in on foot after me. I closed my eyes and squeezed my hands into fists.

When I un-tensed my body the engine sound was gone. Together Lola and I stumbled forwards through a dark world of corn. Up ahead on the track, the tornado was still moving steadily onwards, now parallel with my path, but it looked smaller now. The truck was nowhere to be seen. At the far side of the field, now probably half a mile from the road, I collapsed into a heap by the final row of stalks. Adrenalin was beginning to run out and I started to shiver. My body wilted with exhaustion and this seemed as good a place as any to spend the night; certainly much better than risking being back out on the open road. The tornado didn't seem likely to come back around. I lay back and flattened an area big enough for my torso, and I slept.

CHAPTER 23

THE MORNING AFTER THE NIGHT BEFORE

Come, my friends,
'Tis not too late to seek a newer world.
Alfred, Lord Tennyson

Sunrise woke me and brought with it a calm that made the previous evening's events seem like a wild dream. I trudged back towards the dirt track, then rode the four miles towards Boulder Rapids – the very same place where twelve hours earlier I had jumped in a truck with Michael. I had to retrace our steps back to town in order to pick up the highway again – there was no other road close by that could take me west. Around me now was a post-apocalyptic landscape of flattened trees and houses without roofs. A row of telegraph poles were scattered across the road like matchsticks. Every engine sound that came from behind sent my heart fluttering; I'd hold my breath until it had passed and I'd been able to confirm that it wasn't a Dodge Viper full of guns.

I had no real frame of reference but this seemed like a bad storm even by Midwestern standards. Along the highway, houses and grain silos were crumpled and crushed like balls of paper. Just after lunch I began to shake uncontrollably. It lasted for about fifteen minutes, and the rest of the day I was on edge. Fear had caught up with me.

For the next two days I rode looking over my shoulder and slept with one eye open. The headwinds were back, but I could largely ignore them now; I was more concerned with raging gunmen. I felt as low as I ever had since leaving New York and the idea of taking a lift seemed ever more appealing (assuming the driver wasn't from Iowa and didn't have a goatee or a Harley Davidson vest). This felt like a turning point. All I wanted to do was to give up. Nothing was worth this sort of danger. I thought about my family and how they'd feel. I thought about everyone who told me the trip would be dangerous; I had arrogantly swatted away any suggestions that I'd get into trouble. Now I could see that maybe they weren't being negative but perhaps just realistic.

Yet wasn't this the essence of adventure? Of being in that zone where things happen beyond your control? Despite everything, this wretched scenario seemed to have played out OK in the end and I was alive and well. An inner battle raged as I rode towards the western boundary of Iowa, reaching a climactic crescendo when I got my first flat tyre of the ride. I could feel that my reaction and decisions at this point were now of critical importance. I'd come a long way on a bicycle. No one could say I hadn't tried, and few would argue with my reasoning for quitting. There was so little enthusiasm left for continuing that I began to doubt I would even regret it if I did quit.

But what if I did call an end to it here, by the cornfields of middle Iowa? How would I feel in five years, knowing I'd let this dream slip away at the first sign of true hardship? I sat in the dirt and took off my front wheel. *One step at a time*. Getting a puncture had previously been a worry, my insecurities panicking at the thought of having to rely on my own ability to complete even such a simple task. Now it seemed so triflingly inconsequential, and absent-mindedly I levered off the tyre, replaced the tube, felt for thorns and then put it back together on the bike.

Perhaps it was all a matter of perspective. If I was to look at the situation in a new way, then it would be possible to argue that I was very unlikely to encounter anything as dangerous as the gunmen and tornados again. I might well have just overcome the biggest challenge of the journey. I had wanted to see what I was capable of and how I reacted to real life-challenges, and here one was, as big as they get. I'd beaten it. All I had to do was keep going and things should get better from there.

The skills I learned were acquired so slowly that it was barely possible to notice them, yet they were there. I'd become infinitely more confident at dealing with strangers. I thought nothing of camping on my own, only occasionally scaring myself in particularly odd locations. I was sticking to my budget and had made it over a thousand miles across the continent of North America. Decision-making happened automatically now and I'd learned a great deal about perseverance. Of the people I'd encountered, 99.9 per cent had been wonderful.

I tightened the bolt on my front wheel and pumped it back up to full strength. I couldn't quit, not now. There was nothing to be gained from choosing that path – only regret and disappointment. What might lie ahead if I continued was a mystery but it was unlikely to be worse than that which I faced if I quit. I heaved myself up and back onto the saddle. West, again. There would be no hitchhiking quite yet.

CHAPTER 24

BOXCAR HOBO

Not far from the state border, Highway 9 crossed over a railway line. I stopped for a peanut butter break and sat on the low wall looking down over the tracks. A small town lay up ahead on the road but I was still actively avoiding settlements and people for fear of maniacs. As I sat there a large freight train came steaming through below, heading north. Carriage after carriage of shipping containers rolled by, some full and closed, others lying open and seemingly empty.

At a signal in the distance the driver slowed down and the train pulled to a halt. In that moment it seemed to make sense to jump aboard. I needed a break from this road, that was for sure, and hopping a freight train seemed fun. It was a possibility I may not encounter again so easily, or more likely, one I may not feel brave enough to accept. When opportunity knocks, only a fool doesn't answer the door.

I pulled Lola off the road and we skidded down the gravel embankment. The two carriages nearest me were locked but ahead one gaped open. The only way in was through the container door, which was level with my head; there was no way I could get Lola up that high. Did she need to come? Maybe I could hide her here and come back in a few days to pick her up. Time was running out so I made another snap decision.

I pushed Lola back up the bank and into the thickest bush that I could find. Quickly I gathered some warm clothes, some water and my 'valuables' bag with passport, camera and wallet. I ripped a page out of my diary and wrote on it: 'Please do not steal me. My owner is coming back soon, and needs me to ride across the country. Thanks.' Then I slid down the bank, looked back at her one last time and hopped into the container. Minutes later we started to chug forwards, slowly picking up speed until soon it felt like we were flying, gliding north out into the open country.

I rode in the boxcar through the following day and night, nibbling at my peanut butter, rationing water and wondering why the hell I was there. Sometimes the tracks ran directly through the middle of endless plains of corn and bean crops. Wind whistled in, but it was cool enough to sit facing out with my legs dangling over the side. At times we moved parallel with a road and I'd hide inside in case a car saw me. I didn't know anything about 'riding the rails', except what Bob Dylan songs had taught me and what Susie had said. She'd done a lot of freight-hopping and thought it was pretty easy. So far she was right. I pushed to the back of my mind some half-remembered stories I'd read of the train-yard 'bulls'; grizzled security who would beat the living hell out of any vagabond they found illegally stowed away. There was a buzz to breaking the law, but more than anything I was just glad to be breaking my routine. Lola's position was a little precarious but I tried not to worry. It seemed unlikely that anyone would venture to her hiding spot.

Just before sunset the land opened up to reveal magnificent lakes of deepest blue. The sun disappeared slightly behind me to the left, telling me we were roughly headed north-east. During the night I slept fitfully, vaguely aware that we had stopped from time to time but never for very long. When I woke it was still dark and I watched lights from isolated homesteads and far-off cars battle to be seen.

Not long after the sun rose we slowed and I could see up ahead a large group of buildings. This was probably far enough; I was running low on water and my manna-esque jar of peanut butter was empty. I hopped out when we stopped, glad to have been in a boxcar so near the back. Squeezing through a fence I crossed two flat green fields and walked a short distance down a road. I was in a small city and I'd ridden there in a boxcar. 'Boxcar Leon', they'd call me, I thought.

At the first corner store I asked where we were. 'Willmar, son!' laughed the clerk. 'Willmar... Minnesota?' I guessed. I asked to see a map and gave vague answers to his puzzled questions about how come I had no idea where I was. 'I never met someone who didn't know where they was as bad as you, son,' he concluded. I took it as a compliment, though it's unlikely that was the intention.

Willmar, Minnesota looked to be a couple of hundred miles north-east of where I'd hopped on. It was roughly level with Minneapolis, the state capital, to the east. Apart from that I knew nothing about the place. I bought some bread and apples and filled my water bottles and spent a couple of hours stretching my legs wandering around town. It was pretty small for a city and looked like the rest of the Midwest: mostly boring. My mind turned to the matter of getting back to Lola. There didn't seem to be any reason to hang around. There hadn't been a reason to come in the first place. When asked why he wanted to climb Everest, Edmund Hillary famously answered, 'Because it is there.' The freight train had been there, the right place at the right time, and it was the adventure and escape I'd needed. Now the buzz had worn off and the next task was to get back south without having to pay for it.

While I waited by the roadside with my thumb out, I thought again about why I was doing any of this. I exchanged emails once in a while with friends back home, and by all accounts things were still bad for the young professional. Of all my close pals from university, only one had a job they really wanted. The rest pulled pints and dished out pizzas while bemoaning the wasting of youth. How cruel a hand to be dealt, they said. I felt sorry for them – sure, it was ruthless, but we were all the same, and ours were first-world problems – a case of not being who we wanted to be, or thought we might be.

I was proud that I'd taken the plunge and quite sure that, whatever else happened in life, I could look back on that decision and be absolutely certain it was right. I knew also that there was not a hint of superiority in my decision; we all choose our own paths whether for better or worse, and I had no place to feel like I was greater than those back home for leaving it all. Fear and ambition drive us all our separate ways, and who knows where paths will collide down the line.

My life, I mused, revolved around an increasingly serious peanut butter addiction and sleeping in a different hedge every night. I showered (at most) once a week, and owning a tent was about as far up the property ladder as I was going to get. This lifestyle felt formative, but was it sustainable? Whatever way I was wired, I felt more at home waking up in a hedge than a house. A curious thing. Perhaps the desire for those material things would come.

I remembered listening to an interview with the author and adventurer Rory Stewart who said he felt heavy on his shoulders the weight of privilege, as many of us do, and that anyone in a similar position must launch themselves wholly into positive work to justify the good fortune they received in the lottery of life. That I could agree with, and it didn't seem to sit well with riding a bicycle across America. Yet Rory spent two years walking across Asia, and that didn't seem like wasted time. Afterwards he returned to working for the Foreign Office, set up a charity in Afghanistan, and became a governor of an Iraqi province. Perhaps I would find my purpose through this ride, and any legacy I might create would benefit or indeed be initiated by what I learned on the road. That thought provided much solace.

* * *

It took me two hours on the extreme edge of town to get a ride. Partially this was because only six cars passed me by in that time; not many folk had much business driving through Willmar on a Tuesday afternoon, it seemed. When one car finally stopped and reversed back towards me, I quickly ended my self-indulgent analysis by concluding that the thirst for adventure is to a large degree selfish. Its essence can be boiled down to reveal personal desires for self-improvement, but the result is something that can benefit a much larger demographic, whether by the actions subsequently taken by that adventurer or just through that person's drive and achievement being visible as an inspiration. I was not alone in hearing the call of the wild in my ears. Many know the sound, as clear as the sharp whistle of a steam train, but not all can or will answer it. My greatest blessing perhaps was the luck and judgement to heed the cry and jump aboard.

My drivers were a serious-looking middle-aged couple in a green sedan. In the back seat beside me was a boy of no more than ten years old. I told them about my bike ride but was reluctant to admit riding the rails. Instead I said I'd come north to Willmar with a friend but decided to stay longer, alone, and take some photographs. It was a lame story, we all knew that, but no more questions were asked. The solemn father turned from the driver's seat and asked, as if having read my thoughts of the previous few hours, why I wanted to take on this cross-country ride. But before I could answer him, his young son piped up. 'Don't be silly dad, it's obvious. He wants an adventure!' The perfect summation, much better than mine would have been, from the unburdened and spontaneous mind of a child.

I slept in the back all the way to the outskirts of the family's destination city and from there I caught a second ride, much easier this time on a busier road, and profusely thanked a very perplexed businessman as I hopped out in the middle of nowhere by a railway overpass. Lola was safe and sound in her bed of trees and I pulled her back to the highway we knew so well.

Iowa, the most boring place on the planet, had pulled out all the stops for me. I could no longer claim to have had a dull time, but I still wanted to get the hell out of there. And so I rode west, my natural orientation, refreshed from a northern jaunt. The sun was in the correct place in the sky once more and I was hungry to follow the white line. The life of cycling had regained its appeal.

CHAPTER 25

THE MOUNT RUSHMORE STATE

All I ask, the heaven above,
and the road below me.
Robert Louis Stevenson

Growing outwards from the Big Sioux River, Sioux Falls is the largest city in South Dakota and the eastern extreme of the so called 'Great Plains'; a vast area of prairie, steppe and grassland which was once populated by millions of American bison. Nowadays, since the European settlers killed them all and either displaced or did the same to the Native American population, the land west of Sioux Falls is even less densely populated than Iowa.

Just a few miles before entering the city I took a slight detour off my road to visit a point where three states – Iowa, Minnesota and South Dakota – all meet. It was a poor use of my energy. A 'tri-state marker' consisting of two concrete breezeblocks and a small plaque marked the spot. Even by Midwestern standards this was extremely low-quality tourism; I'd seen more exciting roadkill. The only benefit was that I could join a new road in Minnesota for an hour or so before crossing into South Dakota, meaning I spent one less hour of life in Iowa.

Sioux Falls was busier than I expected, full of trucks and people and noise and lights. Wide streets shone silver in the sharp afternoon light, and swaggering men in plaid checked shirts filled the sidewalk. Signs for a 'Beer Festival' drew me down to the river. Hordes of intoxicated Dakotans who had all been drinking wildly since the morning set the scene. A lithe man with an impressive beard – he introduced himself as 'The Kernel' – told me he was a long-distance cyclist and that I had to make sure I rode through the Badlands National Park. I'd read about the place – a bizarre, lunar landscape of eroded buttes and pinnacles. I'd even heard it was where NASA used to send their astronauts to train and I assured the man I would make the trip.

As I left town the wind picked up once more, driving into my face and making me work for every inch of progress. It barely seemed possible, but South Dakota was even *flatter* than Iowa. There were some new crops by the roadside now, perhaps wheat or oats. Maybe alfalfa. It didn't matter, because it was still exceedingly dull. I was riding Highway 42 and I was having a miserable time once more. The road surface was poor and the shoulder of loose gravel impossible to ride on; it had the consistency of porridge and brought me to an instant halt when I veered onto it. But the road was quiet and so I weaved in and out of cracks and potholes. When a car came past I pulled as far into the side as I could and hoped the driver would see me before passing. Increasingly often I was getting honked at in anger, and sometimes insults would be hurled out the window. I left them to get lost in the wind.

On a better section of tarmac I heard a vehicle approaching from behind and steered in towards the shoulder as normal. A horn was honked, annoyingly loudly. I turned to wave them past and saw an irate white-haired man in a cream Cadillac. He was shouting and gesticulating with gay abandon; soon he pulled alongside and wound down the passenger-side window mid verbal-stream: '... goddamn road is for vehicles, not for goddamn bikes. What is wrong with you? Get the hell off this road and ride at the side, you stupid sonova b*tch. What...' I lost a few words here and there because he was still honking away. He looked a very respectable sort but he could swear like a trooper. After a while I pulled onto the gravel shoulder and stopped. He idled too, then with a final honk sped off down the straight, empty highway.

A few other cars honked at me but I made sure to always be as far off the road as I could. The rest was their problem. Just as the sun was getting low enough to be right in my eyes, I saw a police car screaming towards me. The lights were flashing and the driver was clearly in a hurry. He passed by, and then skidded around in a semi-circle, and put the sirens on. Was I being pulled over?

'Pull over!'

'I see.'

I pulled over onto the shoulder, perplexed and somewhat amused. Out of the car came another character from the Oxford Book of Stereotypes, this one the best of my journey so far. Small and bald, wearing a bushy moustache and with a gut busting over his gun belt, this man was the quintessential American cop (based on my knowledge of Hollywood movies). His mouth bulged with chewing tobacco (I hadn't known people still used that) and before he spoke he spat out a dirty black lump beside my feet.

'And where'r you goin', son?' he asked.

I told him I was headed for the Rocky Mountains. 'Is there a problem, officer?' I asked.

'Yessir, there is a problem. We've had reports that you've been driving all over this here road. Driving about like someone under the influence, they's said.'

I explained the road-surface issue.

'Well, we'll see. I'm gunna have to ask you to stand by my car here while I run a few tests.'

I tried very hard not to laugh as he made me touch my finger to my nose and walk along the white line. Just when I thought it was over, he brought out a breathalyser machine.

'Are you serious?' I asked, incredulous. 'Clearly I'm not drunk! Your roads here are just a mess. And… is it even illegal to ride a bike drunk?'

'Please breathe into the tube, son. If it's over the limit, I'm gunna have to ask you to come with me.' He spat again. He was serious! I humoured him. I'd had one beer in Sioux Falls and for a brief moment I suddenly worried that might show. What would happen if deemed to be riding drunk?

Alas, I was never to find out, as I passed the test with flying colours and he put the machine away. 'Listen, son, you need to drive right while you're in this country. Bikes have to stay off the road. There's a shoulder there that's just for you. You stay on that, y'hear?'

I didn't argue.

'I don't want to see you again, and I don't want to have anyone else calling me up sayin' you've been causing trouble,' he said as he got back into his car.

Goodbye to you too, sir. *I bet it was that idiot in the white Cadillac*, I thought.

Just before dark that night I passed through a small truck-stop of a town, with nothing more to offer than a gas station and a diner. Parked outside 'Bertha's all-American' was a white Cadillac. *It has to be the same one.* In my head I fantasised about clever and mean things I could do to the Cadillac, knowing I wouldn't dare to ever actually key the side of it or take a dump on the passenger seat. I would inevitably let the moment pass and then camp just out of town in a field by the road as always (I rarely put much effort into campsites now; much easier to move 10 feet from the road and sleep there). Slumped at the fringes of the reach of the neon lights, I lamented my lack of chutzpah.

Five peanut butter and jelly sandwiches later I saw the white-haired man coming out of the diner, talking on his phone. I didn't want to run into him, so I quickly jumped on Lola and pedalled off out of town. After a mile or so he still hadn't passed me; no one had. The Dakotan roads were dead at that time of night, and under a moonless sky I pushed Lola off the road into the soybean plants. Then I walked back to the road, and stopped by a large road sign, waiting.

It was only minutes before I saw lights coming my way. It must be him. Using the sign as a shield until the last moment, I jumped out from behind it, pulled down my trousers and stuck my arse out in full view. As the car came close I gave it a bit of a waggle. The vehicle passed and slowed, and as I looked over my shoulder I saw a white Cadillac veering into the centre of the road. I ran back into the fields giggling like a schoolboy, hoisting up my trousers as I bounded away.

CHAPTER 26

WHERE NOBODY KNOWS MY NAME

Baring my bottom and having encounters with the police had added a little spice to my days, but South Dakota was still getting to me. Route 42 was the straightest, fastest way across the state, but it was leaving me utterly depressed and bored. Not far ahead, my map showed that rarest of things in the Midwest – a diagonal road. It led inevitably to another straight highway, but it might provide some excitement for a few hours, I reasoned. It also led through the town of Mitchell, notable in that it was the only place of any significant size around.

The diagonal road was also uneventful, save for the surprising amount of joy there is to be had from watching the sun cast its light at a different angle. In such a sparse landscape, the shadows which fall from a single tree can create an entire world to the passing cyclist with an active imagination. The hard, angular shapes I'd grown used to – cast by a sun which was born behind me and died in front of my nose – were now replaced by kinder, softer, longer forms that seemed to reach out and stroke the tarmac. It was a more amiable road by far. Too soon I was back on a straight east-west stretch, just half a day's ride from Mitchell. The highway was empty and I felt like I hadn't seen another human being in a lifetime.

'Leon!' A voice came from behind me.

'Leon!'

I turned around on the deserted road, very confused. I knew two people who were from South Dakota, and they were living in New York. My list of people who might be shouting my name in the middle of this state was not extensive.

'Leon!!' Three men on squat donkeys rode out of the heat haze and stopped alongside me. Their donkeys were strong and sturdy, and loaded with panniers. I then saw they had wheels... they weren't donkeys, they were bicycles! *Tourists!* All three wore neon-green riding shirts and Lycra shorts.

'Hey man! I'm Matt, this is Alex, and that's Bryan. We're so glad to have found you!'

'You were looking for me?' I asked, not quite sure how that could be true.

'Sure!' said Matt. 'We saw you on TV back in Iowa, then read about you in the *Estherville Daily News*. We've been keeping an eye out for you for days now hoping to catch up! We thought we found you a while back actually. Bryan saw a tent by the roadside in the middle of nowhere and we went to investigate, but it was just an angry lady dressed in bin bags. I'm not sure what she was up to, but she chased us away pretty quickly – we all agreed that definitely wasn't you!'

Matt and Alex were brothers from Pennsylvania, and together with Alex's friend Bryan they were riding coast to coast to raise money for a well-building project in Uganda. Matt was the eldest; average height and built like a football player (of the American variety) with strong muscular limbs. Alex was taller, with an all-American smile and the physique of a track runner. Bryan was tall and lean too, but with a few days' worth of stubble and an altogether sad disposition. He reminded me of Eeyore from the Winnie the Pooh stories.

'Listen, I don't know which way you're going from here, but we have someone to host us in Mitchell. Fancy coming with us there tonight and maybe we can see if we're going the same direction tomorrow?'

I didn't think twice. Together the four of us rode down the highway towards Mitchell, and South Dakota now felt a lot less lonely.

Matt and I instantly hit it off. He was relaxed, with an easy laugh, and had an enormous interest in the world and people around him. He asked question after question, out of real and rare curiosity. That night we stayed at the house of a church pastor in Mitchell; Matt and Alex's father was a pastor himself in Philadelphia, and using a combination of his connections and Google to search for other churches, the threesome had so far managed to make it across the country with a host for every single night. Aside from not having to worry about camping, this meant regular and large home-cooked meals and for one night I joined the club.

Their contact database, unfortunately, ran out after Mitchell and they were preparing for a section of wild camping and fending for themselves until the other side of South Dakota. We agreed to cycle together as far as the Badlands; they were keen for a new dynamic to their group and I was desperate for something to break up my Midwestern monotony.

CHAPTER 27

A MILLION MILES OF CYCLING

We quickly settled into an easy rhythm, riding often in pairs. Mostly I would cycle alongside Matt, with Alex and Bryan ahead. Alex was a natural athlete and seemed to be carrying most of the equipment for the group. He was cheery but focused, and kept a strict watch on the group's finances and schedule. 'Every cent we spend is one cent less that goes to Uganda,' he told me. He and Matt bickered as brothers are prone to do, and Alex would usually come off worse being younger and smaller. And finally, there was Bryan.

Quite what Bryan was doing there I wasn't sure. He'd originally helped Alex design some flyers for the ride at a Pennsylvanian university, where they were both in their second year. Then, he'd asked to come along. This came as a surprise to Alex as Bryan hadn't seemed the active or outdoorsy type. And, as it happened, he wasn't. Bryan's life, I gathered, was spent watching TV and eating pizza. When I chatted to him we got on well but there just wasn't much to say; conversation ran dry before long. I noticed that Matt seemed to avoid him and I assumed that this was because they'd both discovered long ago that forcing conversation is a very unnecessary waste of energy on the road. I figured that Bryan maybe did have his reasons for being there but didn't feel the need to share them, or didn't know how. Perhaps it didn't matter to him whether anyone else was aware or not. I got the impression sometimes that this ride was his rebellion. Against whom, I couldn't know, but he cut the figure once in a while of a man on a mission, internally, just by the very act of being there on his bike, and for all his apparent apathy he never once appeared to consider giving up. He rarely seemed to enjoy it, but he was sure as hell going to see it through. I had a lot of respect for that.

I found now that the days passed much quicker. Hours could be easily spent talking with Matt or Alex, and if for some reason silence descended (or was enforced by having to ride in single file on narrow roads) I had so much more to ponder and analyse than before. There are few things which get your brain working overtime more than the thoughts or actions of another human with shared experiences, and I could happily pedal along thinking over some past conversation or musing the character of my new companions.

As we passed through the far side of Mitchell we made a brief stop-off at the extremely well signposted 'Corn Palace'. A neo-Moorish building boasting domes and minarets, it looked a cross between the Kremlin and Disneyland. It served dual purposes as an arena for the local community and a tourist attraction, drawing people in from all over the state (and all over the country, if you believe their literature – I didn't). The facade was covered with designs and murals made out of corn and other grain. 'Crop art, we call it, isn't it just the neatest thing?' beamed the woman at the desk.

Inside the various halls and rooms, the primary goal seemed to be selling corn-related merchandise. Amongst postcards and keychains I found some information boards which told me that the palace had originally been built in 1892 as a showcase for the rich soil of South Dakota. *Surely even for a Midwesterner a soil museum is dull*, I thought. The palace was still maintaining a similarly riveting level of attraction, now boasting a contemporary display of local grains. I couldn't help but buy some postcards of such an odd place and on the way out read that it cost $130,000 a year to decorate the place. Money well spent, seemed to be the general consensus of the patently happy tourists milling around.

'Are they smiling ironically?' I whispered to Matt.

'I'm quite enjoying myself,' he said. 'And you've just bought some postcards. There's something about this place that's… well, unique!'

It was a good point – I had never before or since been to a palace made out of corn. It's not going to make it into the highlights reel of my life, but I'd still much rather have seen it once than not. We passed on the opportunity to view a photo archive of other corn palaces that once existed in the state, and made haste back on to the road.

* * *

The following day brought a true joy, the sighting of a first hint of elevation in months, by the banks of the Missouri River. The Missouri held for me a status similar to that of the Mississippi – semi-mythical, and symbolic of wild, authentic America. It is the longest river in the USA, one of two waterways that divide the country, and for thousands of years it has provided life to those who live in its watershed. Rising in the Rocky Mountains, now less than five hundred miles from

Lola's front wheel, it runs south and east eventually joining the Mississippi at St Louis where together they flow out to the Gulf of Mexico. Here it looked broad but calm, bubbling along contently, having already spent much of its fury in the wilder sections to the west.

We sped down a steep and straight hill and over a low bridge crossing the river. I'd forgotten how good hills were – the simple pleasure of closing my eyes (briefly) and freewheeling at full speed into the onrushing wind, hearing the world whistling past my senses at phenomenal speed. As Lewis and Clark had done two hundred years before, I looked upon the crossing as another beacon reached in the quest for the Pacific Ocean. On the far side we experienced the downside of elevation, which (ironically) was going back up. My quadriceps muscles screamed in agony at the unexpected effort of climbing onto the plateau. By the time we reached the town of Winner all of us felt like losers.

The town looked like every other similar-sized settlement in the Midwest, but its main street was enlivened dramatically by the arrival of yet more cross-country cyclists. Over the crest of the hill there came two hunched and lithe figures, backs horizontal as they stood on pedals to generate power. Their bikes were bare, but both towed large single-wheeled trailers. One was much older, fifty maybe, while the second rider was younger even than Alex and Bryan – eighteen at most. We waved them down excitedly and asked them where they were headed.

'West coast,' said the older man. 'Do you know where's good to eat around here?'

'Eh, that restaurant, maybe?' offered Matt, pointing to the only eatery around. The two new cyclists disappeared inside and we stood around wondering if they were coming back to chat. They eventually emerged, but talking didn't seem huge on the agenda.

'So, do you do a lot of big rides?' I asked, persevering. I felt like we were all a unique and intrinsically connected bunch, us long-distance riders, and I hated to have that image broken.

'Ever heard of RAAM?' he asked, looking at me from below his sunglasses. I told him 'no' and he seemed to growl.

'Race across America. World's longest continuous, non-stop bicycle road race. Three thousand miles.' He jammed a huge lump of pizza into his mouth, and simultaneously squirted in a hefty amount of some sort of energy drink. Still chewing, he continued. 'I won it. Twice.'

His tone suggested I had made a grave error in my line of questioning, like meeting Stephen Hawking and asking if he knew a little about physics.

'No way! That's crazy. How long did it take you?' Matt asked.

Pizza grease oozed down his chin and he took another huge bite. 'Well, I entered eight years in a row. Best time I got was eight days, seven hours, fourteen minutes. Rode three hundred and more miles a day, and slept three hours a night. Except for the first night, when I didn't sleep at all.' He stopped chewing, and looked up at us. 'I've been riding bikes for forty years, did my first century when I was ten. They call me the "Million Mile Man".' With that, he went back to his pizza.

'Why do they call you the "Million Mile Man"?' asked Bryan.

We all looked at him. No one bothered to answer, and Matt shook his head in embarrassment.

It seemed we were in the presence of cycling greatness, although he wasn't particularly interested in us. I turned to the kid, a shy figure hiding in the shadows. He was very skinny and rather unsurprisingly was happy to let the Million Mile Man do introductions for him. 'This is my nephew. He's only eighteen, but this year he's ridden ten thousand miles already.'

Ten thousand miles? Even this kid is a machine! I thought.

The Million Mile Man and his nephew were an interesting case – they saw cycling as an athletic endeavour. I'd never approached it like that. They found adventure on the way in fits and starts, no doubt, but it seemed a shame to move so fast. It was impressive, of course – they must be covering at least a hundred miles a day even in South Dakota – but it seemed to be missing the point. Part of the appeal to me was in the slow-going, as much as I'd found it hard work in the repetitiveness of the Midwest. Lola was a means to an end, a way to explore. For the Million Mile Man the enjoyment came primarily from the riding itself. With the same tools we were carving incredibly different results.

CHAPTER 28

KINDRED SPIRITS

Alex was up front and first to spot the crickets. To begin with there was just a handful scattered across the road; however, this proved only to be the vanguard, and as we pedalled the tarmac became littered with literally thousands of the insects. A strong wind gusted across us, and blew them out of the grasslands from the south. As they were swept past they leapt and hopped frantically. I wondered what we'd done to warrant such a plague. I donned sunglasses and shielded my face. The crickets still got everywhere, landing on shoulders, heads and bodies. One made it inside Bryan's shirt. Three simultaneously landed in my crotch, the ensuing panic of which led me to accidentally punch myself in the testicles. Our tyres crunched over the unlucky ones. I briefly considered whether a dead cricket could give me a puncture. For twenty minutes they rained down upon us, then slowly the road cleared once more.

By now we were covering somewhere in the region of sixty to eighty miles a day, which I thought acceptable considering the headwinds. When I set off from New York the idea of riding eighty miles even in the most perfect of circumstances was unthinkable. Now my body was highly tuned to the job and did it without complaint. The human body is such an incredible machine, one that we are very lucky to own. It is much more complex than even the most advanced supercomputer, yet so easy to take for granted. Riding across America was a good way to remind myself just what an adaptable and powerful tool the body is, and I made a mental note to be more thankful for it.

* * *

Wood, South Dakota: Population 84. Another place to pass through and forget. A few houses lay off to the right, but all our needs for refuelling could be serviced by a small pub on the main road. Ensconced at the bar were two cyclists and I was surprised to find that they weren't the Million Mile Man and his nephew. These two were young brothers on a simple and evidently gratifying summer adventure. One looked straight out of school, and the other maybe midway through university. Their bikes were a sight to behold, full of all sorts of ingenious additions and contraptions. Two large orange bins, bought from Home Depot, were attached to the rear racks as panniers. Some wild apparatus protruded from a bottle holder (although I had no idea what it might do). It didn't surprise me to learn that both brothers were Eagle Scouts, the highest level attainable in the US Scout hierarchy, and now they were being well looked after by two burly Dakotan farmers who rather uncomfortably reminded me of my Iowan gun-wielders.

Fifteen minutes later a wiry, bearded character wearing thick spectacles and carrying a small video camera came in through the door. I could tell immediately that he was another cyclist. He went straight to the Eagle Scouts, then came over to us.

'Hey guys! What's up? I'm Sean.' Sean was instantly the friendliest guy we'd met all day and seemed more akin to my approach to cycling than any of the other riders. He asked us if we'd seen the Million Mile Man.

'Crazy, eh? This tiny town of eighty-four people in the middle of South Dakota – *South Dakota*, man – and there's nine cross-country cyclists passing through in one day! I met the Home Depot twins over there earlier on today. Dude, isn't this just wild?'

Sean's own story was pretty crazy. He had a manic quality to his speech and movements, as if he'd been drinking coffee all day. I could tell he was someone who wouldn't engage in bullsh*t. The wild look suited him but it also seemed like this world, adventure and outdoors, wasn't a natural fit for him.

'I'm a computer geek, man, through and through,' he confided. 'I work at a college as a video editor, and I film a bunch of bands around Philadelphia. But I wanted to test myself, y'know? I felt I needed a journey, a rite of passage to get to know myself. So I planned to walk across the USA.'

'You started walking?' asked Matt. 'How far did you get?'

'About thirteen hundred miles or so. I walked from Philly to Iowa, but man, walking is super tough. I just got so down, I was seriously depressed. After a while, I just hated everything, every single day. So I was just gonna give up, 'cuz I was worried about how down I was getting. But then my buddy told me about this girl cycling across the US, and I checked out her blog. She was supercool, and I got hooked on the idea of getting a bike as soon as I could, and then biking from there. I know nothing about bikes, man, I haven't had one in years. But this bike shop I was at in Des Moines, Iowa recommended one and here I am!'

'That's a cool story,' I replied.

'Yea, you guys would love her. Susie, she's called – an Australian chick.'

Susie! What a small world. Shared passion is a powerful tool for connection, regardless of geographical boundaries. The unpredictability of it all and the coincidences among like-minded people were at the root of why I loved this life. People like Sean and Matt and Susie – I felt they too were experiencing something similar to me, some desire to discover their own limits. 'To answer the call of the open road,' as Susie often said.

Sean was shooting a documentary about his journey and when the Eagle Scouts said they were heading back to the ranch with their new friends he decided to tag along. 'They're going to rustle some cattle tomorrow – that'll make great footage!' The brothers got in a truck with one farmer, and the other truck was loaded up with all of their bicycles and belongings. Sean hopped in the front. His driver staggered out of the bar and got in beside him, looking haggard in the way only a lifetime of Bud Light bingeing can bring about. I remembered what Michael had told me back in Iowa about how people in the Midwest were used to driving drunk. The trucks rolled away, Sean waving out the window.

In the morning we pushed on west and talked about how jealous we were of Sean and the brothers rustling cattle on a ranch somewhere and having a much better time than us. As it turned out, we couldn't have been more wrong. Later Sean would tell us that on the way to the farm it became quickly apparent that the driver was seriously inebriated, and was struggling to keep his eyes open. At one point he said, 'I sure hope we don't hit any corners, because if we do, we're screwed!'

Not long after that, they hit a corner, without turning, and were screwed. The truck rolled twice, Sean's camera recording the whole time. They could easily have been killed, but both somehow escaped without any serious injury. Eventually the other rancher came looking for them and took them home, where Sean passed out in drunken and terrified exhaustion. In the morning they returned to the crash site to salvage what they could; Sean found all his stuff, including his camera, but when he opened it up the memory card was missing. There was only one explanation – someone must have taken it out manually. The camera itself was almost completely intact, and there was no way the card could have fallen out. Sean figured the ranchers had taken it to hide any incriminating evidence of drunk-driving. When he voiced this theory to them they admitted freely that they had done so, but seemed confident that there was nothing Sean would (or could) do about it. That's where they were wrong. Sean – bearded, bespectacled, video geek Sean – pulled a Special Forces-issue baton from his rucksack and said he'd fight for it. The two beefy ranchers, outsizing and outnumbering him, decided they didn't fancy their odds and gave back the footage. Sean set off riding again with the Eagle Scout Brothers, unharmed, and with bike, gear and pride intact.

CHAPTER 29

TO SHARE THE ROAD

Summer had by now fully taken hold of our world and as we pushed westwards Matt reminded me that Fourth of July was fast approaching. Weeks on the road had become months, and roughly two thousand miles of cycling separated me from my Brooklyn apartment. Matt, and by extension all of us, had an invite to spend the holiday with an ex-girlfriend and her family. They were coming out from California to the town of Custer on the far side of the state. If we pedalled hard we could meet them there in time for a party. Matt assured me it wouldn't be weird to hang out with the parents of someone he used to date.

Independence Day is one of the biggest events in the American calendar and, as we rode, Matt filled in the gaps in my knowledge about the holiday. Stemming from 1776, it marks the day Thomas Jefferson's Declaration of Independence was finally approved by Congress, sealing the legal separation of the thirteen British colonies on the North Atlantic coast from the rule of Great Britain. The day America was born.

It is now a national holiday marked by excessive displays of patriotism. American families whom I had met all seemed able to recount with great accuracy where they had been on each and every Fourth of July, and what they had done. ('Oh yes, 1986 was a good one, John and I took little Alfie to see the fireworks by the river and he was so scared from the banging and flashing that he cried all the way home.') This would be my first experience, and I hoped to mark it in suitably over-the-top style, with pyrotechnics and beer and loud cheering. We pushed hard into the wind, now with the goals of good food, good company and a wild party providing requisite energy.

The approach of the Badlands National Park was announced by a gradual change in topography. Slowly the ground passing beneath our wheels began to undulate, and on occasion the horizon rose or fell a little. The land we were crossing was labelled as Pine Ridge Indian Reservation, designated for and given to the Oglala Lakota people. At one time, before the colonial powers arrived on the continent, all the lands in South Dakota and beyond had belonged to the Great Sioux Nation, of whom the Lakotans and Dakotans were part. As happened in the rest of the country, these tribes were slowly and methodically engaged and defeated by the armies of the US government as part of the westward expansion in the 1800s, and eventually those that were left were rounded up into the Pine Ridge Reservation.

There are over three hundred Indian reservations in the US – areas of land that are managed by a Native American tribe under government guidance – which make up roughly 2.3 per cent of the entire US landmass. Even to my uneducated brain, that seems a raw deal, to go from full ownership to such a small percentage. Even that remainder is significantly tainted. The federal government subsidises the living costs on the reservations, but those residents that we met complained there were no prospects. Alcoholism, drug abuse and domestic violence were rife. Without an outlet, without hope, the government handouts seem to do little more than feed the problems.

Passing through the settlements was a deeply disturbing experience. Pine Ridge is the poorest reservation in the country, and poverty screamed out all around. Houses were little more than tumbledown shacks, and there was practically nothing in the way of industry or infrastructure. Judging by the amount of men and women wandering around or idly leaning on the walls of their tattered homes in the shade, employment here seemed little more than a pipedream; something other people could enjoy. Old men with deeply ridged faces puffed on pipes and watched us go by, sitting in the same seats by the roadside that they have probably sat in for fifty or more years. Cherub-faced kids danced around, kicking stones. They smiled at us, but I couldn't help feel that unless something dramatically changed they would eventually end up like the old men nearby. Like the Australian aboriginals, or the Moroccan Berbers, the indigenous people of America have had it rough, and it's not getting any easier.

An additional oddity was that occasionally we would pass through these rundown, sorry-looking towns only to find within a few miles an enormous, glittering casino up ahead, all flashing neon and kitsch Native American stereotyping. Due to a complex legal scenario, gambling is permitted on the reservations without the restrictions that apply in the rest of the USA. As a result, casinos and bingo halls are popping up all over Indian lands, and tourists flock in from around the country. It's seen by some as the future of the Native Americans – a path to regaining some ownership over their revenue and industry. That revenue, of course, is substantial.

I never saw fit to stop off in any of them; I'm not a gambler (financially, at least) and casinos have never appealed. I suppose I don't care too much about winning or losing, which takes the fun out of it. Nevertheless I was impressed, or at least taken aback, by the size of these complexes. Often they would be the only noticeable building as far as the eye could see – a modern-day neon oasis in a dusty, barren land. They seemed garish and ruthless places to me, but what did I know? If they offer a better future for the people on the reservations, then maybe it's a gamble worth taking.

* * *

By now I was used to the daily rigours of riding a bicycle indefinitely. I woke each morning at around 6 a.m. and tried to be on the road within an hour. I loved nothing more than pedalling as the sun rose behind me. Some people enjoy evenings and late nights, but to me that is a time for the young and the carefree (a niche I no longer fitted). The middle of the day is the realm of the busy man with much to do. I am an enthusiast of the morning, of being on the move as the world gradually awakes, when light filters into the sky and slowly the day begins to take shape. From the prelude of birdsong to the coda of rush hour, I love it all.

Travelling with company, however, always slows and delays the morning process. I shared a tent with Matt who habitually stayed inside his sleeping bag for as long as possible. Usually I had to start taking the tent down with him still inside before he made a move. In the other tent Alex was up before any of us, while Bryan shared Matt's penchant for lie-ins.

The first few hours of proper cycling were almost always difficult and slow. Before the heat crept into the day there would be a slight chill in the air and I'd ride with a hooded top on, slowly spinning the pedals through muscle memory more than any desire or energy. I tried to ride fifteen or twenty miles before the first break, as a pre-emptive strike on the inevitably sluggish progress once the wind and blistering sun arrived.

The Badlands marked the start of what would be the most tourist-orientated section of my journey across the USA so far. By the very nature of following no set plan or structure, I'd struck a somewhat unusual route across the country. As such I'd missed almost all of the big draws for sightseers and travellers, an exception being the Niagara Falls, and possibly the Corn Palace, at a push. A real push.

The Badlands are not quite on the same commercial scale as Niagara in terms of visitor numbers, but they do draw an audience of hundreds of thousands each year. I knew now that I could also expect a similarly bustling experience in Yellowstone National Park; the bubbling, boiling supervolcano that attracts gawpers in their hordes to see at first hand its geothermal wonders. In between I'd pass Mount Rushmore, where visages of four past presidents are proudly and gigantically carved into stone, as well as the lesser attractions of the Black Hills, and the site of General Custer's last stand at the Battle of Little Big Horn.

I was all set to see a different side of America. Historically the West has represented the frontier, pushing ever further towards the coast; a land of roaming buffalo, free-spirited Indians fighting valiantly against their colonial oppressors, cowboys wheeling round muscular horses and lassoing cowgirls with abandon. So the stories and stereotypes go. Now, however, the

West seems a place which serves two very important, but very different, purposes for the American population – a location to vacation in, or to retire in.

The Badlands were my introduction to those who practised the latter (and quite often simultaneously the former). It also marked my initiation into the New World order of the Recreational Vehicle (RV). I'd seen a couple back east, but out here they seemed to have proliferated in the dry heat. As the four of us pedalled in single file along broad blacktop highways, hundreds of these rumbling beasts of the West would pass us by.

There are three main categories of RV, to my mind. The first was the rarest – a humble, traditional 'camper van' as we call them in Europe. These are relatively small with just enough room for a small living area inside, plus a couple of beds and a toilet. Hippies were the most regular exponents of this particular category.

The second group is a larger version of the first – slightly bigger, slightly more brash and with a few more bells and whistles. These are driven by regular, all-American families and are the hardest to predict in terms of their tolerance regarding bicycles.

The final category, and my real pet hate, were the monstrous lorries that seem now to be an acceptable mode of transport despite hogging entire roads and being larger than a vehicle anyone in their right mind would desire. Stretching around 40 feet in length they are the size of a passenger bus, and so awkwardly cumbersome to drive on minor roads that they usually tow a small car behind to take the 'campers' on day trips once they've 'pitched up'. Along with an entire apartment complex housed inside, these colossal fiends often contain myriad bicycles and motorbikes hidden away to provide the merry vacationer with the whole gamut of options for recreation. Believe me when I say these vehicles are far beyond necessity. Guzzling gas at a horrendous rate, spewing fumes out with abandon, and causing enormous tailbacks on winding mountain roads, they are generally driven by a subspecies of quick-tempered, dim-witted, intolerant and overweight morons, with the hand-eye coordination of a small, blind rodent – these were not friends of the cyclist, as I would soon find out.

CHAPTER 30

A CHANGE IN SCENERY

Aside from RVs, the road to the Badlands was characterised by many enormous signs advertising the nationally famous 'Wall Drug'. Wall Drug is little more than a glorified shopping mall which houses a pharmacy and a few other gift shops and restaurants. There is nothing particularly noticeable or impressive about it, aside from the aura that surrounds it – it is a phenomenon so wonderfully and uniquely American that it is enough to bring a smile to the face of even the most cynical critic.

Its reputation and status as a tourist attraction stems from when it first opened in 1931. The wife of the then owner, pharmacist Ted Hustead, came up with the idea of giving their small-time pharmacy's slow trade a boost by advertising free ice water to travellers passing through. The timing was perfect as the Mount Rushmore sculptures had just been unveiled, and the small town of Wall where the Hudsteads had their store was en route. Business boomed. Since then it's become something of a novelty and grown into the mall it is today. During the hot summer months in South Dakota, Wall Drug gives out up to twenty thousand free cups of water a day and, according to the *New York Times*, draws over two million visitors a year. Much of this is due to the wonderfully bizarre and excessive advertising campaign. Billboards line almost every major road in South Dakota, spilling over into neighbouring states for good measure.

Having been caught out by the Mitchell Corn Palace, I was quite happy to give Wall Drug a miss. The billboards and – the *pièce de résistance* – an 80-foot plastic dinosaur branded with the Wall Drug name, which we had seen by the roadside earlier that day, were enough for me. At a small diner, a rancher on his way home from the west coast told us that after Ted Hustead's death, the governor of South Dakota described him as 'a guy that figured out that free ice water could turn you into a phenomenal success in the middle of a semi-arid desert way out in the middle of someplace'. Put that way, that's something to be proud of. Perhaps a classic example of the American spirit, and the ability of this country to produce and endorse the utterly bizarre in an endearing and rousing manner.

A few miles before the real hills of the Badlands we encountered a sizeable tailback, stemming from the small collection of buildings by the roadside that constituted the official entrance to the park. We freewheeled past the idling traffic, drawing looks of consternation from sweaty, frustrated drivers and hopelessly bored kids who bounced around in back seats. Most vehicles, inevitably, were RVs. Squeezing onto the furthest extreme of the hard shoulder to get past one particularly fat model, a voice from the passenger seat high above our heads called out.

'Hey sh*theads! Who says you get to jump the queue? Wait in turn like the rest of us!'

A middle-aged and slightly balding man with a red face leaned out from the driver seat. Beside him a younger and quite attractive lady looked slightly embarrassed by the whole thing. There didn't seem any point in arguing so we just rode on. He continued to shout after us. As Matt pedalled past he greeted the woman with a nod and a wink, then rode off at full speed. 'That'll really give him something to think about...' he laughed. 'And her!'

Soon we were swallowed by the Badlands. What had been flat prairie (and continues to be so on the land to the south and north) was now a curious mountainous scene of sharply eroded buttes and pinnacles of browns and greys. The spires were brightly coloured in a layered effect, each strata of rock and soil clearly separated and defined from that above it. We rode amongst the gullies, climbing up and over and looking out across endless canyons.

Initially it seemed our opportunity for adventure was limited by the blacktop road that picked the path of least resistance through the ravines. Cars and RVs passed constantly, somewhat ruining the impact of the geography around us. A driver told us the temperature had hit 105 degrees Fahrenheit, and I could well believe it – the tarmac beneath our wheels was scorching to the touch and radiated black heat back onto our boiling bodies.

We had been encouraged by the park officials at the entrance to stick to the road, but that now seemed terribly dull. Instead, at a pull-off, we left our bikes by a line of parked RVs and made our way into the pinnacles. A well-tanned couple wearing oversized polo shirts sat in the shade of their RV nearby, watching. It was a Category One model (the humblest available) and so when they called us over I was not too distressed to have to talk to them.

I often forgot quite how ridiculous we four looked – dirty, sweaty, bearded, me in slightly torn and stained clothes and the other three wearing neon green shirts and skintight shorts, giving anyone who cared a good idea of what they were packing. Looking back, I wonder how some people kept a straight face whilst talking to us.

Bill and Lou had just retired and moved to Flagstaff, Arizona. They'd seen some other cyclists a few days back in one of the southern states. Driving their RV across the country was part of their lifestyle now – for six months they'd tour around, criss-crossing the country on northern latitudes, and then return to Arizona to see out the winter with some southern heat.

'We've been here maybe ten times. Just can't get enough of it. You know why this type of place is called the Badlands?' asked Bill.

We looked at each other. Bill took this as a no.

'It comes from the Indian word.' He said Indian with such a drawl that for the first time I could see how 'Injun' had become the shorthand nomenclature in the nineteenth and early twentieth centuries. 'I can't quite remember what the word was, but it was the Lakota tribe who first came up with it. Anyhow, it translated as "Bad Land". Then the French trappers who came through here got the same idea – "the bad land to cross," they called it. Well, I guess it was. For ten thousand years the Indians lived around here, using it for hunting. They could climb to the top of these peaks and get the locations of the buffalo, the rabbits and what have you. Pretty good for spotting other tribes that might want to come get you when you're not looking, too. I bet you boys are pretty keen to have a scramble, eh?'

We nodded and set off up for nearest mound like kids to a sweet shop. Ahead and above was a wall of layered brown rock, topped by church-like spires; clay crumbled in my hand as I pulled myself up the steep embankment and I felt a slight pang of guilt as I accidentally kicked away a huge lump of soil. *People have been doing this for thousands of years*, I told myself. A series of small holes were carved into the narrow ridge near the top, like portholes on the side of some great ocean liner, and I squeezed through and onto a tiny ledge on the far side.

Beyond me a vista opened up like no other. The wall of rock had been beautiful from the far side, but now I saw that it was little more than an ornate doorway to this kingdom. As far as I could see, the wild and twisted oddities of the Badlands sprawled their way across the landscape; afternoon was leaving us and the sun made its eternal cyclical journey down towards the furthest spires on the horizon. In between the lumps there were occasional snatches of flatter prairie land. The literature I'd been given said it was the largest mixed-grass prairie in the USA. I tried to imagine having to cross this topography without the use of a road and I was suddenly more grateful for the easy access of the highway. Yet it still seemed a travesty to me that 95 per cent of the visitors to the park would not experience views like this. The road took in some beautiful sights, but just a ten-minute scramble from the road in any direction was a place where one could feel alone and wild. Just a short distance from any busy path, perhaps, there is the quiet and rewarding route waiting to be trod.

CHAPTER 31

'THREE MILLION?'

We spent the rest of the afternoon making our way along Route 240, pausing for additional forays into the lands beyond the tarmac. I had a vague plan of camping on top of a butte and waking to the sun rising over peaks to the east, but after stopping for the obligatory mid-afternoon peanut butter sandwiches, it materialised that none of us had much food left. Water, too, was not in abundance. Someone hit on the idea of cutting south-west out of the hills. Alex, for whom logistics came naturally, spoke between mouthfuls of sandwich. 'There's a little town on the map here. "Scenic", it's called. Sounds nice. We could get there in about three hours, load up on food and water, and then ride west until we find a nice camping spot with a view of the Badlands.'

We followed a small paved access road that wound along the canyon floor and then up and over a small plateau. Soon it turned to loose gravel on which we crunched our way slowly south. Riding a heavily loaded touring bike in gravel such as this requires quite a bit of skill, something that none of us really possessed. Regularly one of us would fail to hold balance and end up face down on the grit. Travelling as we were at only seven miles per hour meant that luckily nothing was hurt except pride.

The further away we got from the Badlands, the more impressive they looked, dominating the sky behind us. The land ahead levelled out again as if compressed with a large rolling pin and we rejoined a paved state road. Little on the landscape bore the mark of human hands, which made our destination town of Scenic all the more noticeable. It sat in a small cluster less than a half-mile from the main road; to the south verdant green fields interspersed with dusty undulations, and to the north a stunning view of the National Park. By the time we reached the first group of buildings we had clocked up nearly seventy-five miles for the day. It was slightly above our average and felt a good time to be close to stopping.

The town was built around a dusty T-junction with a well on the left, and to the right the Longhorn General Store boasted 'Buy, Sell, Trade'. In painted red letters hanging above a rusted wagon wheel, the shop's motto adorned the awning: 'Ashes to ashes, dust to dust, if we don't have it, it isn't a must.' Wooden steps led to two large, handmade saloon doors, which were firmly bolted shut. The windows had been boarded up, and gravel and dust layered everything. Further along was what at one time must have been the centre point of the town – the Longhorn Saloon. The sign was written in the type of slanted font we now associate with the 'Wild West' and dated the wooden building to 1906. 'INDIANS ALLOWED', it proclaimed proudly. On closer inspection the sign had originally read 'NO INDIANS ALLOWED', but some recent bout of conscience had led someone to paint over the first word. Two rows of animal skulls completed the decoration.

Beyond this core there wasn't much else; only a small temporary-looking structure sitting by the route back to Highway 44 looked like it was from this century. It also looked like it might be open. Alex went to fill our water bottles from the well while Matt and I pulled open a corrugated iron door to let ourselves into what we hoped was a convenience store. There were two large wooden counters in the open room; on those just a few dusty packets of crisps. An old woman was bent double over a crossword puzzle at a low table, and beside her writhed two screaming young girls. They looked about five or six years old, and seemed caught in the grip of an eternal tantrum (though I had no idea what for). Every so often the old woman would reach out without looking and try to slap one of the girls, and they'd cry some more. A man in the very back corner played on a fruit machine, his head hung low.

'Excuse me, do you know who runs this place?' asked Matt to anyone listening. A small table by the door seemed to constitute a rudimentary counter, but for now it lay empty.

'I run it!' came the snapped response from the old woman, pausing briefly from beating her children.

'Eh... can we buy some food, please?'

'Sure!' she barked. 'What do you want?' As if there was a choice.

We chose our flavours of crisps and located a small but valuable packet of trail mix lurking at the bottom of the pile. Alex and Bryan walked in, now accompanied by a second woman, slightly younger than the first. This one had more energy and seemed on a mission. Her face bore pockmarks of years spent facing the elements. She looked tough, and she looked like she didn't have much time for us.

'We're closing up,' she snapped at Alex as she followed him through the door. He started saying something but she wasn't having any of it. 'Closing up!' she bellowed.

Unceremoniously we were pushed out the door. The screaming children were shoved onto an odd-looking dune-buggy-like contraption and the shady man from the fruit machine climbed onto the back. The two women jumped in the front. 'Where is everyone else?' asked Matt, with more than a hint of desperation.

'They're gone! No one lives here no more. This store is closing next week. Nothing left here.' She started the engine.

'Why?' Matt persisted.

The woman paused and cocked her head. She didn't like us, and sharing a few more seconds of conversation seemed to frustrate her. 'No work here, not for a long time. People moved away. Then a few years ago everybody started falling out, arguing with each other. And that was it, they all scarpered. We're the only ones left and we live 'bout five miles down the track now.'

She relaxed a little, with a hint of fallen pride in the town. Matt continued gently.

'How many used to live here?'

'Back in 1916, that was our high point,' she began. 'More'n a hundred and fifty people then. Once upon a time we had two restaurants, a hotel, three gas stations. Anyone driving east used to stop off here on the way from Rapid City. But since the freeways came, there're not many folk using Highway 44 any more.'

'So what happens now? Who owns all this?' I asked.

'Well, I do!'

'All of it?' asked Matt. We looked at each other.

'Sure! I been buying it up bit by bit since 1963. I got fifty-six acres in total now. So I'm gunna sell it,' she said.

'You're going to sell the town? How do you sell a town?' Alex asked wide-eyed.

'Well, it's up there on that eBay, and there's a few realtors looking at it. Plenty of folk driven here from the West Coast, but no one's shown me any cash yet.'

'How much are you asking?' I posed the question with a sudden and overwhelming sense that she might say she was sick of the whole process and that she'd sell up for a dollar. Just like the sale of Manhattan Island. Imagine what I could do with my own town!

'Three million.'

Bugger. The other woman interjected, saying, 'She'll never get that much. People will only pay half that, at most.'

'The hell they will!' was the response. 'I'm not budging for no one. It's three million, or no sale.'

'Well… good luck,' said Matt. 'If we come into some money we'll be in touch.'

'Don't go messing with anything, you hear? It might all be boarded up, but it's still vandalising if you mess with it.' With that she drove off, leaving behind a cloud of dust and us four rather dumbfounded cyclists.

Scenic, South Dakota. My first ever ghost town. I'd heard about these before – mostly they were mining or Old West towns; sometimes settlements that had sprung up to support the influx of prospectors during the California Gold Rush in the nineteenth century. All across the country these spectres of America Past lingered on, the dying breath of a time and place long gone. Since 1920 the rural areas of the Great Plains have lost a third of their population. A slow but steady migration to urban centres is the legacy of railroads that failed to materialise, and of freeways and industrialisation that promised jobs, prospects and a variety of potential futures to excite many a Dakotan farmhand.

We ambled around wondering what it would be like to own a town. The views were spectacular. I was surprised that some Californian billionaire hadn't yet decided to buy it as a holiday home, or to turn into a 'Wild West' theme park. Behind the saloon we found an old jail, the rusty barred entrance gate swinging in the wind. How many people had languished inside this very cell, and for what crimes? Logistically, the town's defunct status meant we were likely to go hungry that night. I wasn't too bothered – hunger would pass, but I was sure that I'd remain intrigued by Scenic for a long time to come.

I have since found out that Scenic, South Dakota was finally sold, although not for the three million dollars desired. Instead, an agent stepped in, cut the price to $799,000, and the competition went wild. The eventual buyers were a Filipino church, *Iglesia ni Cristo*, or 'Church of Christ'. Ostensibly an independent Christian movement (although notably rejecting some key Christian doctrine), they are one of the fastest-growing religions in the world and have gathered a following of nearly two million people, including six hundred congregations outside the Philippines (in sixty different countries). Following the purchase of Scenic they have refused to say much about their plans, which is unsurprising as they are renowned for secrecy. Inevitably this has led to a few concerned ranchers in the local area worrying about possible cult activities. The saga of Scenic, South Dakota, continues…

* * *

It now seemed a waste to just set up camp when we could harness our newfound enthusiasm to make more miles. The Badlands were beautiful, but my mind had drifted to the food and company that awaited us in Custer with Matt's contacts. If we made it to Rapid City before the day was out, we could be eating and drinking in the campsite with them by the following evening.

Together we decided that another forty miles wasn't a problem. Well, three of us decided – Bryan wasn't in agreement, but he was overruled. The sun set by the western extreme of the Badlands and darkness swept over us. For the next three hours we crossed the Buffalo Gap. There were no towns to be seen anywhere, nor in fact any signs of civilisation at all. Stars speckled the sky, the brightest I'd seen anywhere in North America. We rode in the darkness, watching shooting stars and listening to the silence of the Great Plains all around. I was in pain, suffering from the long hours and the heavy bike. But I also felt like there was nowhere I'd rather be. I was especially happy to share the experience with Matt and Alex (and Bryan). I still didn't know what I was looking for on this journey, but gradually I'd been accumulating a sense that I could deal with the road and what it brought. Perhaps after a while longer I'd be ready to deal with life. The companionship brought me out of my tendency to focus on negatives and reminded me to appreciate this experience for what it was. It's unlikely that I'll ever ride across the Buffalo Gap in the darkness again. I'm glad I did it once.

CHAPTER 32

TRANSITIONS

Split in two by a longitudinal mountain range, Rapid City seemed a picturesque and bustling place, the latter aspect at odds with what I'd seen of South Dakota so far. It serves as a gateway to the Black Hills, and when gold was discovered in these isolated mountains in 1874 the region was overwhelmed by an influx of prospectors with their worldly possessions over their shoulder and dollar signs in their eyes. Rapid City was born to house the hopeful. The Gold Rush inevitably dwindled, but not long after the city found a new purpose as the railroad hub between mountains and plains. For many people over many years it had been the launching point for expeditions to find fame and fortune, and equally a place to return to for licking wounds and accepting defeat.

For us, it was merely a brief stop-off on the way to our own landmark of Custer National Park. While Matt, Alex and Bryan stocked up in the Walmart (by this point frugality was defeating higher morality), my attention was caught by a large outdoor store in the middle of an industrial park. Lola was doing just fine, but I figured I could use a spare inner tube. In nearly two thousand five hundred miles of meandering since I left New

York I'd had just two punctures, yet still my insecurities couldn't quite shake the feeling that I was overdue a bad spell.

I pottered around for a while looking at this and that, and thinking of all the money people spend on outdoor gear that never gets used. Men in smart shirts and slacks looked at expensive tennis rackets and golf clubs, and an overweight couple were deep in conversation with a salesman about a frame for doing sit-ups. In their hands they held the remains of a McDonald's lunch; judging by the size of their behinds, it was not their first. I squeezed past to find the cycling section, resisting the urge to point out the sizeable flaw in their proposed fitness regime of eating McDonald's burgers and doing (at most) the occasional sit-up.

The first row of cycling paraphernalia that I saw displayed an array of tight, Lycra cycling shorts. On special offer. Up until this point I was still wearing regular running shorts while I rode, often with boxers underneath. I had a poor-quality leather saddle and the combined effect was one of a rather sore and raw arse. Matt, Alex and Bryan all had riding shorts. Even Susie had been wearing padded shorts. Still, the idea of joining their chamois crew seemed a compromise – a move away from my idealistic low-budget, amateur approach. Rather than a cyclist I had identified myself as a traveller who chose to move by bicycle. I also got an oddly gratifying boost out of showing people how much stuff I'd hauled across the country and how poorly prepared I was. It seemed a counter-intuitive way of thinking, but I liked the applause for succeeding against the odds. Yet if all the hindrances I faced were self-inflicted, at what point did I become the fool for not changing them in the face of increased wisdom and experience? Did cycling across America in inadequate clothing pulling three times as much gear as necessary make me a heroic and courageous adventurer, or a moron who didn't learn his lessons?

I paid forty dollars for my first ever pair of cycling shorts. An attractive saleswoman helped me choose and then, embarrassingly, stood outside the changing rooms while I tried them on. When I stepped out I felt completely naked. Leon Junior (so to speak) felt squashed into a very awkward position, and glancing down I could see the outline perfectly. *How are these an acceptable thing to wear in public?* Marie, as her name badge read, said they looked perfect. I did a twirl for her and she commented on my muscular thighs. I felt far too self-conscious to be flirting (or to be made fun of, I wasn't sure which), so I quickly paid and left. As soon I was outside I put my regular shorts over the top. I wasn't quite ready to strut around town showing off the outline of my willy – that seemed like something I should save for a special occasion.

I walked back to Lola through a small park, set against the backdrop of the mountains rising to the west. On a solitary bench, an elderly man sat facing the hills; indigenous, his face lined with thick creases, long black hair flowing to his waist, torn sandals over gnarled toes. When he called over to me I was hesitant. I wasn't even sure what I should call his people, and was worried I'd get it wrong and seem disrespectful. 'Indian' I knew was a mostly antiquated term, now seen as not much better than 'savage'. Native American seemed to be only used by the middle-class white tourists we'd met. I was out of the Pine Ridge Reservation boundaries and what little history I'd gathered on that region was now rendered obsolete. Back east the people I'd met had identified themselves as Lakota, one of the three groups of the Great Sioux Nation (along with the Nakota and Dakota), but I was unwilling to hazard this as a guess.

As per usual, I was overthinking the situation. He shook my hand and his face broke into a smile, the lines around his mouth and eyes dispersing like a river breaking its banks.

'Beautiful, isn't it? Are you headed to the Black Hills?'

I told him I was.

'They're very special, the Black Hills.'

'Why?'

'Well, there's been people here since 7000 BC for starters. The Lakota people came over from Minnesota in the fifteenth century. Those are my folks, the Lakota. They drove the other tribes out and settled there. It's beautiful in there, man. We got bison, deer, Bighorn sheep, even mountain lions. There'll be people tell you to watch out for them, but you won't see a mountain lion, don't worry about that. The creeks are packed full of trout. The trees you can see from here are ponderosa pine. That smell, it stays with you a lifetime.'

'Was it these mountains where gold was discovered?' I asked.

He laughed with a low rumble. 'Gold is a bit of a touchy subject!' he said. 'The US government once signed a treaty that said the Black Hills was property of the Lakota, forever. Then about ten years later General Custer came strolling through here and announced to the world that he'd found gold. Well, that was that. Miners came from everywhere, from Montana and Colorado where the gold had run dry, and from further afield too. There was a few battles, you've probably heard about those, and when the Lakota were defeated the government reassigned my ancestors to the reservations.'

'And that was it?' I asked.

'As far as the US government was concerned, it was,' he replied. 'Because they'd violated the treaty, the Lakota never officially recognised their actions, but what could they really do? About thirty years ago it finally came to court. *United States versus the Sioux Nation of Indians*, they called it. A settlement was offered, just over a hundred million bucks, but we want the Black Hills back. They're part of our history. And, well, that's how it is. We didn't take the money and it's still being debated. But I realised a long time ago that I wouldn't be around to see the day that the Black Hills are given back to my people.'

I was silent for a while. 'I had no idea.'

'Well, the tourist board don't exactly shout about it, it'd put a bit of a downer on some folks' holiday I s'pose!' He laughed again with that low rumble – a chuckle without mirth.

* * *

With panniers and water bottles stocked once more, Matt, Alex, Bryan and I set off towards the hills. Immediately the ground began to undulate. 'Watch out for them prairie rattlesnakes!' yelled a helpful passer-by in the suburbs. Granite peaks stretched skyward before us and as we entered into the forested foothills I quickly found that this was the hardest riding I'd done since the Catskills in New York. The roads were narrow and twisted devilishly around canyons and gorges, and RVs passed within inches of our pannier bags on blind corners.

In Keystone, a former mining town that had restyled itself as a resort at the entrance to the Mount Rushmore National Memorial, we stopped to make the most of tourist-ville.

Mount Rushmore was now the key draw to this area for holidaymakers. Beautiful scenery and sites of nineteenth-century battles were all well and good, but what the American public really wanted to see was four enormous faces carved into a big rock. Ice cream (for morale) cost us a day's budget each, and with the clouds blowing away on a soft wind to the south the heat gathered and merrymakers revelled.

It is my firm belief that once a place is publicised as a tourist attraction it begins a downward trajectory in beauty and authenticity. I was glad that I'd avoided tourist traps so far. My nature is far from antisocial, but as we rode back out of the Keystone Valley I became convinced that I'd rather find my own private piece of 'moderate' beauty, rather than share a stunning location with a million sweaty families with cameras and cellphones and a complete disregard for why they are there.

I am generalising, of course, and I knew then as I pedalled and pondered that I was overreacting. But on the hard pushes uphill it helped to work myself into a frenzy – the anger released adrenalin, which pumped me up the climbs all the quicker. The fact was I was also jealous. I missed the ease that came with motorised travel, and the lack of concern required about where you might sleep or what you might eat. I loved this life of vagabonding, but I was also struggling to let it become natural. There was still a part of me that clung onto my worries and fears and desires and on some level I would have given anything to jump in an RV, crack open a beer and ride to California. Of course I would soon regret it, but the urge was there now and again. To accept a life of regular physical and mental trials and challenges required constant work and readjustment.

Despite all this, I couldn't ride directly past Mount Rushmore without joining the masses to see what the fuss was about. My first sighting was at the top of a forested pass, steep granite on my left and earth falling away to the right. A valley opened out below and at the far end a large grey compound sat nestled below the four chiselled faces of immortalised US presidents: George Washington, Thomas Jefferson, Theodore Roosevelt and Abraham Lincoln.

Each face is around 60 foot in height and all were carved by a Danish-American sculptor called Gutzon Borglum. To many Americans, I am led to believe, they are an institution – as recognisable as the Washington Memorial or the Brooklyn Bridge – but I must admit to finding them quite peculiar. Inevitably, tourism was at the heart of the idea from the beginning.

Borglum gathered four hundred sculptors to work on the likenesses. He chose Washington, Jefferson, Roosevelt and Lincoln to represent the first hundred and fifty years of American history, and in 1941, fourteen years after starting, carving ceased. Despite plans to add torsos, funding had run out and so they stayed as we see them now. The celebration of the presidents' role in defending the Republic and expanding its territory seemed in particularly bad taste, given what I'd been told about the land-ownership history of the Black Hills.

We rode down to the visitor centre and paid our fee. Alex was concerned that an opportunistic thief might try to rifle through our bags and he was right to be wary; I had grown complacent. But the fact was that in two months of riding I hadn't had a single negative encounter in this regard. I never locked my bike any more, even giving away my heavy chain lock in Iowa. I doubted anyone could ride my loaded bike if they tried. Balancing it was a skill that quickly became second nature, but on first attempt most people will fail desperately, usually falling off almost instantly and ending up trapped under the panniers or mangled by the frame. Complacency won out in this instance and we left our unlocked bags behind, parked beside the visitor-centre staffroom for a modicum of security.

Up close the heads seemed even more bizarre, towering over the crowd below, each set of presidential eyes staring to the middle distance. There's no doubting the impressive nature of their scale, nor of the depictions themselves – the sculptures certainly elicit a powerful sense of authority. I suppose to many Americans that sense might be read as patriotism. To look up at the visages of four such founding and formative influences on the country you call home. I can see the appeal, but it was lost on me.

Matt and I trekked up the side of Rushmore, where a brass plaque told me the mountain was named after Charles E. Rushmore in 1885, a New York lawyer. Or rather, renamed; it had previously been known as Six Grandfathers by the Lakota before the land grab. At the top I was disappointed to learn that I couldn't walk right to the edge and look out over Washington's vast nose. Instead the trail stayed well back, but I could still see the crowds below, looking up at us looking down on them, with four enormous heads and a wealth of complex history between us.

My three companions were also unimpressed with the overall effect of the site, yet still recognised it as a part of national history. 'It is what it is,' said Alex. 'It might have come about in less than admirable circumstances, but it went ahead, and it's quite a feat.'

'Wasn't Borglum a member of the Ku Klux Klan?' chipped in Matt.

'Really?' I asked. The Ku Klux Klan: the infamous and outlandish hate group who spread messages of white supremacism through terrorism and fear mongering, and reside in the shadier side of American history that is almost as intriguing as it is disgusting. I find it hard to believe that anyone could have been a member of the KKK and retained any sort of reputation, but again my ignorance displayed a large failure to grasp American history and its complexity. In the tough economic and social climates in the 1860s (and again in the 1920s) the Klan appealed to certain sentiments among large numbers of people, especially in the south of America. Most, I'm certain, would not have approved of the lynchings and other physical terror, but were swept up in the intimidation and general consensus.

'That was a rumour,' said Alex. 'It's pretty clear Borglum was proud of what America had achieved by 1941 and he had no qualms about how it happened, but beyond that is speculation.'

'And what about Crazy Horse?' asked Matt. 'I was speaking to a guy on top of the heads who says they're building a Crazy Horse memorial to "placate the Indians" – his words. He didn't seem impressed.'

'Yea,' said Alex, 'they're going to carve an effigy of Crazy Horse, on horseback. It's gonna be huge, if they can ever find all the funding. I think it's got the backing of the Sioux people… maybe not wholly, but generally I think they're up for it. A Native American answer to Mount Rushmore.'

I found out later that the monument to Crazy Horse, the Lakota warrior famous for leading a war party to victory against the US government troops at the Battle of the Little Bighorn, is projected to be the biggest monument in the world and was commissioned by a Lakota elder. The site is just seventeen miles from Mount Rushmore. Whatever monuments and memorials find their home in the Black Hills, I think I will inevitably be more impressed by the natural aspects of the landscape.

Riding away under the gaze of the presidents, I felt a burst of pride at our efforts over such terrain. By this stage I was fitter than I ever had been before, and all four of us were able to pound up and down the rolls of the Black Hills like road cyclists on unloaded steeds. That isn't to say it wasn't painful – my thighs screamed and my chest vibrated with effort. But my limits were so far beyond anything I'd known before.

Unfortunately, cycle-touring fitness is extremely specialised, and leads to a certain type of physique. I found myself out of breath when having to walk for more than a mile at a time. My upper body has never been particularly weighed down by muscle, but now there was nothing there at all. A weedy torso led to a disappointingly untoned belly. It is perhaps for this reason that cycle tourists are not known for their shirtless cover-model-like attributes. From the waist down however, I became an array of bulges and firm lumps. Thighs had expanded to fill out my shorts with ripping quadriceps and my calves looked carved out of stone. For any women with a particular interest in men's legs, I was a heartbreaker. And at least I was good in strong winds – my legs were like an anchor that bolted me to the ground while my flimsy torso flailed around.

With hours to spare until darkness, we arrived into Custer National Park and found the pitch of our hosts, the Waterman family. Custer, with its beautiful setting and historical significance, is a hugely popular getaway around the Fourth of July and pitches are booked out years in advance. To have the freedom of camping in an open space without worrying about being found or told to move on was in itself luxury enough. I had no dreams of five-star hotels, just as I had no desires for any of the other expensive extravagances that surplus money could buy. My joys in life were increasingly to be found in the simple places: a flat patch of land to sleep on, a sip of fine whiskey to usher in the night, and an endless ribbon of tarmac to pursue day after day.

CHAPTER 33

A WORK THAT'S OPEN TO THE SKY

The Waterman family took us under their wing and on a rare day off our bikes, we were driven around in the impressive family wagon with DVD players on the back of the seats. The build-up had all been gearing towards the Fourth of July fireworks over Mount Rushmore (for the 100 per cent patriotic experience) but high winds rolled in and the large amount of high explosives was deemed a fire risk; in the Black Elk wilderness adjacent to Mount Rushmore, over 75 per cent of the trees have been killed by an influx of pine beetle, leaving tens of thousands of tonnes of dead wood as, essentially, nothing more than kindling.

Instead we all drove to Custer to watch a much more parochial display. The granite peaks of the Black Hills glinted green and pink and orange from the fireworks over town, and we joined a few hundred other revellers snuggling under blankets and drinking wine from plastic cups. Everyone was in a merry mood, passing along home-made cakes and sharing jokes. This wasn't what I expected from my projected Fourth of July experience but perhaps it was much more fitting and relevant to my journey through the USA to date. Previously

I'd thought that the kindness and hospitality lavished upon me by strangers was due to my vulnerable status as a cyclist, but now I wasn't so sure. Here I encountered the same level of generosity from the other patriots. Maybe I'd just been closed off to such experiences in my life before, or perhaps it was something exclusive to America. Whatever the cause, I liked it, and, more than that, I craved it. Starved of friendship groups and loving relationships, the people I met on the road became, for a short time, my family and my community, and I could pour all of my energies and love and uncertainties into those connections for a short period. This was almost certainly the meaning of home; somewhere to dump your baggage at the door and relax into being your natural and unassumed self.

Before we departed, Tess Waterman drove us to see a cabin in the woods not far from our campsite. It was a simple affair – a two-roomed structure, set in a small clearing on a slight slope. Wooden steps from the porch formed an alcove, underneath which firewood was still stored. In the early twentieth century this had been the home of Charles Badger Clark, a writer for whom the term 'cowboy poetry' was coined. Matt knew a little of his work but I had to admit complete ignorance. The nick-nacks and possessions inside meant little to me, but I did like the idea of a rugged cowboy living out here in the woods, catching food in traps out the back and whiling away his days drinking high-percentage alcohol and writing poetry. A kindly lady, smiling so hard her nose had gone red, was stationed on a chair by the entrance and I gathered from her that Badger Clark was the son of a Methodist minister who had moved to the area during the Gold Rush. In between stints as an Arizona rancher he began to write and carved a career of sorts by touring the West on speaking engagements.

His poetic productivity increased and he was to become South Dakota's first poet laureate, yet he refused to get acquainted with fame or any of its trappings. His work was doomed never to make it beyond the state lines. By the window there hung a reprint of his most famous work:

The Cowboy's Prayer
I thank You, Lord, that I am placed so well,
That You have made my freedom so complete;
That I'm no slave of whistle, clock or bell,
* Nor weak-eyed prisoner of wall and street,*
Just let me live my life as I've begun
And give me work that's open to the sky;
* Make me a pardner of the wind and sun,*
And I won't ask a life that's soft or high.

Reading it and looking out to the wilderness beyond, I thought that maybe he wasn't far wrong. Perhaps these western lands drew kindred spirits to their bosom.

We left the Watermans with long embraces and promises to meet again somewhere further west, and strove west once more descending out of the Black Hills. Through Custer we pedalled, through the same sights as we'd taken in on the night of the fireworks. Now that I was back on two wheels, I thought how much the scene changed. It was interesting to me to see the difference in experience from being driven through a place and then pedalling the same road. On the Fourth of July I was dimly aware of some houses, a few stores and the land opening up to the south of the fireworks. Mainly I was interested in the chocolate almonds on offer in the car.

Now wind blew through gaps in my bicycle helmet and the smell of pine was overpowering. I could see the topography for miles and pick out every boundary between house and field and road. The most striking difference of all was the large amount of buffalo roaming the roadsides. A herd of around one and a half thousand resides in the state park, and they do pretty much as they please (a fact which escaped me when in the comfort of a reinforced steel car). At least twenty now ambled across our path, and we paused to let them do so in peace. Who's going to argue with a 1,000-kg animal of pure muscle, after all? I gave them a wide berth.

The town of Custer, Tess had told us, is the oldest (European-American) settlement in the Black Hills and the site of a major encampment of the Black Hills Expedition that led to discovery of gold and the resultant rush. The gold is long gone but the town still crawls by on mining, now relying on industrial minerals extracted from the nearby hills.

I learned I could supplement my basic knowledge of places I encountered by reading information boards at the roadside. The other way, of course, was to talk to the people that propped up street corners and park benches. There is, in America, a wonderful breed of old folks who potter around their local area just waiting for a stranger to come by so they can unload some wisdom. Those people had thus far shaped much of my understanding, and could be found in pretty much every small town and city in the entire United States. If ever you want to see one for yourself, then try this: stand alone in small-town America for a few minutes and just wait – inevitably these oracles will appear.

A man of at least two hundred years of age (bent double and using two sticks to keep himself vaguely vertical) told me that 'here in Custer we have the widest high street anywhere in this whole darned country! That's a fact, son! Built big enough for a wagon pulled by oxen to turn right around without anything getting in the way.'

None of this information was going to change my life, but it seemed like a more fulfilling way to experience a place than in a fast car with the air conditioning on. The life we lead shapes us in ways that are maybe not always apparent immediately. I'd much rather take the adventurous option every time, I thought, for better or worse, and be content in the knowledge that I left myself open to fortune and misfortune; to chance and experience and the possibilities therein.

* * *

On Highway 16, on a quiet valley road slicing between steep cliffs on either side, we reached another state boundary. 'Welcome to Wyoming – Forever West.'

'Woo-hoo!' yelled Matt. 'This is real cowboy country, lads!' A South Dakotan car careered past at top speed propelling us all into the ditch for safety. The vehicle screeched to a halt in front of us, narrowly avoiding sending itself into a spin. 'F*cking cyclists – get a f*cking car!' On the back windscreen was a sticker depicting crossed rifles and it read: 'South Dakota Gun Association. It's a right – not a privilege.' The driver revved his steed and sped off once more.

I hoped this was not an example of the modern-day cowboy. As a kid I'd played with toys of cowboys and Indians, innocently sending them into fearsome battles with one another; cowboys are right up there with spies and astronauts and dinosaur experts as the aspirational vocations for little boys. And now here I was, in the real thing, seeing it with my own eyes. Canyons loomed over me, there were bullet holes in the road signs. The seven-year-old me would be proud, I thought. And what more can we ask for in life but to grow up and fulfil the childish dreams we had from an age where we still ate crayons and stuck Cheerios up our nose? I still needed bourbon and a ten-gallon hat for the full experience, but this was authentic.

We pulled ourselves out of the ditch. 'Screw 'em,' I shouted, buoyed with adrenalin. 'Saddle up, boys, let's go West!'

PART THREE –
INTO THE MOUNTAINS

The mountains are calling, and I must go.
John Muir

CHAPTER 34

THE COWBOY STATE

The first thing I noticed about Wyoming was that, although it barely seemed possible, there were actually fewer people around than there had been in South Dakota. In a way I guess this shouldn't have surprised me – the fact is that Wyoming is the least populous state in the entire USA – but the scale of my surroundings surpassed even that of the Great Plains. Empty roads led through deep gorges, not a scrap of human life around. Officially we were now riding the High Plains which would take us to Thunder Basin National Grassland and then, finally, the prairie would meet the Rocky Mountains via smaller rangelands and foothills.

On our way into Newcastle, WY, I stopped to read a small wooden sign blowing in the wind by the roadside. Between lines of peeling paint it told the story of Tubb Town, the saloons and houses of which had once filled the clearing where I now stood. The name made me chuckle, remembering a boy at school who had been seriously overweight – other kids in our class referred to his house as Tubb Town (home of the tubbiest family around). It seemed very funny at the time, I guess.

Tubb Town, Wyoming, had been built in a flurry of hope and dreams, right on a site marked out to serve a spur of the Burlington Railroad. This railway was planned to come from nearby Newcastle to serve the Cambria coalmines just north, and speculators with dollar signs for eyeballs jumped in headfirst to claim the precious land alongside the tracks. The promised tracks never materialised and the men in fancy clothes moved on – Tubb Town's existence only lasted a matter of months.

That was enough, though, for it to get a reputation as a hard place, hard and mean. Anyone unlucky enough to be passing through was harassed and threatened, then forced to buy a round of drinks for everyone in the saloon – even the first town ordinance that was passed stated as much: 'No one shall pass through without paying sufficient toll to set 'em up to the bunch.' The passer-by could consider themselves lucky if this was all that was extorted – normally some money and a few teeth followed. The residents eventually abandoned ship and moved to nearby Newcastle. I wondered if there were still other similarly debauched places around. Tubb Town sounded wild and unpleasant, but it didn't seem short of excitement.

The present-day people in Wyoming and South Dakota, I was beginning to worry, may be quite dull. Interesting, yes; generous, certainly. There was even the odd psychopath on the road. But so many just seemed very, very boring. In diners old men would sit in circles scratching their necks and talking about the weather for days on end. ('Clouds today. Clouds yesterday. I'll tell you what, Joe, I'll be betting you that there's some clouds coming in tomorrow.') Small-town sidewalks had housewives gossiping outside the store about inflation. ('Over a dollar for a box of washing powder! Jesus, Annie, what the hell next? I mean, what does it say about this place when I gotta pay one dollar and nine cents just for this here cleaner! Bandits in powder, that's what it is, bandits! Apples is cheap today though.') At gas stations drivers gave each other endless advice about which roads to ride and places to pass through. ('Highway 65 leads you onto 34, and you want to ride that all the way through Chundersville. If you hit Massive Rock City you've gone too far. You'll wanna take the 23 cut-off across to the 144b, and wind up the windows through Weiner Rapids 'cuz they're a funny bunch there, then go straight on to Crudmanstown, where you'll be just about ready to chuck it all in and head straight back home.')

There are a lot worse things to be in life than boring. I'm often guilty myself (get me talking about dinosaurs and I'll bore the arse off a baboon). I wanted more, though. Now I wanted action and wild stories. I wanted characters from Kerouac and Hemingway to jump out and slap me round the chops. The scenery was great, but I needed more. John Keats had it right on when he said 'scenery is fine, but human nature is finer', although he probably didn't mean that in reference to dullards. It's funny how quickly I could forget an act of kindness, but would remember with annoyance something that bored me.

When the four of us reached Newcastle, only rain waited to greet us. I wondered what the men in diners would have to say about this. I even found cause for a pretty dull conversation myself about it – I couldn't remember the last time I'd seen rain. It'd certainly been dry as a bone since I entered the Midwest over a month ago. The temperature dropped. I felt it in my fingers first, curled around the handlebars and slowly crystallising in the stinging wet rain. It was easy to forget that we were riding now on high-elevation grassland; at night significantly colder than we'd experienced in a while.

I pulled on a windbreaker jacket and we set off across Thunder Basin, passing to the north and west of the USA's largest coalmine. There'd be wild characters there all right, there always were around mines, but we wouldn't get any closer than this and would have to take our chances on this road west.

The cycling had become muscle memory and I was completely apathetic about it. Mostly I found no enjoyment from spinning the pedals. Equally, there was no dread or angst about another day of riding. It had become a way of life. I enjoyed the company of Matt, Alex and Bryan, and, though I occasionally longed for time by myself to re-catalogue my brain, I knew that I could ask to ride alone for a few hours. There would be plenty of solitude ahead, and for now I was still grateful to them for 'rescuing' me from that highway in Iowa.

Often days and miles seem to pass in a timeless state. My lower body would push and pull, us four cyclists silently turning our legs in endless circles. Winds blew, grasslands changed from green to brown and the endless white line led us seamlessly from one road to another to another. There was little emotion, nor concept of scale. These were the empty moments, the gaps that needed to occur between moments of incident – the body of water on which our raft of adventure floated along. In their own way these were every bit as necessary and meaningful as anything else I saw or did. These were the times when my brain processed and formed opinions, and during which I covered the requisite distance to move ever farther across this vast land.

* * *

I was first over the threshold into Gillette, proclaimed by a too-large-by-far road sign to be the 'Energy Capital of the Nation'. We were now firmly in coal country. The Powder River Basin area is a hotbed of resources including, alongside coal, enormous quantities of oil and methane gas. Wyoming alone produces 35 per cent of America's coal, and cities like Gillette thrive on the industry. In recent years the population has exploded, and Gillette is so symptomatic of the problems that this rapid growth causes in boomtowns (increased crime, high cost of living and weakened social bonds) that it has lent its name (I imagine somewhat unwillingly) to a psychological term for the phenomenon – Gillette Syndrome. I wondered also if the town had anything to do with the brand of razors that have all those annoying TV adverts, but I never did find out.

As with most centres of industry, it made for a pretty crummy place to ride a bicycle. Air was thick and traffic was heavy with coal-laden trucks, trundling through with loads bouncing and spilling out the top. The world glittered gold as if lit up by a million paparazzi when the afternoon sun hit the nuggets of black that littered the highways.

I visited a local library to ask if there might be a better way out of town, but my only success was in kicking a small dog in the head after it humped my leg at the entrance. The owner looked as angry as if I'd just kicked his mother and I felt guilty (although the dog looked fine – just randy) so the lads and I quickly set off once more. Our options had run dry – we'd spend the next hundred miles or so on the freeway until a minor road picked up again.

We'd actually graced it once already – the last few hours of riding into Gillette had been done along I-90; a three-thousand-mile-long cross-country highway running from Boston to Seattle. The longest in the USA. In theory, it's illegal for a bicycle to be on the freeway. These are the arteries of a nation – huge, straight roads of four to eight lanes that strike through the country carrying millions of speeding cars, trucks and freight every day.

The government deem them too dangerous for dawdling bicyclists. It's not an entirely bad idea (the roads are not overendowed with exciting features for cyclists, so the regulation actually does us a favour in that respect), but what lawmakers don't necessarily understand is that rural roads and lesser highways can often be even more dangerous. When there's no verge by the side of these tiny thru-ways, being on a bike is never a pleasant place to be. What freeways have in their favour is that they come complete with huge paved hard shoulders which are separated from the 'slow' lane of traffic (a particularly relative term in this case) by 'drunk bumps' – a series of ridges on the road designed to shake a vehicle which strays onto them, reminding the driver to wake up, or pay more attention, or sober up quick.

The loophole in the law is that where there is not a reasonable alternative route for cyclists or pedestrians, they may use the freeway until the next point at which smaller roads are viable once more. It seems to be generally a pretty subjective loophole, but in Gillette the decision was clear. The freeway to Buffalo would take a day on a bicycle. The detour via state roads would be three times as long, and involve a section of easterly (backward) travel. No contest.

We rode in single file, positioning ourselves as far away as possible from the traffic that whistled past our left ears. More empty time. I passed the hours by counting colours of cars or musing at shapes in the rockfaces we passed, gnarled forms hewn out of the sandstone. Slowly brown became a predominant feature of the landscape, eclipsing the greens and yellows that had characterised the Midwest. One hour. Two hours. A break, a spoonful of peanut butter. Another hour. Another two. Life ticked by and the High Plains, Great Lakes and East Coast slipped further behind my back wheel.

The freeway undulated a little before leading down into a long, wide river valley, and at the bottom an RV was parked on the shoulder, hazard lights flashing. A family of three stood around, their van having blown a tyre coming down the hill. All looked a little shaken from trying to keep the vehicle on the road at high speed. Boston accents were immediately noticeable: when they said car it came out 'kaaa'. The poor souls were clueless, standing around looking glumly at each other.

We stopped and introduced ourselves, and quickly Alex and Matt were scrambling underneath to release the spare wheel, while Bryan and I heaved at the rivets. Thirty minutes later and we'd switched the mangled tyre over to a brand new one. The Bostonians were ecstatic. I was impressed too – I could barely fix a puncture on my bike. Our reward was a $100 donation to the building of the wells in Uganda that Matt, Alex and Bryan were raising money for. Less important but more instantly gratifying was a haul of biscuits and sugar-laden fizzy drinks.

The family hadn't wanted to call out their insurance company because it would've cost them eighty bucks. Yet they happily donated more than that to us, for what was surely a worse job. I liked their attitude – it wasn't going to do them any favours financially, and I hoped it wasn't how they ran their businesses, but their spirit was excellent. Susie had spoken of 'karma of the road' – to my mind a hippy-ish notion of shared energies amongst those who inhabited the same space. Do good by fellow travellers, and good will be done unto you. A biblical concept in origin (aren't they all?), it only differs here by being applied specifically to the road. Now was a good time to be reminded of this, and it was a worthy model by which to measure yourself. Accepting good deeds with grace and humility, then paying them forward.

CHAPTER 35

HIGHER THAN THE CLOUDS

June was midway gone, and the mornings had taken on that inescapable smell of warm summer air long before the sun came into view. Weather and scenery had settled into a familiar routine and one day was very much like the next, or at least it had been until now. With little warning that change was afoot, we crested a lump in the landscape to be met with a horizon violently broken by jagged mountain peaks, snow dusting their tops. The blinding white of icy summits was an alien feature in this land of brown and yellow, and your eye was immediately drawn to it. It is a strange thing to stand still in sweltering summer heat and look upon the fruits of winter.

The first climb looked like it would begin not much further than a day's ride away. The range nearest to us was the Big Horn Mountains, the highest peak of which climbed over 13,000 feet into the thin, wispy clouds above. Beyond that the Rockies – the three-thousand-mile-long spine of North America running south from British Columbia all the way to Mexico – promised a greater challenge still. Unlike the gradual and humble transitions that had occurred on my journey to date between coast and hills and plains – each of which had rather shyly introduced themselves and their key features over the course of a few hundred miles – the western ranges of the USA screamed out, obliterating their predecessors with dramatic demarcation.

We rolled into Buffalo and in a run-down General Store on the main street I found a second-hand hip flask that had seen a few battles. I paid ten bucks for it, and Matt and I filled her up with a bottle of Bushmills whiskey. That distillery is located only a couple of miles from where I grew up; it's a damned good dram. I love seeing a bottle on a shelf anywhere in the world. I don't even have to drink it and it makes me happy. When I was young and suffering from one of the many ailments little boys are afflicted with (scraped knee, falling-out-of-a-tree injuries, upset stomach from trying to eat grass), my grandmother would gave me a little sip of Bushmills. I'd down it and she'd give me another. 'Don't tell your mum,' she'd whisper. On cold winter nights I was allowed a (small) hot toddy – whiskey, sugar, hot water and cloves, one of the most warming and most comforting drinks known to mankind. Bushmills is a fine whiskey.

The climb towards the sky was slow and steady for the first few hours, winding us up through the coniferous forests of the lowlands. In the wilderness beyond the road were black bears, mountain lions, elk and Bighorn sheep. They were stalking about somewhere in there, but knew much better than to come out and sniff around the road. Looking into the heart of the forest, all I could see were drops of dew glinting right back at me. Not much further along and we'd be into grizzly territory too.

Ever since I left New York, a lot of people I met had been extremely anxious to impart wisdom about various ways in which I would meet death on this trip. Back east it was black bears that would find me in the night and rip my head from my shoulders. Should I happen to disturb the highly venomous copperheads and rattlesnakes (which I surely would), then they would happily inject me with enough poison to kill a small elephant. Further across the country now and, as well as watching out for bees and hornets ('You mightn't think bees will do much, son, but theys'll sting yer head silly till you don't know which ways's up'), I'd enter the territory of mountain lions, wolves, coyotes and grizzlies. They'd take it in turns to hunt me down and tear me apart, finally leaving me for the scorpions and venomous lizards. Vultures would pick at my bones. If, by some miraculous series of serendipitous events I stayed even remotely alive in the wilderness, I could expect to be shot at and robbed on a daily basis by rednecks. God forbid if I strayed into the Deep South where the cast of *Deliverance* lay in wait with toothless grins and lengths of rope.

I wondered what it was that made people so wary and fearful. As far as I could see, most of the folk that handed out warnings had never been within ten miles of a bear, and didn't look like they'd been mugged or shot too frequently either. So why the excessive cautioning? Even before I left England I was being warned about the numerous, faceless dangers of America. I supposed it to be a result of our increasingly sterile and safety-obsessed society – a world in which we must wash our hands every few minutes to avoid germs and where children aren't allowed to climb trees for fear of falling. In the past, even when I was a kid, none of these things were of much concern and as such people were naturally bolder. Now we are encouraged to be risk-averse in every aspect of life, and that in turn breeds fear.

There are real dangers out there in the world of course, I'd found that out the hard way, but on a human level the vast majority of people are willing to help and look out for each other. And I don't believe that to be a naïve sentiment. As for the natural world, with a decent dose of common sense and a respect for the environment you're in, maulings and snakebites can mostly be avoided. It is important to remember too that there is an inherent thrill to be found in the act of engaging with some real danger out there in the Unknown, and only by entering into that can we take ourselves out of and away from what we know.

If we can predict how every second of every day of our life will be, then where is the fun in living it out? On windy nights when twigs snapped outside my tent, or when hooded figures lumbered past in unknown cities, it was easy to feel the fear and hear again every one of those worriers' warning words. But mostly, with a positive attitude and a modicum of good judgement, there was nothing to be afraid of. The world is without doubt a more exciting place when we have been through and come out the other side of those situations. I was determined not to let the misplaced or exaggerated fear of others be a barrier to my undertaking this (or any other) journey. The best intentions of others can have disastrous implications if followed too closely.

* * *

Rocky Mountain juniper and limber pine grew in timeless rows by the roadside. After ten miles of steep gradient my thighs burned and lactic acid built up in the muscles; this was not the flat or gently undulating landscape that my legs had grown so used to. The road wound us round yet another switchback and in a lay-by we saw a mess of camping gear and a bearded man crouching by a bicycle.

'Sean!' I called out.

'Hey guys, what's up?' Sean grinned behind his thick glasses and dense beard. 'I wondered if I would see you again.'

Our last sighting of Sean had been as he waved out the window of the pickup truck in Wood, South Dakota. He now recounted the story of the crash and how he regained the missing memory card. He seemed no worse for wear after the crash and it was good to have fresh blood in the group again. Alex and Bryan led the vanguard while Matt, Sean and I pedalled behind, three abreast on the quiet road. Somewhere in the distance there were cities and offices and industry and people, but none of that mattered to us now; our world was the smell of pine and the turning of pedals.

'I really gotta stop smoking if I'm gunna do the Rocky Mountains after this. These hills are killing me!' Sean wheezed as he spoke. He was lithe, a natural athlete, but the transformation to touring cyclist was still recent and his body had yet to adapt fully to the rigours of the long, hard days. The bike he bought on a whim in Iowa was designed for city commuting and instead of panniers he had his hiking pack strapped onto the rear rack.

'Dude, that pack on the back is crazy. I'm impressed you made it this far!' laughed Matt.

'It's way, way better than walking, Matt. That was just so hard. Not physically – the physical side was tough, but definitely manageable. The mind games were madness, though. I can daydream like a trooper, y'know? I thought I'd be fine. But moving so damned slowly, it felt like it was crushing me. Each step became hell.'

'And cycling's easier then?' I asked.

'Yea, for sure! It's way more enjoyable. The sweetest thing is being able to just blast a huge distance if it's all getting too much. I love it, man.'

Spinning my legs methodically up the winding strip of blacktop that would take us over and out of this range, I agreed with him wholeheartedly. I took joy from the beauty around, and solace from the shared effort and pain of fellow riders.

A storm rolled in and we sheltered behind a dry stone wall, watching clouds gather and empty and disperse. They floated away on the wind as quickly as they arrived, clearing fog and revealing snow-capped mountaintops just across the valley to our left. By afternoon we reached the snowline, past small clumps of hard-packed ice cowering in the shadows. A few false peaks raised and dashed our hopes before finally we pulled into a viewing area by a sign reading 'Powder River Pass, Elevation 9,666 ft'.

Alex bounced off his bike and ran to the sign. 'This is amazing, guys! I've never been this high before.' He cupped a few handfuls of snow and let it melt in his grasp, dripping through his fingers back to earth. 'I've never even seen snow-capped mountains before either. What a privilege, eh?'

'I never want to live too far away from the mountains ever again,' I enthused.

'Hey, listen, I don't know when I'll next be up this high, and it seems a real shame not to get over ten thousand feet. So I might just go run up that scree slope. Watch my bike, will ya?'

With that Alex was off, bounding across the road and scrambling up the loose ground to our right. The kid was like a racehorse. He jumped and ran and slipped and tripped and we shouted to him as he climbed, urging him further on. Once we all agreed he must be past the invisible finish line he celebrated wildly, nearly tumbling straight back down again. Matt and I took a sip of Bushmills from the flask to toast the achievement, and Sean lit up a cigarette. Bryan quietly munched on a biscuit in the background. We were an unconventional group, if nothing else.

A swooping descent of thirty miles took us less than an hour; cold wind cut into our bodies and faces and I couldn't stop grinning. After the slog to reach the pass this felt like flying. The world, until recently such a slow, lumbering beast which I had time to watch and process, was now a blur of snatched thoughts and images: branches heavy with rain that leaned into the road; yellow summer blossom fighting its way through the undergrowth; a pair of eyes, maybe a squirrel, peering out from the gloom. On the western side of the Big Horns the landscape changed again. Red, gnarled rock lay all about and the Wild West seemed ever more present.

In the town of Ten Sleep, Sean met up with his dad who had flown in from Florida to meet him. When we asked how his dad knew where to meet him despite the two not having communicated, Sean replied simply: 'Dude, my dad is ex-Special Forces. He knows where I am better'n I do.'

The rest of us picked up some supplies and rode out of Ten Sleep to camp in the wild open spaces, leaving the white-tinged peaks of the Big Horns glinting in the last light of the day.

CHAPTER 36

BUFFALO BILL COUNTRY

Cody, Wyoming, is the gateway to Yellowstone National Park, and is named after the infamous 'Buffalo Bill' Cody (William Frederick Cody). He was a real character, the type that doesn't come around too often. Buffalo Bill was mythologised for his cowboy exploits, though I wondered whether the lifestyle required for heroic cowboy status in the second half of the nineteenth century might not be quite so respectable nowadays.

It took us a couple of days to arrive in Cody, winding our way through increasingly large canyons from the east. Higher elevation took its toll, and the night before we arrived I woke to a thin layer of frost that had gathered on the roof of my tent. Matt groaned and rolled around, and I warmed up a little by kicking him back over to his side. My woolly hat was either lost or buried out of reach in my panniers, so for warmth I put a spare pair of boxer shorts on my head. In the morning I rode with the boxers still on, underneath the helmet. The chill was still there, why should the underpants be removed? I hoped that from a distance they might look like a bandana.

En route Matt had popped four spokes and by the time we made it into town his rear hub was disintegrating. A local bike store quoted $200 for a new wheel. He was annoyed and paced around in search of a different solution, but there was no choice. If he went any further on the wheel as it was it would soon fall apart completely. Matt bit the bullet and sent the bike in for repair.

I was grateful for how few problems Lola had caused. All her components remained strong and reasonably unblemished, and for the first time I was feeling confident that I might make it. My odometer had recently ticked over the three-thousand-mile marker; I'd seen that almost all problems could be overcome by a bit of creative thinking and decision-making, and crucially by a lack of any alternative other than to get on with it. I wondered again what I might do once I got to the west coast.

Suddenly Seattle, my likely destination on the coast, seemed all too near. Perhaps there was much more riding to be done before my sense of adventure would dull. Or perhaps it would not dull at all. I remembered John Steinbeck's thoughts in *Travels with Charley*:

When I was very young and the urge to be someplace else was on me, I was assured by mature people that maturity would cure this itch. When years described me as mature, the remedy prescribed was middle age. In middle age I was assured greater age would calm my fever and now that I am fifty-eight perhaps senility will do the job. Nothing has worked. Four hoarse blasts of a ship's whistle still raise the hair on my neck and set my feet to tapping. The sound of a jet, an engine warming up, even the clopping of shod hooves on pavement brings on the ancient shudder, the dry mouth and vacant eye, the hot palms and the churn of stomach high up under the rib cage. In other words, once a bum, always a bum. I fear this disease incurable.

While we waited for the wheel rebuild I wandered around the hot, dry streets of Cody and noticed that 'Buffalo Bill' was everywhere – on storefronts and posters, and eulogised in plaques and by large and ugly plastic models of him. He earned his nickname, I read, by killing over four thousand buffalo in eighteen months when under contract to supply the Kansas Pacific Railroad workers after the Civil War. An Iowan by birth, he then made a fortune out West using (at least partially fabricated) stories of past work as a trapper, bullwhacker, Indian fighter and Pony Express rider to propel him into the spotlight and launch his famous 'Wild West' shows. From 1870 onwards he toured first the US, then later Europe, with the circus-like attraction. In the mid 1890s he came to the site of the current Cody, Wyoming, to found a town and single-handedly began to build the place up. His early vision of tourists sustaining the place had now come to fruition, surrounded as I was by thousands of holidaymakers on their way to or from Yellowstone National Park.

'Hey, look at this,' shouted Matt. He was standing beside one of the many Buffalo Bill information boards.

'It says here he became quite a friend of the Native Americans in the end. Apparently Sitting Bull [the Sioux holy man who was eventually to lead his tribe in resistance against US government forces in the mid nineteenth century] turned up in his shows sometimes. There's a good quote here – he calls the Native Americans "the former foe, present friend, the American". I like that thought.'

'Looks like he supported women's rights as well,' chipped in Alex.

'And conservation – he was a fan of creating a hunting season to protect stock and rallied against hide hunting,' added Bryan, joining in.

Buffalo Bill, it seemed, was quite the philanthropic hero. I guess all that stuff is true, though I found it hard to grow too attached to a man who slaughtered bison, or anything, so freely. There was something about his helping hand in the decimation of almost a whole species that disturbed me. In a world where we are still very much on the path of destruction – cutting down rainforest, polluting oceans and bringing countless other species to the brink of extinction – reminders like this from the past chilled me; a sure sign of what can happen when those in search of money or power are allowed to act freely.

I told this to Matt who in turn teased me for overthinking the situation, and reminded me that I was still wearing underpants on my head.

CHAPTER 37

RIDING ACROSS A SUPERVOLCANO

Yellowstone National Park was somewhat of a bonus. Originally I hadn't given it a second thought; hell, I hadn't even been sure I would make it out of New York City. Time passed and now here I was, so close I could smell it. It would've been criminal to pass by without visiting; snatches of overheard conversations and the occasional picture in a brochure had filled me with a sense that this place was something remarkable. The ride over the threshold of its eastern boundary certainly fitted the bill – a deep-set road on the canyon floor led through steep cliffs, which in turn fell away to reveal the mountainous vista stretching out beyond. Forests of lodgepole pine blanketed low-lying foothills, while on higher reaches I could see subalpine firs and clutches of spruce balanced on rounded peaks. Jagged rock leapt out towards the sky at irregular intervals, and even now in summer a smattering of snow could be seen on the highest reaches.

A long climb ensued and as the sky darkened we took shelter amongst the pines. Hours passed as nature blew her fury out across the park, huffing and puffing, reminding us just how much at the mercy of this environment we were.

Hardy Yellowstone leaves battled to stay attached to their branches, fluttering wildly, then losing and floating down, like confetti, to eventual rest on the calm of the forest floor. Matt, Alex and Bryan returned to the road but I lagged behind, watching three small figures pedal ever so slowly across such a vast and eternal landscape. There was a sense of privilege to be here, but even more an underlying discomfort at just how insignificant we were – four miniscule dots painstakingly traversing a continental landmass. These breaks from the pedals were pause for thought; a timely reminder that we cannot ever be fully in control of that which is around us. At times, perhaps, the best we can hope for is to react positively to life's storms and hope that they blow over rapidly.

That night we slept at a campground on the fringes of the 'tourist zone'. A retiree warden let us pitch our tent by the banks of the Yellowstone River and after a hearty meal of lentils, rice and beans we all stripped to our underwear and bathed in the icy waters. Days, weeks even, of dirt and grime washed away downstream where they intersected with the reflection of the full moon beaming over a sleeping wilderness.

Yellowstone was created as a National Park in 1872, the first in the USA and maybe even the first such designation in the world. Native Americans resided in the area for thousands of years but exploration by the settlers did not begin in earnest until the 1860s, relatively late in national terms (Lewis and Clark bypassed the area during their journey of 1804–1806, and so it remained the domain of indigenous peoples and a few wild mountain trappers for a further sixty years). It's huge, officially sixty-three miles long by fifty-four miles wide, but to me it felt huge in a way that numbers just can't explain. It's the type of huge that makes your eyes hurt. It's everywhere and when you're in it you forget there was ever anywhere outside.

What draws the crowds are spectacular geothermal features, as well as extensive flora, fauna and unusual geographical features – if it's weird, and natural, it's probably right here in Yellowstone. I suggested this to Matt as a new tagline for the park, but he wasn't impressed.

Much of the park is essentially three giant calderas, hotspots where molten rock has risen to the surface from the supervolcano below before collapsing in on itself. The caldera where we pitched our tents and rode our bicycles was created by an unfathomably huge explosion 640,000 years ago. Experts in 640,000-year-old volcanoes reckon it was a thousand times more powerful than the eruption of Mount St Helens (in Washington State) in 1980. I guess that was big too – both happened before I was born so I had a hard time getting my head around either. If you start to factor in free-roaming buffalo, elk, grizzly bears and wolves, it makes you begin to wonder why this place draws such vast quantities of visitors in a culture otherwise so risk-averse. Lying in a shallow pool by the riverbank, staring up at the subalpine forest silhouetted on the foothills, I could only feel glad to be one of those visitors. Glad too that there is still enough curiosity in the American psyche to draw so many others to such wild spots.

We rode first to Yellowstone Lake, the largest 'high elevation' lake in the world at over 7,700 feet. Our wheels skirted around it to the south while crystal-blue water reflected the mountains beyond, though the warden had told us that it had only finally broken free of winter ice just a few weeks previously. A horribly busy visitor centre greeted us at a fork in the road and we were outraged at having to pay six dollars for a jar of peanut butter. *That is more than a whole day's budget, you roaring madwoman!* I thought as I handed over my money, timidly and politely, to the lady at the counter.

As with most spots of scenic beauty, I discovered it was best to stick with nature itself, rather than any of the other pomp that grows up around it. When people are involved, things become infinitely more unpleasant. I felt a pang of guilt at the thoughts that passed through my head when I watched hugely overweight people clamber out of their RVs to investigate the snack stand. What bothered me was that I'd seen so many RVs pull in to the roadside or lay-bys so those inside could admire the view, yet they rarely saw it as worthy of the effort to exit their vehicle. Candy replenishment was another matter. I reprimanded myself for my criticising mindset – I guess I was brought up not to judge – but time and again the thoughts resurfaced.

Riding west past Yellowstone Lake, we crossed through the broad and panoramic Hayden Valley. A queue formed on the road, and with just one lane in each direction we were forced to stop. We freewheeled carefully past the build-up of traffic.

'This car has just stopped in the middle of the road!' Alex reported back to us, turning his head to shout at us. With a silly grin he moved past.

'Eh, Alex… they've stopped for a reason,' said Matt, and pulled his bicycle in behind the nearest car. 'You might wanna come back here!'

Alex turned to find himself just yards away from the nose of a large and curious-looking American buffalo. It appeared to be mainly shoulders – a huge beast of an animal with a humped back leading to a long oval head, eyes and horns protruding out through a shag of fur. The American buffalo, technically a bison, is a very front-heavy animal (although its 1,000-kg frame is packed with muscle all over), and if there's one place you don't want to find yourself, it's staring straight into his red eyes with nowhere to escape to.

Alex slowly walked backwards on his bike. I thought I heard him cooing gently, 'Good buffalo, nice buffalo.' The buffalo stared at him and blinked, bemused by this odd piece of theatre. Car drivers peered out through their window, eyes shining with bloodlust. Eventually Alex and his bike made it behind a large estate car, much to the annoyance of the driver (who presumably wasn't keen on being used as a shield).

The buffalo, as it turned out, had no interest in either the car or Alex. I guess the animals of Yellowstone, at least those that graze near the roads, must have grown used to human interaction over the years. This beast ambled slowly past, ignorant of the tailback, and lumbered down the bank to join his pals on the valley floor.

Two hours later we had a similar scenario, and that afternoon a further encounter. After a while we became used to it and the fear began to dissipate slowly. There are over three thousand buffalo in the park and we were unlikely to steer clear of them, but despite their fearsome size there was a certain buzz to be had from sharing a space with such a wild and powerful animal. I'd read online of a buffalo's ability to gore a man, their incredible speed, and apparently their enjoyment of chasing cyclists. Our experience showed this to be an exaggeration as usual, at least in the busy areas, but we agreed it would be prudent to keep our wits about us when in more remote stretches.

With buffalo very much on my mind, I disappeared that evening into the woods for a pleasant 'dump au naturel' only to be rudely disturbed by a huge clatter of branches behind me, and a loud braying sound. I fairly sprinted straight from the squatting position, running ludicrously back towards the road with trousers around my ankles. Chancing a quick glance back, I saw not a fearsome bison in full charge, but Matt bent double in hysterics holding two branches to his head as makeshift horns.

* * *

The Yellowstone tourist experience is facilitated by a thirty-mile loop of road taking in the key sites, with a few offshoots for further points of interest. I'd learned already that it was exceedingly hard to motivate myself to visit anywhere that happened to be even just a mile or two off my planned course, no matter how wonderful it might be. There is something that grows in the mindset of a long-distance cyclist, regardless of how fast or slow they move, which makes the idea of a detour to anywhere utterly abhorrent (even worse is a return journey). I think it's something to do with the idea of wasted energy, or perhaps it's just that enough satisfaction is garnered from the riding itself that additional miles and destinations are not required. Whatever it is, I've found the same tendency in all other cyclists I know. It was therefore decided that upon arrival we would set up a base camp, of sorts, and then hitchhike around the park for a day or two.

Camping in the park is only allowed on organised sites unless you obtain a special permit that requires money and hassle. With over six hundred grizzlies and an unspecified number of brown bears wandering freely through the forests this seems reasonable enough, at least for those uninitiated in bear-country camping. Bears, of course, are not inherently dangerous. Grizzlies have a pretty accurate reputation for being more aggressive than brown bears, but it seems to me that it's most often an unhelpful mix of ignorance, complacency and stupidity on the part of humans that leads to them getting eaten.

In Yellowstone the bears have learned that where humans congregate there can often be found food. Why stand in a river all day trying to catch fish when you can poke through hikers' luggage and find sandwiches and Oreos, and perhaps a tasty limb or two? To counter this, campsites are provided with 'bear lockers' – large steel containers that require opposable thumbs to open – and rangers wander nearby to keep a watchful eye.

At the entrance to our Madison Junction campground, a lean figure with crooked spectacles and a haggard beard was sat on a wall by a familiar sleek-looking bike.

'Sean! You're just hanging around now hoping we turn up, or what?' I shouted. He grinned, face shiny with sweat.

I was amazed once more at how such coincidences could occur on a landmass as vast as this. In New York City I had never once run into anyone I knew at random, yet here in the expanse of Middle America I couldn't stop crossing paths with a fellow cyclist. A band of five once more, that night we ate well and sat around a campfire. A ranger came over to yell at us a little for setting up our tents in the wrong place, leaving food out and making too much noise – in one fell swoop breaking almost all the rules of the site. Once he left we rectified the serious issues, the ones that might cause a bear scenario, and got back to the business of drinking whiskey and making noise.

I looked upon the time in Yellowstone as a mini-holiday – a break from the rigours of cycling every day. As much as I enjoyed riding a bike, professing it to be the best method of transportation around, I was also very keen to have at least one day every couple of weeks when I didn't have to look at the bloody thing even once.

The following morning, Alex and Bryan went to the road first to hitch a lift and were quickly picked up; Alex's beamingly earnest face and winning smile surely set any driver's mind at ease. Next up it was Matt, Sean and myself. Sean and I sported wild, scraggly beards and stained clothing, and Matt, with his cropped haircut and stocky broad-shouldered figure, looked a little too much like an escaped convict for comfort. Unsurprisingly, it took us a while to get a ride, and when our saviours did eventually come, it was in the form of two middle-aged hippies driving a VW camper van.

'Hop in!' said the driver, looking at us from behind his purple sunglasses. 'When we were your age, we had some crazy adventures. We criss-crossed the country just like you guys are doing! It's a rite of passage, seeing this place.'

Now, without our bicycles, we were just another group of young travellers bouncing around the USA learning how the world worked; three more pilgrims of the road. We'd lost our unique selling point – cycling. For the time being, that was actually pretty pleasant. It was nice to blend into the crowd a little easier once in a while.

'Do you guys smoke, man?' asked the passenger.

'Yea, you got anything with you?' the driver chipped in.

'Uh… cigarettes?' offered Sean.

'Never mind,' the driver replied, then glanced at his pal. 'Listen, we're gonna take this cut-off right here so maybe you guys should jump out now. You can walk down to the geysers, it's just a couple of miles.'

'Uh, OK,' I said. Evidently we'd looked like the sort to have a stash of weed to share, and were now being jettisoned. We hopped out and the VW pulled away. Sean looked at a crumpled tourist map.

'I think we just take this path up here for about a mile. Then there's a fork, we take the right one, and it's another mile or two down to the big geysers.'

Matt, Sean and I walked off the road and looked back at the space where the VW van had once been. Suddenly I was very aware just how alone we were. A tingle of excitement rippled through me. With nowhere to be and no one to answer to, we had one of the wildest and most volatile landscapes at our fingertips, ripe for exploration.

Alongside the trail were regular clearings occupied by steaming pools. This is the truly remarkable thing about Yellowstone – these geothermal features are absolutely everywhere. Around every corner it seems there is yet another geyser, hot spring or some other dangerous feature which could happily scald a man to death in seconds. Warmed by magma below, superheated water rises to the surface then cools upon contact with the air and sinks to be replaced by the next batch. The effect is a haze of steam and an occasional bubbling under the surface. It's like being on the set of a 1970s horror movie.

'How hot do you think it is?' asked Matt.

'Boiling temperature?' I guessed, a pseudo-scientific guess based on the fact that water was bubbling, and therefore boiling.

'Think I can touch it?' Matt asked us.

'Eh…'

'You won't do it!' laughed Sean.

Matt walked tentatively to the edge, and reached down. Very cautiously he dipped a finger in.

'Aghh!' he squealed. 'That's bloody hot!'

After a few brief seconds of mock concern, which ended when Matt revealed his finger was fine, Sean and I burst out laughing. Sean did a very good impression of mimicking Matt's high-pitched squeal, and Matt chuckled along good-naturedly.

'I figured it was worth checking out!' he laughed, 'at least now I know not to try it again!'

As we walked on, we read in Sean's brochure about how much of the ground around hot springs and pools was unstable due to underground caverns and the hot, volatile rock and magma below: *Stay on trails at all times, and never approach a pool or spring unless there is a purpose-built platform in place. Failure to adhere to these guidelines could result in unstable ground giving way, exposing you to the magma below.*

'Who knew?' Matt mused.

At the end of the trail, we found the complex that has grown up around 'Old Faithful'. There're a lot of geysers in Yellowstone National Park, thousands probably, but Old Faithful is the original – the old mother hen of the park. What's most impressive is how perfectly suited it is for tourism. While most geysers go off whenever they feel like it, with hours, days or weeks passing in between spurts, Old Faithful is as regular as clockwork. She always has been, too. The National Parks Authority must've been chuffed with that fact when they started bringing in the droves. A visitor clock is set (and reset, and reset again) to ninety-one minutes and counts down to show time remaining, allowing everyone time to wander around the gift shop uninterrupted until it's time to step outside.

With just a few minutes to go when we were there, thousands of people swarmed out of the store and the nearby hotel, and Matt, Sean and I climbed a nearby rock to get a bird's eye view. When it erupted it was indeed spectacular – a sudden rush of air (a 'geothermal fart', according to Sean) pre-empted the event and shortly after an explosion of water blasted 150 feet into the air. The ferocity continued unabated for at least a minute. A stunning feat of nature, yet I found sharing it with two thousand sweaty tourists tarnished my enjoyment, and quickly I got frustrated by the crowds. I preferred that lonely trail, with its less impressive geysers but ultimate peace.

Below us a man explained how the geyser worked to his younger daughter: 'the water seeps slowly through the ground until it hits hot magma, then it heats so quickly and violently from the impact that it's sent rushing back up through a narrow chamber, making it erupt out the top. See?'

'Can I watch my Justin Bieber video on the drive home?' she responded.

For the rest of the day we hitched rides between acidic bubbling mudpots, hissing fumaroles and more geysers and hot springs. Many had wonderfully evocative names like 'Dragon's Head' or 'Roaring Mountains'. Entire cliffsides exuded steam, and lunar landscapes with fizzing caverns stretched off into the distance. The most enjoyable moments I found, though, were those spent walking along the back trails with Matt and Sean, watching scattered elk roam free on the grasslands, or peering through the undergrowth hoping to catch sight of a bear. We only ever saw one, a grizzly, and that from the back of a pickup truck that gave us a ride back to our campsite, but the idea that they were out there was exhilarating. So often it is that reward lies in the hunt or the journey, rather than the discovery or destination.

As we watched the sun set over the Rockies in the distance, wind whistling around my head in the back of the pickup, I couldn't help but feel that I'd rather be here than anywhere else in the world, despite my antisocial grumbling and my own ignorance. Often I beat myself up for lack of knowledge and understanding of the things I encountered. I felt so uninformed, watching as people around me discussed flora and fauna, culture and history, technology and science. Much of what I'd seen and done in America had been new to me and I hoped I was learning something, but mostly I was learning how little I knew.

Right now, though, those gaps in my knowledge didn't seem to matter so much. What mattered was that I kept going and kept appreciating that which was around me in whatever way I could. I decided there and then that the moment to end this journey was when I became jaded with all of this. That was still a long way off. Tied into this, perhaps, is the interesting dichotomy of America – it seems that the real beauty to be found is in exactly the places where other people do not gather. To truly find what is worth seeking we must travel to the lesser-known spots, taking on the challenges that confront us to get there.

CHAPTER 38
THE TREASURE STATE

The time came to finally part ways with Matt, Alex and Bryan. They were riding south to the Teton Mountains and I was headed north-west to Montana, the Rockies and finally the Pacific. Faced with both offers, Sean finally decided to join me for the western venture. Another chapter to explore. We hugged goodbye and I rode off alongside Sean. I felt a real sadness to be leaving the lads behind – they'd been the best company I could have hoped for.

The nights in Yellowstone had been cold; underpants on the head had become standard fare for us all. Sean and I now rode fast to warm up and I explained to him my plan, making it up to a certain degree as I spoke. I'd been given the phone number of a friend's uncle who lived in Seattle, and had called from a ranger's cellphone to ask if I could stay. Of course I could, he said. The only issue was that my host-to-be was going on holiday in fourteen days' time. If I arrived before then I could have the keys and use the house for as long as I wanted. If I couldn't, well, I was out of luck. I calculated the distance in my head as I spoke to Sean.

'It's just over a thousand miles to Seattle,' I said, 'according to my map anyway. I figure if I ride, sorry, if *we* ride eighty miles a day for thirteen days, we'll make it, and either have time for one day off in between or just get there a day early.'

It would be much faster and more intensive than I was used to at this point. With Matt, Alex and Bryan I had ridden a few big days, but they had been interspersed with the quieter and easier times. This new schedule promised to be relentless, and would take my total distance to somewhere in the region of four thousand miles. I was daunted, and for Sean too it was totally new territory.

'OK, man,' he said. 'The biggest I've done so far in one day is seventy miles, but I'm down to try it. Let's do it!'

I liked his attitude to the ride and to life. Try it, see what happens. If you like it, do it more. If not, then at least you gave it a shot.

As we pedalled, he talked about his girlfriend and the troubles this journey had caused in their relationship. She was supportive, he said, but the time apart had been destructive. He wasn't sure how things would be when his ride was over. 'But I gotta finish this, for me. This is my rite of passage,' he concluded.

For the first time in weeks I let my mind drift back to my own girl back home, Clare, and wondered where she was now, what she was doing. I could see her driving through the streets of Canterbury on her way to or from work. She was a girl who smiled easily, one of those people made to live a happy life. Yet in my mind now she was frowning. A dull ache grew like a knot in my stomach. I'd successfully disciplined myself to avoid thinking of her, in much the same way that I could force myself to get back on a bicycle day after day even though often I didn't want to. Yet just because I could do either of these things didn't necessarily make them right. Now as I conjured a picture and remembered what it felt like to be near, to hold her, the sense of longing flooded back. It seemed to be the only aspect of this new lifestyle that I wasn't content with. I complained about the misery of cycling once in a while, but really I wouldn't want to be anywhere else. The pull of my heart, the call of romance, however – this was the one thing that I couldn't shake.

I determined to repress these feelings again at least until I got to Seattle, then to deal with them wholeheartedly. I had learned that I could survive on my own, and indeed thrive. But at what cost to my emotional welfare in the long term? I wondered if there wasn't yet a compromise that I hadn't thought of – a way to engage with both the journey and with love. More than ever now, I was ready to reach the west coast.

* * *

On our second day together Sean took out his video camera to film me riding alongside, and in doing so pedalled off the road and smack into a large vertical cliff. Sean was a funny guy. Amidst tears of laughter I realised the situation had a serious undertone and I helped pick up popped spokes from his back wheel. Together we botched the rear end of the bike together so that it was rideable, though Sean still had to take his pack off the rear rack and ride with it on his shoulders. It looked madly uncomfortable, but for the thirty miles to Livingstone there was no alternative.

The road wound us alongside the Yellowstone River, a crystal blue cascading energetically beside us. In the National Park we had crossed the 'continental divide', the line that separates the watersheds that drain into the Pacific Ocean in the west from those that run out to the Atlantic in the east.

The divide runs from the Bering Strait north of Alaska to the Magellan Strait at the foot of South America.

The term 'watershed' bounced around in my head. Unlike watersheds in the physical world that are easily identifiable, most internal watershed moments seem so much harder to define, only noticeable in retrospective analysis. I wondered what watersheds I'd marked on this journey so far and how many more would come before the end.

Yellowstone National Park is surrounded on almost every side by the Rocky Mountains and the topography is suitably dramatic for a merry pair of cyclists. Crossing into Montana we were told by a ranger that it was called 'Big Sky Country' because 'well, the sky just seems bigger out here, don't you think?' I couldn't disagree – mountains cut jagged figures all around, yet the blue dome above us seemed to have expanded, lifted. If I had felt like an insignificant speck on the surface of the earth before, Montana was a new level of perspective.

In Livingstone we fixed Sean's bike with the help of a local store and rode on feeling fit and fast. The roads continued to parallel rivers through the valleys, and as we pedalled on ever westwards the Rockies around us grew in size and quantity. Much of the continental divide is pinpointed along ridges of the Rockies – they're the largest mountain range in North America, running three thousand miles from British Columbia to New Mexico, so that's not a surprise. Ever since setting off from New York I had seen the crossing of the Rockies as a true test of my mental and physical abilities. The point at which it may become clear whether I would succeed or fail in my quest.

Lewis and Clark had blazed a trail through these mountains during their exploratory expedition to the Pacific Ocean in

1804, following in the footsteps of just a handful of previous Europeans to have entered the range. William Clark's diary entries from the book I still carried echoed in my head:

Whilst I viewed those mountains, I felt a secret pleasure... but when I reflected on the difficulties which this snowy barrier would most probably throw in my way to the Pacific Ocean, and the sufferings and hardships of myself and the party in them, it in some measure counterbalanced the joy I had felt in the first moments in which I gazed on them. But, as I have always held it little short of criminality to anticipate evils, I will allow it to be a good, comfortable road until I am compelled to believe otherwise.

CHAPTER 39

DRIFTING

We rode the freeway through Bozeman, a pleasant university town basking in the reflected beauty of the backdrop. By the local library we met a tall, stooped man with long hair covering his eyes. He offered us his lunch. 'Next year, I'm gonna set off east from here, on horseback, and see if I can't make it to Florida.'

Two elderly ladies standing nearby came to join us. 'Well, aren't you all so brave! You two on your bicycles, and you planning to head off with a horse! We'd just love to do that. I love this town, Bozeman's been my home for seventy-six years, but I sure would like to see this great country.'

More than once I'd met people in America who were drifting from one place to another, planning to do so soon in the future, or at the very least harbouring a longing for movement. John Steinbeck described the same phenomenon when he travelled around the country:

I saw in their eyes something I was to see over and over in every part of the nation – a burning desire to go, to move, to get under way, anyplace, away from any Here.

They spoke quietly of how they wanted to go someday, to move about, free and unanchored, not toward something but away from something. I saw this look and heard this yearning everywhere in every state I visited. Nearly every American hungers to move.

I get it, Steinbeck, I really do. Yet alongside those who craved to satiate the wanderlust, I encountered a larger majority displaying definite unwillingness to go. Many small-town residents greeted me with warmth and generosity but behind their gestures I sensed no envy. A response of 'I could never do that' trumped any yearning in them to drift or travel, more often than not.

There was now a split between the two camps. What had happened to the country in the thirty years since Steinbeck toured around? Why were increasingly more Americans content to remain stationary? It could be read as defeatism or repression, I suppose; just as a school of fish may be afraid to move into darker waters beyond for fear of monsters, people cluster and bed down in places they feel safe.

I prefer, though, to see it as a mentality born of contentment and a satisfaction in time and place. The United States of America was founded by those who pushed on always a little further, and ever since then those same pioneer-minded types have edged the country forward. Now, maybe more Americans are finally keen to establish roots and communities and have less need to wander. They seem to want to actively grow and create their own legacies, intrinsically linked to the locations that bind them together.

* * *

At the headwaters of the Missouri River we turned our noses north and pedalled the longest day yet – ninety-two miles – to Helena, Montana's state capital. Sean was flagging badly and during each break he fell instantly asleep. These distances were new to him and I wished I could offer respite, but the reality was that I was set on making it to Seattle. So much so, I figured, that I would probably leave Sean. I hoped it wouldn't come to that. He was exhausted, but had the requisite determination of anyone who wants to cross a continent by human power. After each too-short break, without fail, he rose up and was back on the pedals.

We slept in the shadow of mountains, and I was grateful now that the headwinds which plagued the Midwest were mostly a thing of the past. Better still was that our choice of river-valley roads had so far led us deep into the belly of the Rockies with only minimal altitude gain. Local residents continued to show the hospitality that I'd come to expect from small-town America. It is a true privilege to be greeted warmly by a total stranger who offers food or lodging, and I reminded myself always not to take it for granted. In Canyon Ferry Lake Sean and I were taken in by the local minister and given keys to the church. Cushions from the pews made up our bed, and the morning light that woke us streamed down in multicolour through stained-glass depictions of Christ on the cross.

As a compromise to our gruelling schedule I called up some friend's relations in Missoula, Montana, and asked if we might stay with them. I figured we could afford a day off there, and I knew it would do Sean the world of good. Me too – the unconsciously competitive element of riding with others had strengthened my resolve not to complain or lag behind, but I could feel my muscles tender with fatigue. The idea of waking naturally in a comfortable bed and whiling away a few more dozy hours had become the stuff of daydreams.

Barring access to that promised rest day, like Cerberus at the Gates of the Underworld, were three enormous passes across the final section of the Rocky Mountains. Ever since we entered the state, people had talked of them as the obstacle that might break us, especially MacDonald Pass – the most central and highest of the lot. ('I can't even begin to imagine how you'd get a bicycle up there, can you, Jeff?' 'Oh no, not a hope in hell, Susan... not a hope in hell.') It was, however, the most direct route so we set forth into its midst. When we reached the foot of the climb, temperatures had peaked at 97 °F and we'd already pedalled fifty miles.

'Are you up for this, Sean?' I asked.

'Sure I am!' he said, enthusiastic as ever. 'Once we're over this we've crossed the Rocky Mountains, man! I'm pumped – let's do it!'

There was no arguing with that. Despite tired legs and a sore behind, I could rely on the vast leaps and bounds my fitness had taken since that last big climb in the Big Horn Mountains. I shifted Lola into her lowest gear (the 'granny gear') and let my legs spin slowly.

The gradient reached 7 per cent, then 9 per cent, then fourteen miles later we crested the Rocky Mountains with a distinct lack of pomp and ceremony. Nobody arrived to present medals, our bodies and minds failed to disintegrate. If this was another watershed moment, it sure didn't feel like it. Sean had a cigarette and I took a sip of whiskey. Many of life's most important milestones happen in this way, I suppose – understated and underwhelming. The true significance may often be visible only through the lens of retrospection. Looking forwards is crucial, for only by doing so can we hope to see the way. But backwards too can't be discounted, as there's always benefit to be had in remembering how far we have come.

'I'll tell you what, Sean,' I said, 'either that was a lot easier than the Big Horns, or we are just cycling machines now.'

'Can't it be both? Dude... look at that downhill...'

We launched off the top like eagles taking flight, twisting downwards from MacDonald Pass and whooping like lunatics. The sky at the top of the pass had seemed bigger than ever but as we descended the mountains grew back up around us, back to the familiar protective cocoon of rock, and delivered us safely into the bosom of the valley.

* * *

Our only viable route into Missoula was on the freeway. We endured between us six punctures in one day, a new record, caused by the debris and detritus that littered our path (mostly the remains of exploded truck tyres lined with sharp wire). The twin benefits of riding this road were that it saved a three-hundred-mile detour and that we were guaranteed a large hard shoulder on which to pedal. Save for the increasing likelihood of flat tyres, it was overall an upgrade in safety from the provincial roads. Personal well-being was often far from my mind on this journey, but there was an occasional reminder of my frail mortality. Usually it was vehicles passing too close as they overtook, or near misses when speeding down curving mountain roads. What a wonderful country this would be if there was no traffic, or people, I sometimes thought.

As I rode, I admired the Blackfoot River that bubbled alongside. Every so often our straight highway dashed across its coiling, snaking form, the freeway builders having created bridges to span each gap. For one reason or another, however, the construction crews neglected to include a shoulder on these bridges. Maybe it saved money. Maybe it made the structure stronger. Either way, the result was that suddenly, at intervals of every few miles, our wide bicycle-friendly section by the verge disappeared into the void. Traffic flew past almost continuously on the two lanes running in each direction – surely travelling at a minimum of seventy mph.

At the first bridge Sean and I waited fifteen minutes for a pause in flow. Then, with heart beating through my chest, I set off like a streak of lightning. There was no hope of reaching the terminus of the bridge before traffic bore down; all I could do was ride as swiftly as possibly and trust that the chasing vehicles saw me well enough in advance to pull out and around.

Engaging in this once was terrifying, yet also electrifyingly exciting in that way that potential life-and-death situations can be. Going through this fiasco three or four times every hour, however, became tedious and mentally exhausting. Each time I ran the gauntlet I felt I was draining my stores of good fortune. There was surely only a finite amount of times you could take this risk before it went wrong. What were our chances of getting hit – one in fifty? One in twenty? By the tenth time we'd run it I felt like my egg timer of luck was fast running out of sand.

Coming down from a plateau at top speed, I saw yet another bridge up ahead. I was very reluctant to lose terminal velocity again. Glancing back showed both lanes busy with trucks and cars, but they were a way back from me and I was moving at speed. *Fortune favours the brave.* I took a chance and pulled out in one swift movement onto the 'slow' lane of the freeway just as the shoulder disappeared.

Within seconds I felt a hot burst of air as a large logging truck whistled past my shoulder. A horn sounded long and loud. Breaks screeched for a split second and the wing mirror of a white truck brushed my shoulder so gently it could've been a lover's caress. I was less than an inch from the solid stone boundary on my right, and ten yards below I could see the Blackfoot peacefully running its course. All I wanted to do was close my eyes and be taken away, but instead I stared straight ahead, holding my breath. Two cars now veered around me violently, skidding past. None could pull out any further as the traffic in the fast lane was a continuous wave of speeding metal, the drivers out there unaware of the cyclist surviving on a prayer on the extreme edge of the blacktop.

It ended as quickly as it began. The shoulder reappeared and I pulled in, stepping off the bike onto legs of pure jelly. A stream of cars and trucks and metal and life continued beside me. There was no carnage, no crashes. Ten minutes later Sean arrived too, having waited for a gap as we had practised before.

'Sh*t man, I thought that was it,' he said, noticeably distressed. 'Don't do that again… that was… horrible. That first white truck tried to pull out around you and he nearly took out a car on the outside. I can't believe that didn't end up worse. Seriously… I can't believe you're here, and there's not a pile-up of cars with you somewhere in the middle.'

I took in his words, felt numb. Why hadn't I waited? This was the ultimate low in poor decision-making and misjudged risk-taking. In an overarching sense, I thought of my whole journey as a risk. A low-adrenalin and low-risk journey, yet still a risk. Leaving behind what I knew and understood and seeking out uncomfortable challenges and unpredictability. Yet there was much pragmatism that went into the creation of the idea, and it is only through taking risks that we can hope to achieve highly. Narrow down a goal, set in place parameters for action, commit to the attempt. I had a personal value system of what I deemed too dangerous (riding at night on certain roads) and what seemed unsafe but also unlikely to cause me any harm (riding on the freeway). These rules were at the core of my journey, and in essence I was reliant on them to guide me away from perilous scenarios.

Now I was scared and angry; frustrated that I let my own standards slip. I wanted an element of danger in the adventure, of course, but I never wanted to die. Now for the first time I saw that as a very real outcome if I ever made such poor judgement calls again. I pictured the faces of Clare and my mum, and imagined how they would react to the news that I'd been flattened by a truck on a Montana bridge. Silently I said my thanks to whatever powers protected me and promised myself that I'd never make such a half-baked instinctual decision again.

Sean and I rode on, in silence. On each remaining crossing of the Blackfoot I waited much longer than necessary for a requisite gap with which to take my calculated risk. Eventually a turn-off appeared on the outskirts of the city and we pulled onto this new beast, clogged with smoke and traffic but free of bridges. The Blackfoot disappeared out of sight and I pedalled into Missoula, Montana, feeling very lucky to be alive.

CHAPTER 40

A RIVER RUNS THROUGH IT

The world is full of b*stards, the number increasing rapidly
the further one gets from Missoula, Montana.
Norman Maclean

Missoula is a quintessential mountain town, sitting at the convergence of five major ranges. It is also the largest city in Montana and was known to me, along with the Blackfoot River, as the setting for the short story and subsequent film of *A River Runs Through It.* I'd read the book as a teenager and through Norman Maclean's words, from my bedroom in Northern Ireland, I could see the Rockies as clearly as if I was standing right beside them.

It was a book that had long coloured my perception of how the rest of Montana would look too and, to a certain degree, how people would act. I imagined wide valleys, tall mountains and hard lives; people who spent their time outdoors and filtered discussion on life through a medium more comfortable to them, such as fly-fishing.

To an extent, this seemed accurate enough. People in Missoula looked healthy and outdoorsy, and the scenery was

256

certainly spectacular. The men especially were how I imagined them, cut from the 'Gary Cooper' mould – the 'strong and silent' type.

My contacts here were the Armstrong family, relations of a friend from New York. I had never met them before arriving on their doorstep (as happened with so many of my trusting hosts), but to some people there's just no such thing as a stranger, and the Armstrong family took it upon themselves to grasp the mantle of unreserved hospitality. Caitlin fed both Sean and myself to bursting point, set us in front of the TV and offered free-flowing wine. Her husband Jonah told us stories of hitchhiking in his youth, and the couple's two children were delightfully polite and intrigued by our journeys. Our fabled day of rest had come.

They took us the next day to Seeley Lake, a picturesque spot where the bowed light of mid morning danced across the gently rippled water. The family kept a boat at the dock and shared a vacation cabin with relatives from all over the country. Jonah Armstrong concerned himself with the practical tasks of the day – driving us all there, opening the cabin, readying the boat. He seemed at home when working with his hands. The physicality of these simple tasks brought him joy and I could empathise with the easy pleasure that flows into your body when contentedly busy with manual labour. Sitting at desks and typing onto computer keyboards can never provide the same holistic gratification that comes from being in contact with the land, or from making something or other come to life.

As he busied himself stocking the boat with drinks and food, he talked, telling more stories about his past. During college he'd once attempted to post himself in a cardboard box across the state, only to get cold feet at the last minute and burst out of the parcel as it was about to be loaded on the train. As an apprentice mechanic in the 80s, he'd 'borrowed' a Cadillac that came in for some bodywork and used it to chauffeur pretty girls around town for a weekend. Caitlin milled about and laughed good-naturedly, occasionally filling in factual gaps in the tales.

Amongst the telling of adventures and mishaps, I was taken aback to find out that two years previously Jonah had suffered a massive heart attack. He went straight into the operating room and a team of four surgeons worked for twelve hours straight. Caitlin told us that when the doctors unclogged his aortic valves they also removed a haze from within him.

'She's right,' he said. 'I used to be carefree as a kid, but I'd gotten pretty serious over the years. Focused in on being an adult, I suppose, and kinda forgot what I really cared about. I feel like that heart attack helped me a lot. It was touch and go whether I'd make it, but I remember thinking that if I did come out the other side, I'd do things differently.'

'Like what?' I asked.

'Like making sure I didn't miss out on the best bits of life!' he replied. 'I learned more than a few things from that. I changed my ways – I eat healthier now, Caitlin sees to that, I guess. That keeps me in good shape and I can spend more time in places like this. And I figured I should spend more time with the things and the people that I love. No point in working all your life till you die, and then wondering what happened to the stuff that's important to you.'

'That sounds like a pretty good philosophy,' said Sean.

'I reckon so,' said Jonah. 'I spend a lot more time with my family now – I have two of the greatest kids in the world, and a wonderful wife. I try'n see them as much as I can and to enjoy their company. And, well, I bought a boat! There's no substitute for quality time, and no matter how crazy work and life gets, we all come up here to this lake and take the boat out, and everything is good again.'

We left Jonah to take the family out on the first boat ride of the day, and Sean and I lay with closed eyes in the dappled shade of a billowing larch tree, occasionally answering the call to hop in and join everyone for a zip around Seeley Lake. Extended family arrived throughout the course of the day, each group coming from a different corner of the state to convene with nature and revel in time spent with people they loved. These were hard-working Americans, etching out a living in a variety of manners and then putting their downtime to good use by indulging in the best of rich food, wine and company.

Viewed like this, life seemed so simple. There was a compromise to be had, trading hours of life in return for money, but maybe that can be worth it when the pay-off is so close to one's heart. Maybe compromise is not such a bad thing after all. A sense of perspective is key – working hard at a job that you don't necessarily enjoy, one is maybe more inclined to seek to make the most of what time is left. In the same way, Jonah Armstrong had been given a terrifying insight into what he stood to lose. Slowly I felt I was distilling the most important elements of life for me. Freedom seemed key. Adventure – the sense of challenge and unpredictability – was necessary, too. And love – I missed that.

* * *

The next morning Sean and I left with the generosity of the Armstrongs still at the forefront of our minds. Not least of their gifts was directing us towards an alternative route that could take us clear of the I-90 freeway. This rural road would be much more circuitous, and over a hundred miles further, but after my near-disastrous encounter by the Blackfoot River I was only too happy to sign up for more miles and less traffic.

For two days we followed the Clark Fork River until it emptied its tumbling mass into Lake Pend Oreille near the Idaho border. A forest fire blazed in the area surrounding Thompson Falls and I watched as helicopters flew overhead. Each carried below it a large bucket of at least 20 feet in height. The pilots would swoop down to a nearby lake and accelerate forward just above the surface, scooping water into the oversized bucket, then dump it onto the burning area. It was a huge job – the forests on these mountains are as large as some European countries and fires can burn for weeks or months.

Four Scottish students we met in the wonderfully named town of Paradise told us that this blaze was into its third day. 'Aye, it's true,' said the largest, at the back of the group, 'I just hope it doesny get at me favourite mountain around here. See o'er there, straight across the river? That's "Patrick's Knob". Hee hee hee!' He was very proud of that knowledge, giggled like a kid, and my inner child enjoyed the joke as well.

Just before the border with Idaho, Sean cycled into the back of a parked truck. Sometimes this man was like Buster Keaton on a bicycle. Climbing a steep ascent, head down, he was fully focused on pumping his legs to power to the top. Looking up was not on the agenda, so engrossed was he in the moment, and he crashed straight into the rear bumper of a very large and bright-red pickup truck. The driver had pulled over to fix a blown tyre and now he cried with laughter. Sean had been thrown over the handlebars and landed in the flatbed at the back, nothing wounded but pride.

'Man, I was told that when you're going up hills you just get in the zone – head down and pound the legs. Big red trucks were never mentioned!'

He was a liability, that was for sure – in the short space of time we'd ridden together he'd crashed into this truck, ridden into a cliff, left a brand new camping map outside a library and forgotten to pick up his phone from a roadside diner table. But he was a good companion – loyal and straight-talking – and I was happy to have his company for the final few days to the coast.

CHAPTER 41

IDAHO AND WASHINGTON

Leaving Montana, Sean and I briefly crossed the Idaho Panhandle; an elongated finger of land (shaped, unsurprisingly, like the handle of a pan) stretching north to stroke the Canadian border. Our lateral traverse of the state was no more than thirty miles wide; it consisted only of posing for a photograph by the bullet-hole-riddled state sign, taking a short and very naked dip in Pend Oreille River, and visiting Walmart to buy multivitamins.

I had recently enforced a rule that, if we were going to talk about anything of importance (most of our conversations were utter nonsense), we should do it while riding so as not to encourage lengthy dalliances by the roadside. This had worked wonders in increasing our daily mileage and reducing time wasted by lingering longer than necessary. Passing through Priest River, Idaho, Sean suggested we take a break. I objected, and by the time both arguments had been presented fully we'd ridden out the other side and into Newport, Washington – the twelfth US state of my journey.

McDonald's restaurants had, surprisingly to me, become a desirable feature of larger towns for us, at least as a source of free wireless Internet. For the most part I sought out libraries once a week to update loved ones back at home, but I also carried an iPod Touch which had the ability to access wireless networks. If I had wanted to, I could probably have found a hotspot every other day and remained in connection with the world almost as easily as had I been sitting at my desk in England. I tried my best to avoid this.

A large part of the appeal of my journey by bicycle was in breaking the reliance on technology and instead learning to reconnect with the land around me and its people – real, natural and human connections. Even when I did catch up on world news, I couldn't properly get a grasp on it – this bike ride was a bubble and I existed only in that sphere.

The girl who served me coffee said that we'd just ridden across a time zone – I was now in Pacific Time. This was the fourth separate zone of my journey – from Eastern to Central to Mountain to Pacific. More than ever this felt like a watershed moment. It's an odd experience to travel by human power into the future (or past). An aeroplane takes us with such ease from one world into another that is so very different culturally or geographically; time change is just one component of the new beast into which we have arrived. Any form of land travel across a time zone gives some indication of scale, but to rumble through in a motorised vehicle still reduces true impact. To cycle – or walk or kayak or row or crawl – from the border of one zone to another gives us a wonderfully accurate and well-formed notion of distance, scale and the beauties that lie therein. I used up most of my newly gained hour of time pondering this.

I was now only five short days from Seattle; five days from touching the Pacific waters and letting sea lap around my feet.

A Pepsi salesman from Spokane stopped to tell me he'd passed us on the road a couple of times and was impressed with how fast we moved. It didn't feel like it. It rarely does, but one pedal stroke at a time we were getting there.

We trundled through Reardan, another tiny blotch on the Washington state map holding no more than a handful of homes. The sort of place that passes in the blink of an eye yet, conversely, for the few residents that live there I suppose it can constitute their whole world. From time to time I'd meet some or other kindly old soul who'd tell me they'd never left their state, or county, or town. Yet they were adamant about being an American, identifying themselves with people thousands of miles away the length and breadth of the country – people living lives so different in places they couldn't possibly imagine. The notion of patriotism and belonging is a strange one, sometimes.

The Achilles tendon on my right foot twinged and I pulled over onto the Reardan sidewalk. Aside from a sore bottom and the odd muscle cramp I'd been mostly unafflicted by injury, and this ache was an unsettling development. I jumped up and down a few times to try and locate the exact problem. That certainly didn't help. Sean suggested I down a few high-octane painkillers and pedal the last few miles of the day with my right ankle resting limp on the pedal. What a ridiculous thing to have to do, I thought, powering a bicycle with just one leg.

The next morning brought no sought-after relief. Instead I was still unable to put pressure on the ankle and so I set the injured foot on the pedal and strapped it in place using a bungee cord. For the next ninety miles that day I rode using just my left leg, the other spinning helplessly.

To a large degree, the fact that this was achievable at all was a fortunate by-product of a pleasantly flat landscape – the Channeled Scablands of Eastern Washington. Essentially it was desert, not by name perhaps, but in practice certainly. Millions of years ago a large part of Idaho and Montana had lain silent, hidden under a vast ice-covered lake, and when that ice broke every few hundred thousand years the water rushed out west where it was stopped by the formidable Cascade Mountains. After many countless years of this happening, the land in between grew flat and arid and, deprived of the rainfall and fertility that characterise the other side of Washington State, it became desert: scabland. The irony is that, while on the eastern side there is this little-known desert and one of the driest places in the USA, the extreme west of the state boasts one of North America's only rainforests – the temperate Hoh rainforest on the Olympic Peninsula – and one of the wettest locations on the entire landmass.

It made for an easy if dull ride, and I passed the time munching painkillers and singing songs to myself about the lack of scenery. ('The desert bit's connected to the... brown bit. The brown bit's connected to the... crusty bit. The crusty bit's connected to the... desert bit...')

Behind me were the Rockies, ahead the Cascades. Dust devils spiralled violently in the plains. A moment for reflection, and anticipation, between these two great mountain ranges. Another of the liminal spaces necessary to add context to the rest of my journey. I dreaded the approach of the Cascades' passes and knew now that it would be these, not the Rockies, that would constitute the final barrier blocking my way to the coast. The last challenge.

* * *

In hopefully named Coulee City (in reality a hamlet with a small gathering of houses and a solitary gas station) Sean's bike began to give us serious problems. We prodded and poked cluelessly, like small children examining a dead animal, then finally stood with hands on hips hoping the other would be first to admit they didn't know what was wrong. What was clear was that the chain refused to shift between the larger and smaller chainrings, and no amount of derailleur adjustment would help. The teeth on the rings were worn away ('shark's teeth', I learned later, is how this is referred to) but something else was wrong too, something much more serious which caused the whole mechanism to feel unsteady, ready to snap.

At the gas station we upended his bike once more to have another go.

'Got a problem?'

A large bearded man in a grubby T-shirt watched us from the shade. Beside him stood an equally grubby bicycle. In that respect they were the perfect match. His large belly and tight jeans didn't seem to fit quite so well with the small purple bike frame, but each to their own. He looked content, like he didn't care who saw him with his tight jeans and his tiny bike.

'Let me have a look.'

He knelt beside Sean and fiddled with the screws on the derailleur.

'Do you know what you're doing?' asked Sean, a little concerned.

'Sure, I've ridden cross-country twice, which I guess is what you two are doing. I'm actually heading back east right now.'

'On that?' I asked.

'Yep. Don't need much, got all I need. I stop in truck stops at night and do seventy miles a day. Here you go, this should be better for you now.'

We thanked him and watched as he mounted his purple bike and pedalled off unsteadily, knees up around his elbows. On the rear rack was a newspaper, a sweater and a spare pair of jeans. There was a guy who knew how to travel light.

Unfortunately that was where his talents seemingly ended, for it was soon apparent that he knew as much about bicycles as he did about fashion and bike-sizing. His tinkering had left Sean's bike in a much worse state than before. The gears would now not shift at all unless the chain was lifted manually between settings.

The Cascades were now upon us and there was no more time for delay. So, with Sean riding a single-speed – unable to shift into low gears for hill-climbing, or higher gears for building up speed on the flat – and me puffing along on my one good leg, we began our final mountain foray.

CHAPTER 42

THE FINAL HURDLE

*Boys, be ambitious. Be ambitious not for money, not
for selfish aggrandizement, not for the evanescent
thing which men call fame. Be ambitious for
the attainment of all that a man can be.*
William S. Clark

Stevens Pass awaited us at just over 4,000 feet and within
an hour it became startlingly clear that Sean was not going
to make it to Seattle unless he fixed his bike properly. In
Leavenworth, a Washington town inexplicably modelled on
a Bavarian village, we decided to split up. I'd shoot for the
coast alone and Sean, hopefully, would follow a day behind. I
departed with a final image of him eating a bratwurst outside
a lederhosen store, waving me off to the tune of a German
marching band. *Auf Wiedersehen, Sean.*

Highway 2 took me first through the smooth and narrowing
valley of the Wenatchee River. Gradually the dense pines of
the lowlands began to thin out and a first climb to higher
altitude began in earnest. The Cascade Mountains are part
of the Pacific Ring of Fire: a horseshoe-shaped zone running

north from New Zealand, up along the eastern extreme of Asia and then back down the west coast of North and South America. Further west from where I was the peaks of Mount Rainier and St Helens dominate, but here the mountains clustered tighter together in a humble collection of subalpine scenery. By sticking to a strict regime of heavy-duty painkillers I was guaranteed a numb Achilles tendon, free from the sharp pain of previous days; I was no longer one-legged, but still far from full fitness.

Cutting off the main road, I found a much smaller and partially paved track winding through an adjacent valley. There was a certain amount of pleasure to be had in making this final hurdle as difficult as possible. Part of me hoped to fail – deep down, I suppose I was curious as to how I would respond. Only by consistently raising the bar would I know how high I could go. The other part of me scolded myself for making a hard situation harder, and fought viciously to convince me that I should turn back.

The surface was poor and I edged along at just a few miles an hour, pumping pedals rhythmically and counting revolutions. Ten yards travelled required twenty revolutions. I thought of the words of Wilfred Thesiger, that great British desert explorer, who remarked in one book how he enjoyed the very deliberate and methodical nature of his journey, and never wished for anything more. 'In this way, there was time to notice things... [and] the very slowness of our march diminished its monotony.' He pointed to the insects scuttling past, animal trails on the path, nesting birds in the branches overhead – all things I could now appreciate.

I had been caught up in the rush to reach Seattle and now that my breath was upon the city's fine neck I felt urged to slow and absorb what was left of this moment. Delayed gratification played a part as well, knowing the reward would be enjoyed imminently. Mostly, I realised what a large part the small things had played on my journey. I didn't recognise every tree or root or bird or rock, but you don't need to be able to accurately identify a giant sequoia to appreciate its majesty. In a similar way, the whys and wherefores of many significant moments in life are probably beyond the comprehension of a lot of us; maybe it is enough just to enjoy them for what they are.

An hour into the ascent I rounded a corner to see a small wooden bridge over a creek. It was flimsy, used only for occasional backwoods hikers. I dashed across with summoned courage and exhaled. Maybe I was turning into a heroic adventurer after all. Wilfred Thesiger would have been proud*.

Less than five minutes later I slipped and slid my way around another corkscrew in the path, cursing the lack of solid surface, and arrived at a precipice over a fast-flowing river. The bridge, what was left of it, lay in a heap on the far side. Scattered lengths of log and two metal girders hinted at what used to be. It looked to be roughly 20 feet to the far side. The flow was wild, and upstream I could see a small waterfall feeding the frenzy. Downstream the river twisted out of sight leaving horrors unseen.

B*llocks.

Returning back to the main road wasn't an option – it would take me all day. I dipped a long, thin branch gingerly into the water's flow, and was surprised to find it only a foot deep. I

---

* Wilfred Thesiger would not have been proud – he would probably have referred to me as he did Eric Newby when the two first met: a pansy.

stretched my arm out as far as it would go and reached in again with the branch. About the same. Maybe it was shallow all the way across. My mood lightened instantly. It was fast, sure, but as long as I didn't slip I could probably hold my own.

Tossing my depth-gauging branch into the heart of the river I watched as it was swept away within seconds, spinning and fighting, before finally disappearing around the Corner of Doom. That was unnerving, but I was determined not to turn back. I would cross, and just make sure that I didn't slip and get carried downstream. I put together a haphazard safety plan, muttering to myself as I paced back and forth by the water's edge. Eventually, on the riverbank where I stood, I hammered in a tent peg and then cut a guy line from the outer flysheet of my tent. It was the closest thing I had to real rope and, although thin, it was strong. I tied one end to the tent peg and secured it in place with a collection of nearby rocks and boulders. My hope was that I could cross the river once, unloaded, and secure the other end of the line in a similar fashion, giving me a safety line for when I made return trips with Lola and my gear.

Stripped down to my underpants I was suddenly released from internal-panic mode, and began to giggle at my predicament. Once it began I could not hold it back, and I sat for maybe ten minutes chuckling to myself by the riverbank. If this was madness, I thought, it's not so bad. Leon McCarron, wild and fearless adventurer. Rider of small paths up reasonably big mountains, and semi-naked crosser of quite-fast rivers. *Watch out Shackleton, Scott, Thesiger – there's a new hero on the loose.*

The first tentative step was ice cold, the rocks below rearranging themselves under my weight. Four steps in and the water rose from shin to waist. Two more; current lapped at my ribs. Cold, fear and concentration united in a mighty triumvirate that made it almost impossible to breathe. Another two steps, each a mighty battle with body and mind. Another couple of inches closer to salvation.

I reached dead centre, the point of no return. It struck me here like a blackjack to the back of the head that this was a remarkably stupid thing to be doing, even by my own high standards of poor judgement. Nevertheless, there was now nothing to be achieved by turning back, and so I leant into the flow. I imagined I was holding shut the gate of some Great Kingdom, single-handedly bracing the defence against forces of evil who charged repeatedly from the other side. I was over halfway – I knew that from here I would rise out once more, as long as I held my footing. My ankles screamed in pain, perennially readjusting to hold my weight steady. This was a hell of a workout.

Less than twenty steps in total and I was released. The river rushed past unaware, as if the whole thing had never happened.

How many thousands of years had this course of water flowed through this spot, and how many more thousands before it ceases? Here was timeless nature as she always had been and always would be. My success or failure would be of no consequence when measured on that scale. There was an odd sense of solace to be found in that. I took a second tent peg from my mouth and with a rock hammered it in hard to the firm soil, tying the guy rope around it. Now I had a lifeline, of sorts – it was unfortunate that I still had to return to collect all my belongings.

Three return journeys later, I collapsed on the far side of the river with all of my equipment scattered around. Bringing Lola across was toughest, even with all the cumbersome panniers removed. I had to hold her high above my head, and my weedy arms complained mercilessly at supporting 20 kilograms for such a long period of time. Yet here I was. Another challenge completed. I was proud, if still scared. How many more of these crossings lay ahead? A wave of longing for the imagined comfort of Seattle swept over me.

Thankfully there were no more swept-away bridges, and shortly before Stevens Pass I hauled Lola over a gap in the rock and rejoined the main road. The pass itself was another underwhelming affair, marked only by a small sign announcing the elevation highpoint of the road at 4,061 feet. And that was it – downhill to Seattle, I hoped. Corkscrews and hairpins kept me on my toes but I descended like a man possessed, through Skykomish, along the Snohomish River and into Gold Bar township. Sniffing the air brought only scents of pine and damp wood, yet the salt of the ocean could not be far now.

Traffic began to build up behind me on the turns, and I was ready for an argument when a blue hatchback pulled up alongside. Someone was shouting out the window. I looked across to see Sean sat in the passenger seat and a very serious-looking girl in glasses driving, her nose brushing the wheel as she peered straight ahead. Sean smiled at me, but his body was tense and rigid. He leaned his elbows on the dashboard as the car idled beside Lola.

'Sean! What the hell are you doing in a car?' I shouted over the noise of the engine. 'And where's your bike?'

'Don't ask, man. That bike shop fixed me up, but straight outta town on the first climb, the whole derailleur just came right off! So I hitched a ride and Wendy here stopped.'

'Hey, Wendy…' I said. Wendy didn't take her eyes off the road, nor acknowledge me. She looked young, maybe early thirties, and was wearing a large grey cardigan that obscured most of her body. 'So you're both headed for Seattle right now?' I asked.

'Eh…' Sean stuttered.

'Yea, we just gotta call in to a few places on the way,' Wendy chipped in. She had a calm and even voice, but still didn't look up. There was something very strange about her detached manner.

Sean raised his eyebrows. I'd never known him to look so uncomfortable; my guess was that Wendy was an oddball, or perhaps just a very bad driver, and he was beginning to regret his decision to jump in the first car that offered him a lift.

'Listen, we gotta go,' he said, 'but call me when you get to Seattle. God speed, Leon!'

With that he was off. *In a bloody car.* It had started to rain and I thought enviously of the warm, dry interior of the hatchback. No matter how uncomfortable Wendy was making him, Sean would still be in Seattle in a matter of hours.

'Idiot!' I shouted into the wind, not sure if I meant him or me.

By nightfall I felt like a broken man – exhausted mentally from the day and suffering physically from the Achilles injury. I pulled off the road and left Lola on the shoulder while I scouted out somewhere to sleep. I had become complacent and lazy; reluctant to drag Lola into the woods unless certain of a perfect camping spot.

Now I returned from my recce to see the outline of a vehicle stopped by Lola's silhouetted frame. I felt panic rise from my gut; my arms tingled and pace quickened and for a split second I thought just how silly I would feel if she found her way into the boot of a passing car. I half-jogged, as fast as I could go, and found the blue hatchback from earlier was idling alongside once more. Now Sean was in the driving seat, hunched over the wheel with a cigarette in hand and a manic look on his face. Wendy sat in the passenger seat, her hair dripping water onto the lenses of her glasses. Her eyes were shut, her breathing slow, only interrupted by the odd snore.

'Sean... what are you doing driving?'

'This is crazy, Leon! This girl is...' He glanced down, and lowered his voice.

'She's crazy!' he whispered. 'Turns out she was totally drunk. I mean seriously off-the-wall drunk, so I started driving. She insisted we stop at this scenic pull-off by the river. I was like "no way, we just need to get to Seattle," but she started shouting so I stopped. I went to film some stuff, and turned around, and she was just floating downstream past me! I guess she fell in. I had to run down and fish her out, and some other folks there called the police...'

'That's... crazy!' I agreed.

'It gets worse. Now she's talking all sorts of mad stuff. Says she's the Ninth Gate to Hell. I'm not kidding, man. Something about an Angel of Death, too. She made us stop at a bar but they threw her out. I think she might roam around here quite a bit, being all screwed up.'

'Why are you still driving her around?'

'I dunno, I don't wanna hear tomorrow that she's washed up dead somewhere, or crashed into a tree halfway up the mountain, I guess. So I'm just gonna take us to Seattle, and figure it out there.'

'Uh... OK. Well, call me if you need anything. Like moral support, I guess. There's bugger all else I can do really.'

'Thanks. This is crazy...' he repeated as he signalled to pull out.

I walked back off the road to my camp spot, and suddenly felt a lot more content with my lot. It was wet and cold, but at least I wasn't responsible for getting an Angel of Death back home before the cops arrived.

* * *

Only thirty miles remained to the city and I consumed them like an animal. Approaching Seattle from the north I rode through Everett on a green and leafy country road. A sign told me I was close to the small village of Mukilteo, but the air had an even clearer message of its own to impart. The fresh, salty breeze all around could only be oceanic and I stole a first glimpse of the Great Blue between some tall blocky houses built on an outcrop of rock. I looked away quickly, wanting that first proper vision to be perfect. I had never seen the Pacific before.

The road wound south and west and downhill, until finally a gap in the wall of trees appeared on my right and led down again to meet a single track of rusted brown railway tracks heading south in parallel with the road. I hopped off Lola, left her resting by a tree stump on the hard shoulder, and squeezed through the traffic gates at the crossing, blissfully ignoring the 'No Trespassing' sign as I stepped over the wooden sleepers. There was one final rocky mound to climb over, which brought me onto a narrow pebbled beach that dropped away into the lapping tide. The sea. Bits of flotsam danced around in the moving water by my feet. Technically it was an inlet rather than the open ocean, and just a few miles west across the Puget Sound I could see Whidbey Island. It was now nearly three months since I had stood on the shore at Coney Island and looked east over the Atlantic. This lacked the majesty of that view, but I didn't care. At this moment it was more than good enough – clear, blue, viscous and connected to the Pacific Ocean proper. I waded in up to my knees and dipped my hands, then dunked my face. Submerged, eyes closed, I could see clearly each and every moment that had brought me to this spot. Four thousand miles of stresses and uncertainties and defeats and fears came away with the grime and floated out peacefully into the void. I had made it across North America, on a bicycle.

PART FOUR – SOUTH

*A journey is like marriage. The certain way
to be wrong is to think you control it.*
John Steinbeck

CHAPTER 43

SEATTLE

For my first few days in Seattle I slept long and ate often. I drank tea and coffee until it was an acceptable time to have a beer. I sat in my underpants feeling like king of the world, looked out the window at busy people with busy lives, and watched terrible daytime TV. I couldn't care less about anything other than just existing in stationary vegetation. This was a time for indulgence and brainless wasting of time. There'd been a lot of thinking and doing in the last few months.

Robert and Sarah, whose home I was now enjoying, had caught a flight out of the country only hours after my arrival and I was left with their keys. ('Stay as long as you want!') Sean and I met up and sat in a bar drinking cold beers and reminiscing about the ride. He was finished, done with cycling, readying to fly home to Philadelphia the next day. It didn't take us long to turn from talking about 'the ride', a present-tense current activity, to 'the Ride', a mythical and heroic story of adventures past – of mighty rivers, wild armies of gunmen, tornados the size of skyscrapers, and the protagonists to defeat them all.

When he was gone I was left alone with the city and my thoughts. Seattle is pretty, sitting on an isthmus between

Puget Sound (where I first met the Pacific) and the vast Lake Washington, which I had yet to encounter. I stayed in a northern district and although I briefly wandered the main drags, visiting Pike Place Fish Market and staring out at Mount Olympus across the sound, I began to mostly now frequent coffee shops, wondering what to do next.

It had long been in the back of my mind that if I did make it across the country, it would then make sense to continue on down the coast. Well, I'd made it across the country. I was fit and healthy. I still had some money. And, most of all, I had the desire to keep moving.

The old self-doubt resurfaced; guilt, too, came back. Guilt about continuing my jaunt around the USA when everyone else was back home suffering. That situation didn't seem to have improved. I knew of only two people from my university course who had jobs even vaguely related to their chosen industry. Two out of over two hundred. Other friends on other paths weren't faring any better. Many seemed to have gone back to study – a not dissimilar method of escape to mine, I thought. Ride out the recession by occupying yourself with something else. The problem was that Masters degrees and doctorates now brought no guarantees, other than that of increased debt. I dealt in equal amounts of uncertainty, I supposed, but at least my debts stayed put. I was pretty confident, too, that I was learning more out here than I ever would through another year at university. Each to their own arena of education – this was mine.

I was also carrying guilt over Clare, my girl back home. I called her up, finally, and we talked for hours, days. Her voice transported me instantly to a different time and place. The longing for England and a normal life and relationship washed over me. Retrospective amnesia was in full flow; I romanticised the life I'd been so desperate to leave. I sensed that she had dared to hope I would be content with the continental crossing, but it became clear that I wasn't. I told her that I wasn't ready to come home; that, despite missing her and loving her, I still had unfinished business with my journey. I said, out loud for the first time, that I would like to ride down the coast to Mexico. Not only that, but that I'd like to keep riding until every penny of my savings had run out. I'd been spending only five dollars a day, so that might be quite some time. There was a good chance I'd run out of tarmac before I ran out of money.

She made no demands, but accepted my position as immovable; we had known each other long enough to be able to discern things that fell into this category. What was inarguable, though, was that we missed each other; that we were still in love. We had reached a fork in the road after finishing university and had started down different paths. For a while they had struck out in a V, and it seemed we may lose each other as our distance apart increased. Now the paths had straightened out and, although apart, there was still a sense we could be moving in the same general direction together.

I had no immediate plans, other than to start southwards at some point. She was on summer vacation (the major benefit of being a teacher, of course, is the holidays). Quite quickly we discussed the possibility that she could fly out to see me. As simple as that, it was decided. The cheapest flight for Clare arrived into Las Vegas, a result of casinos subsidising the cost of air travel to encourage gamblers, so I stashed my bike and the majority of my gear in Seattle and jumped on a Greyhound headed to Sin City. For two days I had an adventure of a very different sort on low-budget buses with a revolving cast of characters that ranged from drunk to wildly insane (with very little in between). Never was there a time when I missed more the solitary luxury of self-directed bicycle travel.

Vegas is not an ideal place for lovers, unless you are flush with cash or perhaps heavily into burlesque shows and gambling. Clare and I were neither and soon split for the coast. For three weeks we hitchhiked and rode buses, camped and walked along beaches. Mostly, it was perfect. Being together again felt natural, as if we had never been apart. We let ourselves enjoy the time and only talked of 'what next' as the last few days counted down.

I told her again that I wasn't ready to come home yet. She agreed. I was surprised; I knew how painful this was, yet she was encouraging me to keep going – to stay on the other side of the world from her. It wasn't ideal, was her summation (in typically understated manner), but it'd be for the best in the long run, for me and for *us*, if we were to work. And then she flew home.

Later she wrote to me that it felt like a physical pain, the parting, which I think is about as accurate as any description can be. I rode north on another horrible Greyhound, my mind split into two separate and polarised strands, each pulling hard in their own direction; one was on the plane home with Clare, the other back on Lola headed into more of the unknown.

CHAPTER 44

ONE STEP NORTH, TWO STEPS SOUTH

Back in Seattle, I realised what I'd gained from seeing Clare: now I had a destination. It wasn't a location, though, but a person. I would ride until my last dime, with no idea of how long that might take, then I would go home to a woman who loved me.

The west coast of the USA seemed like a good place to start this new journey. To the south lay Oregon, California and, even further beyond, Central and South America. This would be my new direction. It felt strange to reset my natural compass – for so long travelling west had been second nature. Now the sun would rise on my left shoulder and set on my right, a fiery ball of orange dropping into the endless blue ocean each day.

At the start of my trip I'd felt obliged to ride from the Atlantic to the Pacific so I could legitimately claim to have crossed the entire USA by human power alone. For whose benefit, I knew not. Now I felt that if I was going to ride to the southern border of America then it would make sense to start at a northern boundary. That was a couple of days' ride north from Seattle. It wasn't necessary, but then neither was any of what I was doing, if I took that approach. Who knew when I'd be riding north again? If nothing else, I'd have a chance to bid a final farewell to Canada.

It was now over four weeks since I'd rolled into Seattle from the Cascade Mountains. Slowly, and with much groaning, I heaved myself onto the road and into the damp surrounds of northern Washington. Rain patted at my head constantly and my body felt heavy, legs unaccustomed to the motion of riding.

This area of the Pacific Northwest is characterised by an archipelago of islands clustered around the coast. West of Seattle, Whidbey Island is sandwiched in a horseshoe-shaped sound between the mainland and the enormous Olympic Peninsula. Above this and beyond lie the San Juans, a hilly and fertile collection of beautiful islands.

I rode north along the coast, watching various islands and peninsulas pass by, each obscuring from me a view of the as-yet elusive Pacific Proper. At the international border I was waved into Canada with a wonderful lack of ceremony, just as in Ontario. British Columbia, my second Canadian province, welcomed me with a confident and brash statement on its sign: 'The Greatest Place in the World'.

Slight panic ensued on the way to Vancouver when I saw a sign suggesting it was fifty-six miles to the city centre. 'It's only meant to be thirty!' I blustered, panicking that my couchsurfing hosts would lock the doors if I turned up three hours late. All afternoon I was a speeding bullet (or as close as I could resemble one with 70 kilograms of bike and gear) until finally, approaching the outskirts, I remembered that Canada works in kilometres, not miles. I was not late, just a moron.

Vancouver was handsome, a seaport clustered around a few miles of coastline overlooking the Strait of Georgia. Yet now I was here, I was mainly thinking about leaving again. For a few days I wandered around, marvelling at how the plush polished buildings of downtown blended into heavily forested Stanley Park, accidentally stumbling into East Hastings where Vancouver's homeless are congregated. Drifting complete, I got back on Lola, turned my nose south and pushed off onto the tarmac, following a white line that I hoped would take me all the way to Mexico.

CHAPTER 45

SOUTH

My journey back to Seattle was simple – for the first time I knew exactly where I was going and how to get there. In Mount Vernon, midway between Vancouver and the suburban sprawl of the Greater Seattle area, I spent a night inside a cinema when the manager took pity on me riding past in the rain. While I waited outside for the film to finish, I was approached by a lanky fellow wearing taped-up glasses. Tomcat (a name I would guess he had assumed) was an ex-film-industry professional who now seemed to spend his life smoking weed and telling people about his actual cat. When I turned down an invite to go and meet his drug dealer ('You'll love him, man, he digs cycling. Doesn't normally like the British, though... but I'll tell him you're Irish, and I bet he won't mind!'), Tomcat instead went away and came back shortly afterwards with Priestess, the famed feline of his many stories. In just twenty minutes (it felt like twenty days), I had heard how Priestess learned to change TV channels, use a toilet, open windows and even read a book.

'This is the most famous cat in the west, I'm telling you! She knows tricks and everything. And, get this, she goes skiing.'

'She goes *skiing*?' I repeated.

'Well, I take her skiing. She sits on my shoulder. Did a few runs up at Whistler just the other week. She's on YouTube, man!'

As soon as it was possible I made excuses to leave, and was relieved when the cinema owner locked me inside for the night. Tomcat was certainly an odd specimen. It was these encounters, though, which added colour to my days, whether I enjoyed them at the time or not. It was easy to feel annoyed or uninterested in people who were only trying to converse or even help me out. My patience was somewhat less than it should have been. Sometimes I was in luck, and met a character of great wit and intellect, and sometimes it was cat-obsessed potheads. Both had their mark to make. I settled down for the night with two buckets of salted popcorn and a large fizzy drink, and read until my eyes closed on the floor between aisles of reclining cinema seats.

* * *

I skirted around Seattle and Tacoma, avoiding the metropolitan area as much as possible. My maps indicated that if I wanted to visit Portland, the purported cycling capital of America, then I should stay in the hinterland for my first few days south. When I asked directions at a bike shop in south Tacoma, the bike jock in the doorway laughed: 'Look at the road, dude!'

I wondered if this was some kind of bike slang that I didn't understand. I played it cool and tried to seem nonchalant. 'Erm, OK, sweet, man. And... I'll just find it that way, yea?'

'Well, sure! There's a big ride we help organise once a year called the Seattle to Portland Classic. A whole bunch of people get together and do the distance in one or two days. Anyway, most people get lost if they're just following a map, so we spray-painted directions onto the road to help. If you just keep an eye on the tarmac, if you can see it beneath all this rain, then there's a red circle with "STP" inside it and an arrow telling you which way to go!'

For two days navigation was as easy as that, despite torrential weather. It was nice to be directed for a change – no brainpower required. I was on autopilot, riding quiet country roads through southern Washington.

* * *

For the second time on my journey, the Columbia River crossed my path. The first time had been just before I entered the Cascade Mountains, but now it was twice as wide and nearing the end of its 1,243-mile course from the Canadian Rockies to the Pacific. My route across was via the aptly named 'Lewis and Clark Bridge', taking me not just over the river, but also into a new state: Oregon.

In November 1805, more than a year and a half after leaving Missouri on their expedition to find the Pacific Ocean, Lewis and Clark has paused at the point on the Columbia where the bridge now stands. William Clark noted how the river tasted salty and that there were tidal influences at play. He suspected they were close. Four days later they arrived at their goal, having traversed the Rockies and the continental divide, and having survived a harsh winter by weathering in a hut in North Dakota. Clark describes the men 'beholding with astonishment the high waves dashing against the rocks of this emence [sic] ocean'.

I had yet that pleasure to find, but the significance of the spot did not escape me. Many times over the previous three months I had thought of their expedition, striving westwards through unknown territories. It was hard to see them simply as heroes; it's fair to say that their journey set in motion a terrible series of events for the native peoples. Yet (mostly) they themselves treated the indigenous people they met with respect and humility, unlike almost everyone else who followed. Chief Joseph, a tribal leader who gained nationwide recognition in US newspapers following his principled and peaceful response to his people's removal from their ancestral lands, said of the early expedition that 'the first white men of your people who came to our country were named Lewis and Clark. They brought many things that our people had never seen. They talked straight. These men were very kind.' The implication was that Lewis and Clark were a different breed to the merciless settlers who followed.

What's definitely true, and what I could now appreciate a little more, was their skill and determination as explorers. In their diaries I read universal desires and reflections on adventure, on the need to push oneself, and the excitement of discovery of new lands. The Columbia River had meant much to them, and also now to me. America's geography may have changed dramatically in the intervening two hundred years, but while states and political boundaries emerge and drift and shift and fade, the physicality of mountains and rivers and oceans remains relatively constant. It might not have been called Oregon State or the Columbia River back when Meriwether Lewis and William Clark came through, but we each stood on the banks of this mighty river and took from it our own inspirations. I wondered, too, how many others throughout history had done the same.

Their expedition weathered another cruel winter near present-day Astoria, not far from where I was now, before returning east to report on their findings, and subsequently they laid claim to the west for America before the British, French or Spanish could. Lewis and Clark had found the principal river valleys at the eastern and western extremes that would lead to the first overland routes across America, chiefly the Oregon Trail. I was not heading home, nor back east. I was heading further into my own unknown – a 'civilised' and tame exploration incomparable to that of Lewis and Clark's, but one which elicited in me that same buzz and drive, and led me to wake each morning eager to beat the sunrise in the race for the day.

CHAPTER 46

KEEP PORTLAND WEIRD

Portland is Oregon's biggest city and sits at the confluence of the Willamette and Columbia rivers, nestled in the shadow of Mount Hood to the east. It had been recommended to me and lauded like no other city I had encountered. Mostly the reason was obvious: its reputation as a green and eco-friendly place and above all its provision for cyclists. Portland's governors have been extremely supportive of urban cycling, building dedicated cycle lanes and endeavouring to reduce traffic flow. The rate of commuters travelling by bike is ten times higher than the national average (8 per cent of people ride to work in Portland).

The first thing immediately apparent was the impressive array of bridges that span the Willamette as it runs through the centre of the city. Standing by the steel tied-arch Fremont Bridge at the north of the city, I could look south along the river and count at least four more metal beasts stretching spindly limbs up and over and out across the water like the legs of some great spider.

I found the mass of other cyclists around me to be disorienting at first, speedsters whizzing past and cutting across at junctions. It reminded me of London: Lycra-clad road bikers weaving in and out of traffic (and yelling at cars who don't give enough room). Soon, though, it took on a life of its own, aided by the wide bike lanes, and I noticed that it wasn't just 'roadies' cycling the streets. In fact, a cross-section of the whole Portland community could be taken from those out on their bicycles at any one given time. Students with long hair and satchels ambled alongside at my slow pace and chatted, while old women dinged their bells and gave me a smile as I overtook. Lithe, tattooed shapes with dreadlocks shouted encouragement as they floated past on lightweight flying machines, and a few businessmen in suits did a double take. I guess even by Portland standards my bike was an odd get-up.

I was set to stay with more friends of friends, the wonderful two degrees of separation that had connected me with hosts and helpers all across the country. Terry and his housemates looked the part of a folk-country ensemble with an array of shaggy hair, scruffy beards and tie-dye shirts. For four hours I drank locally brewed beers and listened to them jam in their living room, blasting out Led Zeppelin, The Beatles and Bob Dylan. Portland is a cool place full of cool people – microbreweries, food carts, a thriving music scene – and it seemed I'd landed right in the middle of it all. Confirming these suspicions, Terry made a plan for the evening. 'OK, let's head out for some disc golf, then we'll hit up a few of the microbreweries for a bit of a tour, and get some food. We can go see my bar later, too.'

Terry was about my age, and looked exactly like the Canadian actor Seth Rogen. He could've probably made a career out of lookalike appearances. Originally from Sioux Falls, South Dakota, he'd been lured out here by the lifestyle. Putting down roots, he'd now part-purchased a sports bar with a friend and was desperately trying to make it work financially. Portland was full of folk like Terry. Every bar or coffee shop we went into was rammed with hip young things, all talking about their latest band or start-up or film. I guess for the young, the ambitious and the dreamers, for anyone who identified with cultural markers that got labelled as 'alternative', Portland would be extremely appealing (especially if you came from some sleepy town in the Midwest – I knew from experience how little there was to stimulate the mind out there).

As we left for a round of disc golf (like regular golf, but with Frisbees instead of clubs and balls), our group was comprised of two Midwesterners, a New Yorker, a Floridian and three girls from Seattle. Not an Oregonian in sight.

'Don't forget your "walking around" beer!' shouted Terry. 'I love this game whatever the scenario, but it's two hundred per cent more fun with beers...'

The next two days were spent in similar fashion – walking around, drinking beers, and always doing one additional activity to help disguise the fact that in reality we were just spending all day drinking. I found my way, in between this heavy schedule, to Powell's Books. All the cool people talked about it all the time. This independent store in Portland takes up a whole city block, and claims to be America's largest second-hand bookstore. I'd been devouring books throughout my journey and was down to just three paperbacks (from an all-time high of eleven in Montana). Dee Brown's *Bury My Heart at Wounded Knee*, Lewis and Clark's diaries (or at least half of them, I'd ripped out some pages), and John Steinbeck's *Travels with Charley* were the sole survivors, and I'd finished two of those.

For six hours I browsed in a cut-price musty-odoured personal heaven. There is nothing quite like the smell of a second-hand bookshop. When I left, it was with another six books to take me south. For the most part, I tried while travelling across America to avoid any writings that seemed too escapist, in the same way that I aimed to not listen to music for more than one hour a day. It seemed rather pointless (or at least, *more* pointless) to ride around the country caught up in another world, someone else's world. The power of music and books to transport us away from the here and now should not be underestimated, for better or worse. Here in Portland, though, I made a small compromise. I have always had a weakness for hard-boiled detective novels and, as I was soon to enter the California of Sam Spade and Philip Marlowe, I allowed Dashiell Hammett's *The Thin Man* and Raymond Chandler's *The Long Goodbye* to slip into my panniers.

Portland was somewhat of a trap; a little slice of comfort and culture that could easily suck me in. Normally I recoil from places that are branded as 'quirky' or 'cool' or 'alternative' – places like Camden in London always feel too staged, full of people posturing and trying too hard. I'm far too much of a nerd to be comfortable there. Part of it, too, must have something to do with insecurity on my part, a sense of fear of being rejected from that community. The result, more often than not, is that I find it all a little fake and unappealing.

Portland did not elicit that response; instead I felt drawn in. The guys brewing beers in their backyard didn't seem to care what anyone else thought, and the musicians played in their bands because they loved it. I liked being around them, and people were interested in hearing my story. I wasn't sure that I really fitted into this crowd long-term – music, drinking and being cool all seemed a little too sociable and enjoyable for my current tastes of joy through abject physical and emotional suffering on a bicycle – but I could easily have spent another week or two with Terry and his friends.

For a few reasons, I decided not to. Firstly, my budget couldn't handle extended stays in towns and cities. Secondly, this trip wasn't meant to be a holiday. To the outsider looking in perhaps it often seemed that way – gallivanting across America doing as I pleased. That didn't really matter to me – what was important was that I didn't come to view it as such myself. That meant sticking to my plan to keep pushing, to keep myself stretched. I'd recently had an actual holiday with Clare and had no need of another one. And so I moved on, leaving Terry and his housemates to their good life in quirky Portland.

CHAPTER 47

TO SLEEP IN THE TREES

The road running out to the Oregon coast took me through twenty miles of faceless Portland suburbs before finally I emerged into the Douglas firs of Van Duzer Forest. The Salmon River wiggled alongside and it wasn't until light began to fade from the day that I realised I'd been dawdling. My map showed fifteen miles to the coast; I wasn't going to make it before darkness and camping was a much more enticing option than riding these windy roads at night. I wondered idly if I was in bear country yet.

A short driveway cut into a forest clearing on my left and a large, well-kept home filled the space. The walls were pebble-dashed purest white, and a path of smooth granite ran to the doorway. 'Worth a shot,' I thought. Pulling up alongside the 4x4 parked out front I heard the garage door slide open, and a very large man in very large dungarees emerged almost immediately.

'Hey! I was, eh, just wondering if you could tell me how many miles to the coast. I was hoping to make it there tonight and sleep on the beach,' I began. There was deception in my words.

'Fourteen miles to Lincoln City from our driveway, sixteen to the first spot of beach, but I dunno if you can sleep on there, they might have some rules about that.'

'Oh, OK. Do you think I can just camp in the forest?'

He looked at me, large limbs hanging heavy by his side like meat on a rack. A small smile grew at the side of his mouth. I got the feeling he knew that if I really wanted to camp in the forest I'd already be there and would have stayed well clear of his house.

He began slowly, '... most of it's state land, so you can't legally sleep there. But I don't think that's such a great rule...' A pause. 'If you liked, I guess you could just camp beside the house here.'

I was nearly there, but the next move was always the trickiest. 'Wow, thanks! That'd be perfect. I really don't mean to cause any bother, I'll put the tent up well away from the house, and be gone early in the morning.' I shook his hand, three times the size of mine. He introduced himself as Marty and went to fetch his wife.

As they came back around the corner, I heard her gently chastising him, '... oh, now, we'll make sure the young man has some food!' They appeared together in front of me, and she fussed and mothered at me as I spoke.

'Well, that's all just wonderful! How about you wash your hands and come on in for some dinner... we got corn, stew and then some jello. You like jello?'

I nodded enthusiastically. *Success!* This was my basic template for trying to secure either a warm bed for the night, a hearty meal or (ideally) both. Tonight was going well.

'I'll tell you what,' added Marty. 'I got another idea. Follow me.'

I started after him down a trail behind the house, hoping he wasn't suggesting I put my tent up all the way down by the river. It was a prettier spot, sure, but who could be bothered with all that extra walking?

'How about this for the night?' He had stopped in his tracks, and with a triumphant flourish pointed to the sky. Above him, nestled halfway up the trunk of a Douglas fir, was the most perfect tree house I'd ever seen. A wooden staircase, carved from another fir, wound up the trunk from the base and ended on a solid platform complete with balcony. It was like something out of a Disney movie, even down to the tiny window ledges decorated with potted plants. This was someone's dream, right here. Marty led me up to the door.

'It's fully functioning, we got electricity in here, a little TV and VCR player, bunk beds, wardrobe. I just finished building her, actually. Hoping to rent it out soon. Me and the wife were planning to make the whole place into a tourist resort, but… well, it's tough times. Our daughter just lost her job so she's moved home. Plans are on hold while we help her out. But this one here is done, and it's all yours for the night.'

On a trip such as mine it was easy to get sucked into a world of pedalling and sleeping in forests and having fleeting conversations with strangers. It was easy to forget that the country I was travelling through was also in recession. It just wasn't as noticeable as it had been in the UK because I was just a glorified tourist, and lived frugally. Perhaps in Michigan it had been clear, Buffalo too maybe, but without being immersed in any one place I often skirted over issues such as this that lay at the heart of how the country operated. A nationwide (and global) slump wasn't just about the big deficit numbers getting thrown around by politicians on TV news; on a personal level it affected almost everyone. Here, in the middle of a state forest near the Oregon coastline, a family was suffering together through the problems, and it infiltrated every aspect of their lives.

A beautifully carved wooden door opened through to a spacious bedroom. Bunk beds stacked high with blankets and cushions sat at the back, and beside the entrance a window looked out into the forest and onto the Salmon River below. A clunky old TV sat in the corner, fringed with bunting.

'Nothing to disturb you here,' said Marty, 'except the steelheads and cut-throat trout splashing around down in the river. Go get your stuff, we'll put your bike in the garage and then join us for dinner in fifteen minutes.' He turned to go. 'It's nice to have you here. We're Christians in this house, and we try to look after folk. I'm glad we could help you out.'

CHAPTER 48

MY WITNESS IS THE EMPTY SKY

It didn't take long to reach Lincoln City the following morning; a rather sad and tacky-looking town designed to cater for flocks of absent tourists, and haunted by spectres of a more lucrative time. Beyond the rows of empty cafes and peeling billboards, the highway spun to the south and joined Route 101, an iconic longitudinal road running the length of the western coastline. This same strip of tarmac would take me almost all the way to the Mexican border.

I escaped the built-up arena of housing blocks and climbed high onto an escarpment overlooking Siletz Bay. Beyond it the Pacific Ocean, in all its beauty, was finally revealed. White horses rolled into the sands below in unison; rugged lumps of rock jutted out of the blue bay beyond. Ahead of me to the south a dramatic coast wound its way to the horizon. The beach faded and reappeared sporadically, waves crashing into bare stone at every opportunity. To have such a companion as this view for the next 1,300 miles was a dream of Kerouac-ian proportions.

For four days and nights I travelled with one eye on the road and the other watching the eternal lapping of the ocean. The days were long, clear and warm, yet, despite it being the middle of summer, a coastal breeze ensured life remained reasonably cool and comfortable. I slept on bluffs without a tent, drifting off to the sound of waves and waking to the early-morning sun heating up my world. There was nothing to interrupt me. *This is why riding a bicycle is perfect.* When good weather, roads and views combine, nothing can match a bike trip for making life seem an ecstatically pleasurable privilege.

During my night in the tree house I'd received a text message – my first in weeks (I had little use for a mobile phone and only turned it on once every couple of days). It was from Susie, and read:

Crossed Rockies on Northern Tier. Now in Vancouver. Hitching down the coast with bike – might cycle in California. Fancy meeting up?

We had agreed to find each other in the city of Florence, Oregon, not far from the Californian border. Again I marvelled at how small such a huge country could become through communication and communities. How many people had I already criss-crossed paths with across the country? Now Susie, whom I met in New York State and left behind in Wisconsin, would re-enter my life by the Pacific.

During the afternoon a fog with the consistency of a Tweed blanket stole away the Oregon coastline, and I could just as easily have been riding into Florence, Italy, or anywhere else on the planet. The world was one of greyness and rain, only enlivened by an occasional logging truck emerging from the void with a prehistoric rumble. Logging, along with mining and fishing, has long been one of the staple industries of the West Coast and these trucks towing huge lengths of redwood timbers were now as much a part of the landscape as the forests themselves.

I found Susie sheltered under the awning of a cafe outside of town. We hugged and quickly got down to the important business of sharing our journeys' highlights since we parted in Wisconsin, over a month previously. Susie had been on more than a few adventures, which came as no surprise. In North Dakota she'd met a cycling musician and pedalled slowly west with him and his guitar, until eventually they both hopped on a freight train for a change of scenery. That made me smile. Somewhere in the Rockies she'd picked up more cyclists and convinced them to cycle north into Montana, past the headwaters of the Missouri River and almost right up to the border with Canada. Finally she'd reached the coast alone by riding the Going-to-the-Sun highway across Glacier National Park, the road culminating in five epic passes, each seemingly much more exhausting than those that I rode.

Susie laughed and grinned constantly, and her stories told me she hadn't changed one bit – she was cheery, light-hearted as always, with that determined and deeply driven streak shining through. Through the consistency of her character, I was surprised to note how different I had clearly become. I was infinitely more confident and content, and gone were so many of the fears and worries I'd had when we had last pedalled alongside each other. I'd been on plenty of adventures myself, and the unpredictable lifestyle we shared was now so natural to me that I almost couldn't recognise the difficulties any more – this was just the way things were now, and I was happy with that. Susie noticed too.

'It's amazing how gradually we change and develop, isn't it?' she mused. 'It's the best reason I know to keep doing good stuff, exciting stuff every waking moment, because one day you're gonna realise that you're not the person you thought you were, and it's way better to have become a better version of yourself rather than the other way round!'

Full of coffee and cake, we left the cafe and rode south. The world was still grey, and soon the downpour and fog dampened our spirits as much as it did the ground on which our pedals rolled along. We rode in single file, in silence. That night we pitched our tents on the hillside, and I fell asleep to the rhythmic pattering of rain on my flysheet.

Just before the state border we chanced upon the 'Seven Devils' – a section of road so named for its fiendish curves and bends. This was the kick-start we needed to shake our funk. We puffed up around hairpins and squealed our way back down, slamming on worn brake pads to avoid tumbling over into the abyss. By Devil Number Seven we were both beaming, the worries and gloom of the previous day left on the hills behind.

It is a curious thing about bicycle touring. So much of it is, in fact, boring; quite probably the vast majority. Another large proportion is miserable. A smaller percentage is both. Whatever is left over, though: that is superb. I had encountered plenty that was boring and miserable between New York City and the Seven Devils. Yet monotonous days were already nearly faded in my memory, and the truly miserable times became retrospectively enjoyable to recall how I endured or conquered them. The highs – cresting the Big Horns, crossing the Missouri, swimming in the Finger Lakes – were as clear in my mind as if they had just happened minutes previously.

I remembered how, in my brief life as a full-time employee, every weekday faded into one long blur. I automatically lost five-sevenths of the week, and was normally so tired that I subsequently wasted at least an additional seventh during the weekend. Each day of cycle touring was not perfection – I had yet to discover the trick to making every single day memorable. But my ratio was much better than before, and the highs higher than I'd ever known in my previous life. Even the lows were better; on dull days I felt a sense of achievement that I never got from regular employment. On the road, twenty-four hours of boring scenery or bad camping or tough roads felt one day closer to a more exciting time in a new location further down the trail. In England, rather morbidly, the same period of time only felt one day closer to death.

***

'I have to tell you about Issac,' said Susie as we descended to sea level and skirted along shingle beach. Issac – her 'lover' from who she had been parted for three years while they each rode bicycles alone in separate parts of the world.

'He's had an accident.'

I gulped. I didn't even know the guy, but I knew how much he meant to Susie. His fate seemed tied in with hers, and with mine. He was one of us, on the road, vulnerable and at the mercy of the world.

'He got hit by a truck in Pakistan. At first it didn't seem too bad so they just took him to a local hospital. But now the doctors reckon his hip is fractured in a couple of places. He's been moved to Lahore, and they're going to have to operate.'

The only sound was spinning pedals.

'What will you do?'

'I don't know. More than anything, I want to go and see him.'

Her dilemma was that she hadn't been in an aeroplane for nearly five years; an ethical opposition to the damage done to the environment by air travel. Susie lived by a strong moral code, and in many ways her dedication to it defined who she was. She was humble, but commanded respect through actions over words. To fly would be to compromise.

'What happens if you don't go?'

'He'll go through the operation alone and then spend three months recovering, alone.'

'Can you afford to go financially... in theory?'

'I can borrow the money. In theory.'

'Susie... I think you have to go. You don't want to regret anything afterwards, but I think you're much more likely to regret leaving Issac there alone than taking one flight out to Pakistan to be with the person you love.'

'That's what I was thinking too,' she said, almost in a whisper. 'I still need more time to decide though.'

It seemed a battle between principles and love. In her life, principles trumped almost everything else. But there are few forces that can overpower love. Rejecting to fly this one time would not save the world. Neither would going to see Issac, at least not in a grand sense, but it would make their personal world a better place. A compromise for love.

I was now more comforted than ever that Clare had come out to visit me. Our tough times had not been on the same level as Susie and Issac's – neither of us was ever seriously wounded, physically or emotionally. But we hurt in our own way, individually and together, and there is so much in life that can only be communicated in person, through contact and being able to look into someone's eyes as you speak to them. I hoped Susie would go and I knew that as soon as she arrived by Issac's bedside she would know she had made the right decision.

CHAPTER 49

THE GOLDEN STATE

The state boundary passed beneath my tyres and nothing changed. I had become a fan of physical borders: rivers, mountains, oceans. An arbitrary line drawn between grains of sand on a beach, separating two adjacent trees in the same cluster – this did not seem worth stopping to notice. Yet change had occurred, even if I couldn't see it reflected in the land around me. From relatively humble Oregon State, Susie and I had now entered California: a state so powerful that at one point it was said that if it were a country, it would have had the seventh most powerful economy in the world. An arbitrary line the border may have seemed, but billions of dollars said otherwise. The line dividing California from Mexico would be even greater still.

Occasionally Susie and I would drift inland when the road demanded it. These forays took us away from the wilderness of the ocean and into equally impressive blankets of forests that rose up in the foothills to the east. Most of these wooded areas were designated as state parks and received government funding for upkeep and conservation. It also meant that it was illegal to camp wherever we liked, and diligent rangers roamed around looking for anyone who might be thinking of breaking the rules. Unlike the rest of the USA, however, where state-run campsites were much too expensive for my daily budget, here the parks ran an impressively accessible and affordable scheme called the 'Hiker-Biker' sites. The deal was that if you arrived on foot or bicycle you could camp for five dollars. You could never be turned away, so I was told.

We began to spend most nights in these Hiker-Biker sites. They were an easy option – no thinking required. More than that, though, each was its own self-contained community of similar souls, people who had travelled a section of the coast by human power and were looking for somewhere to lay their head before the next day's excursions.

Bicycling down the west coast of America, I was discovering, was not that unusual. In fact it was positively popular. Driving Route 101 has always been on the radar for tourists, but cycling is relatively new, and recent growth has been rapid. Each night I shared my camping experience with anything from three to twenty other cyclists. During the day they were easy to spot at regular intervals, either overtaking or being overtaken by me, the occasional rebel riding north against the flow. My time as an oddity was over. Now I was in kinship with every other soul who took to the pedals and breathed in the salt air.

* * *

The northernmost redwood trees, prehistorically tall and broad, were immediately apparent amongst smaller pines, and it was here amongst them that Susie announced she was going to leave. She would hitch down to San Francisco and organise a flight to Pakistan. I was delighted for her. We hugged and I left her by the roadside at Klamath, waiting to hitch a ride with a small sign saying 'South' and a grin on her face. I hoped Issac would recover quickly but I knew that, whatever the state of his leg, he'd be much healthier with Susie by his side.

The redwoods began to dominate surroundings quickly. These trees are the largest in the world, by height and volume, and are native only to this region of California. For a cyclist, or anyone who passes by their base, the first thing you notice is a total lack of low-level foliage; no branches protrude from the first 30 feet of smooth trunk. This gives the dual impressions of immense space at eye level and a sense of enclosed claustrophobia caused by the greenery above obscuring anything beyond. Entering into a redwood forest was akin to stepping inside some vast gothic cathedral, mighty pillars stretching up and sunlight banished from view.

For hours I would ride through these corridors of giants, specks of sunlight dappling the road. I joined tourists to see the 'Ride-Thru tree' – a lame duck of an attraction, nothing more than a large hole bored through a chunky redwood base. Of more interest was a fallen tree lying beside the entrance to the complex. It had been smoothly sawn so the rings inside the trunk, and therefore the tree's age, were clear to see. A sign alongside claimed it was 2,500 years old and a small arrow pointed at where historic events would have occurred during the tree's lifetime. The founding of America, the signing of the Magna Carta, the birth of Jesus. All came and went as the tree just kept growing. The USA may have just a couple of hundred years of 'civilised' human history, but its natural world boasts an antiquity that has silently watched from afar as the world at large developed and civilisations rise and fell.

Before leaving I scribbled 'Leon arrives in California' onto a piece of paper and wedged it into a crack just after the 'Declaration of Independence'. Perhaps my legacy could live on here, if nowhere else.

CHAPTER 50

CARRIED AWAY

Along with logging trucks, recreational drivers and cyclists, the roads of California boasted a large smattering of hitchhikers and vagabonds. Eureka, Garberville, Fort Bragg – all had streets full of wandering hippies, shoulders hunched under duffle bags and unkempt hair poking out below wide-brimmed sunhats. The atmosphere was not that of expectation and wanderlust, as I had expected, but rather a musty and sad feeling of desperation. Some of those that paced by the sidewalk showed scars from needle marks, and more than once I saw fights break out. Greyhound bus stations served some of these towns, and perhaps the cheap ride north brought an undesirable element of drugs and hopelessness from the sin cities of Los Angeles, San Diego and San Francisco. I only ever saw them from a distance, though, so my impression was just that; a view from afar.

The cyclists were a different bunch, and one that I came to know well. They came from all walks of life but most seemed to be young folk just out of college, or parents who had finally packed their kids off to school. People for whom a natural window of opportunity had arisen. Perhaps because of this, most were cheery and pedalled with wild smiles on their faces.

I rode for a number of days with Stan, a broad-shouldered blond and gentle giant with a Viking beard that hid the creases in his face when he smiled. He was cycling from Portland to San Francisco before starting a Masters degree in Urban Planning. Making cities more sustainable was his passion, and Portland the template.

'In Portland, they don't build a mile of road without thinking about where the next mile of bike path will go too. It simultaneously builds a community that way, and takes away that stigma of being odd. You can ride your bike to work and be sweaty or smelly, and that's OK.'

We rode apart most of the day but met up for lunch, and again as evening fell so we could camp in the same spot. After one particularly exhausting day we splurged ten dollars on organic beers and an array of vegetables from a local market, then spent the night in Humboldt County making chilli over a fire and getting increasingly tipsy.

To the east now were the Sierra Nevadas, a four-hundred-mile-long coastal mountain range that reaches almost as far as Mexico. Brown bears and grizzlies roam in the wilderness areas that stretch to caress the ocean, and evenings in the forests were again a time for caution. In Hiker-Biker sites, food was stored in communal bags and thrown over high branches on a rope. The company and jovial atmosphere at these campsites was a comfort, and without ever seeing or hearing the bears it was hard to imagine they were even around. Nevertheless I followed procedure when it came to food, even on the rare nights that Stan and I camped wild. It seemed only wise. The land was beautiful and I was nearly in San Francisco. Life was good.

Route 101 became a freeway and along with Stan I was syphoned off onto Highway 1, the California State coastal road. We climbed high over an escarpment to see the first signs of city life encroaching. The density of villages increased and a haze filled the sky ahead. Screaming down a hill at top speed into Sausalito, just a short ride across the bridge from San Francisco, I felt inspired by the scenery and the whistling wind to let myself go wild. I'm still not sure why I let go of the breaks, though.

The first mile of descent passed in a flash on smooth tarmac, ocean glistening to my right and steep bank stretching vertically to the sky on the other side. Then, without warning, the surface deteriorated and became a mess of potholes and loose stone. On a tight turn I saw in front Stan's trailer rise onto one wheel, balance precariously and then mercifully slam back down into the correct position. I was not so fortunate, and squeezing the breaks led Lola to squeal and wobble. I wasn't going to make the turn, and only a small metal retaining barrier separated me from an undoubtedly liberating but ultimately terminal flight into the Pacific. The cliff wall on my left seemed (slightly) more appealing so I pulled all my weight to that side, hoped for no cars, and careered into the rock.

A few minutes later I came back to consciousness and found that, aside from mild concussion, all seemed well. A kindly lady stopped her jeep and gently reprimanded me for going too fast, then pointed out the large patch of poison ivy I had narrowly avoided. A large deal of skin was missing from my left forearm and Lola needed a bit of front-rack readjustment. Aside from that we'd survived pretty well. A timely reminder not to get carried away, perhaps, and it would certainly have been a shame to become critically injured so close to a city that offered as much respite as San Francisco.

At the bottom of the hill Stan was waiting. He laughed it off and gave me a high-five. 'In Portland one time I was coming down a hill on my racer at full speed, and this guy cut straight across my path. It was like a catapult for me, I just went flying, straight over the handlebars, straight over him. Another poor dude was just standing close by, and I went bang! Straight into his head, with mine. We both ended up with fractured skulls. Ha, pretty funny now though, eh?'

CHAPTER 51

THE LAND OF MILK AND HONEY

San Francisco is said to have its own microclimate, and this was patently obvious as Stan and I rode out of the sunshine into the gloom. The entire San Francisco Bay was obscured from view by a heavy, wet cloud that clung around us. My world extended as far as my front wheel. One of the icons of modern America, the striking red Art Deco towers of the Golden Gate Bridge, was in there somewhere. I think I saw a flash of colour as I cycled onto it. Then I saw nothing beyond its heavy steel railings until I reached the other side. Microclimate in action.

I thought San Francisco a pretty city, skyscrapers glinting in the summer sun and handsome people walking hand in hand along broad streets. I stayed in the suburb of Danville, in the house of a friend's parents. One day became two, then three, then a week. My hosts left to visit a son in Georgia and once more I found myself in a new American city with a house to myself. Almost to myself – for company this time I had a cat named Goose, who was perhaps the inspiration behind the saying 'curiosity killed the cat'. For ten days Goose and I watched television and ate all the food in the house, and I helped him get out of the washing machine when he got stuck, or removed his paw from the sink when he'd prodded too deep.

The cultural highlights of the city mostly escaped me. I rode a tram up the obscenely steep streets and watched the expensive yachts dock in the marina. But my mind was elsewhere. I was now only ten days' riding from the Mexican border. The thought of what I might do after that began to wake me up in the depths of night – sometimes I came to in a fearful cold sweat, on other occasions my eyes jolted open bright with life and excitement.

* * *

South of San Francisco the landscape softened noticeably. The Sierra Nevadas still dominated, crashing down from their high peaks to meet the sea, but now long beaches of golden or white sands were increasingly prevalent. Gone were the isolation and wilderness. Cars passed, sending lilting music drifting out the windows while tanned surfers sang along inside. It was still technically illegal to sleep on beaches here, but once the sun dropped into the Pacific the hidden coves were a safe bet for an undisturbed rest. Often it was feasible to rise early from my sandy bed, take a dip in the cool dark waters of the ocean, ride south as the sun arced over my head and then finish the day as it had begun, suspended in water staring at a starry sky.

Santa Cruz, when I passed through, looked like every California-based television show I'd ever seen. People with oddly perfect physiques and square jaws lay side by side, and everyone seemed to have a lifetime membership to the gym. Men with arms the width of my face strutted beside girls bursting out of bikinis, saying things to each other like

'Rad, dude, that wave was super gnarly!' and, I imagined, 'Who's that pale skinny dude with those tiny little muscles? They're so... tiny!' Embarrassed by my weedy, pale body and intimidated by the amount of biceps on show, I kept pedalling.

Less threatening was the Salinas Valley, just inland from the surfers' paradise. I'd heard this region called 'the salad bowl of the world', and riding in through the city of Salinas I found myself on a thin corridor of tarmac surrounded by the endless rows of broccoli, peppers and lettuce that filled the broadening valley floor. My interest, however, lay not in agriculture, but rather in the valley's history as home to one of America's favourite literary sons, John Steinbeck.

The Grapes of Wrath, East of Eden, and, most of all, *Travels with Charley* had had a profound effect on me, the former two drawing me into Steinbeck's world in Salinas and making me wish to see it one day for myself, and the latter galvanising me into attempting my own jaunt across his fair country. I couldn't vouch for the characters he wrote about so well, nor the social commentary that gave his work such power, but the landscape was just as he described: 'on one side of the river the golden foothill slopes curve up to the strong and rocky Gabilan mountains... on the valley side the water is lined with trees – willows fresh and green with every spring.' In Monterey, too, I paid only slight attention to the sights of the city and instead rode along Cannery Row, wondering where Lee Chong's Heavenly Flower Grocery might have been.

My self-guided literary tour of Southern California continued not far south, at Big Sur, where a most dramatic meeting of mountains and ocean takes place. Big Sur is perhaps the most famously scenic spot on the entire coastline. You can stand on a bluff looking up or down the coast and watch the Santa

Lucia Mountains roll gently towards the west before finally they hurl themselves into the sea. The result is a coastline of rugged power and beauty, where the spectacular trumps the parochial every time. It was here that Jack Kerouac fled to following the unwanted fame he acquired when *On the Road* was released. His novel *Big Sur* describes a fictional character (based on himself, of course) deteriorating physically and mentally in a cabin in the mountains.

'What a place to go mad,' I thought.

Before I left the area I spent a night with the Watermans: the same family that Matt, Alex, Bryan and I had camped with in Custer over the Fourth of July. They lived in a beautiful and spacious home set in the foothills of the Sierra Nevadas, where at night coyotes could be heard from the hot tub on the porch. Tess and Charlie, whom I'd last seen on the far side of the Rocky Mountains, were another couple of people whose lives I had developed an intrinsic link with, even it was for just a short amount of time.

It seemed an ideal time to finally cut loose the rest of my excess baggage. Gradually throughout the journey I had been jettisoning belongings that no longer seemed necessary – an extra T-shirt, a second cooking pot, a selection of lenses for my camera. Now I could finally fit everything I needed into four pannier bags and a small pouch on the handlebars; my trusty trailer had become redundant. I had of course never actually needed it; in reality it only facilitated the carriage of surplus luggage. But it had served a purpose, and saved me from having to cut ties with all of those possessions too early. This was the time for them to go.

I was left with a sleeping bag, a camping mat and a tent. One set of clothes to ride in, washed in rivers or occasionally in the house of a host, and another 'posh' set for evenings and days off (posh because they were slightly less sweaty and grimy). A cooking set and some tools, a stack of books. A hip flask of whiskey, a camera and a diary. Finally, a picture of my family, and one of Clare. This was all I needed – the world and myriad options still lay beyond my front wheel, and I had, balanced on Lola's broad frame, the necessary tools to go and find them. Slowly but surely this journey was teaching me how to remove superfluous baggage from life, and how to appreciate fully that what is left over is as essential as food and liquid and air.

* * *

Many pretty and stylish towns were dotted along this final stretch of road, and San Luis Obispo was the cream of the crop. Whitewashed Spanish-style villas gave way to palm-lined avenues and shady parks full of pretty girls. Thought had gone into this place, that was for sure – every street and shop looked like someone had stayed up all night planning it out. It is, however, possible to have too much of a good thing and I was beginning to find hordes of tourists a little tiresome despite the coastal beauty.

The Los Padres National Forest includes nearly two million square acres of land along the Californian coast, and south-east of San Luis Obispo it grew to fill my horizons entirely. With the cities of Santa Barbara, Los Angeles and San Diego all lying in wait whatever route I chose, I took a final foray into the forest for one last shot of the wild.

The twisting mountain highway was infinitely quieter than its counterpart on the coast, and for the first time in days

I believed I had the whole world to myself, save a solitary falcon circling high above. A small trail appeared leading into the depths of the forested hill beside the road and it seemed a shame not to break early and enjoy a night alone in the woods. I set up my tent and cooked a simple dinner over my gas stove – lentils, carrots, broccoli and a dash of chilli powder to liven it up. Dessert, as always, came in the form of a sip from the hip flask.

Stuffing the remaining food into a rear pannier, I looped a rope around the whole thing and trekked for a few minutes into the forest. The trees, tall thin Jeffrey pines, were like firemen's poles; hard to find a branch that I could reach to sling the bag over. When I did, eventually, it came at the cost of scraping my elbow while scrambling a trunk. *All this for bears who never even show up.*

For two hours I read *Big Sur* and watched the sun dip behind the hills. Another night in paradise. Coyotes howled somewhere in the distance, but I had no fear of them any more – many nights on the trip I had drifted into slumber to the tune of their mournful wail.

At 4 a.m. I woke with a start to hear a large branch break outside the tent. Another followed it, and a third. Too much of a definite 'snapping' sound to be wind. Perhaps deer? I vaguely recalled reading something about them around here. I also remembered reading about mountain lions, but this sounded too heavy-footed for that. I calmly thought through the options, until a snort inches from my head sent my bowels into panic mode and I had to stifle a shout.

'Jaysus!' I whispered.

The footsteps circled again. This was either a large bobcat doing a very good impression of a bear, or…

But why? Why would a bear come here? My food was at least three hundred yards away, safely stored high up a tree. It was then, with all the clarity of a new dawn, that a realisation descended upon me. With it came the chill of fear that we know only when we have done something terribly, terribly wrong. I groped in the dark for my riding shorts and felt silently at the pockets. As expected, half a Snickers bar lay melting in its wrapper. It had been a gift from a friendly elderly couple in San Luis Obispo. It had seemed prudent to save half for later. Now that decision seemed downright life-threatening.

The bear, probably a black bear, did another lap of my tent. On his third pass he came a little too close and tripped on the guy rope. The tent shook, my bowels took another hammering, and I heard him (or her) snort. *Now it's angry as well as hungry.* I let out a small and involuntary whimper and tried desperately not to soil myself.

What a stupid reason to get eaten, as I now surely would be. Getting mauled for not finishing a chocolate bar would not factor on my chosen list of ways to go. If ever I had harboured dreams of being heroic and mighty, like the adventurers of the Golden Ages, those were now to be dashed. What would Wilfred Thesiger have to say about this?

Disbelief turned to real fear. I had to act or I was pretty sure I knew how this would end. If I did something, then maybe I stood a chance. I've always believed inaction to be at the root of continued misfortune. My options, however, were limited. I could make a break for it. I could fight the bear. I could create a diversion. Option three seemed mildly preferable to the other two, and I closed my eyes in the darkness willing an idea to come to me.

There is always a decision to be made, even in the most uncomfortable of circumstances. I chose to take matters into my own hand. Thus far my journey had been characterised by fear – fear of everything, everyone, even of myself. Fear of bears and buffalo and muggers and murderers. Fear of the very things that brought me out here in the first place – of the open road, independence and responsibility. Slowly my experiences had taught me that I was capable of more. If I was striving to be all that I could be, I was surely on the right track. Now a real threat was upon me, and a new challenge.

Summoning all my courage, and an additional amount from the ether that I had no right to claim, I zipped open the inner compartment of my tent. Then the outer. I jumped out into the blinding blackness of a moonless mountain night and ran twenty yards to the treeline. Wearing nothing but my underpants, stumbling and cursing as I trod on sharp pine needles and undergrowth, I must have looked quite a sight. I turned and bellowed back, 'Hey, Bear!', then threw the offending chocolate bar, until now grasped in my sweaty palm, deep into the woods behind. And then, after a momentary pause, I ran back.

I zipped up the outer flysheet, then the inner compartment. I told myself it was my inner sanctum and in here nothing could harm me. I pulled the sleeping bag over my head, and I waited. Perhaps to be eaten, perhaps for a saviour. Mostly, for a conclusion.

None came. Two minutes passed, my body shaking. Five. Ten. The sleeping bag muffled any sound so I took it off my head. Nothing. Fifteen. Twenty. The bear had gone.

I got out gingerly, and turned on my head torch to make sure I was alone. And then I packed up, retrieved my food from its branch and made an unplanned early start to my day at 4.30 a.m., pedalling as wildly as if a horde of hungry black bears was rampaging behind my back wheel baying for blood and chocolate.

CHAPTER 52

THE END OF THE BEGINNING

The Bear in the Night, as it came to be known in the many retellings of the story, was a timely reminder of just how little I knew about this world of wilderness survival and how easy my journey thus far had been. There was an argument that said I could have avoided gunmen and broken bridges and Bears in the Night altogether, but I preferred the one which said I was fortunate to have encountered all three and come away safely.

Santa Barbara came and went, my mind still lingering on the bear. In Malibu I saw the movie star Adam Sandler pushing his kids around a parking lot in a shopping trolley. He didn't notice me. Multimillion-dollar houses clung to the cliffs above, no doubt one of them his, and everything hinted at the megacity to come. Before long it was upon me, Los Angeles's imminent appearance marked by the herald of smog claiming the sky.

LA, the second most populous city in the USA, sprawls for nearly a hundred miles along the southern coastline, with the iconic districts of Santa Monica, Venice Beach and Long Beach nestled on the shore. It began to rain as I approached from the north and didn't stop until I was well beyond its southern limits. Those famed beaches were empty and I was left with a soulless, traffic-ridden bicyclist's nightmare to negotiate. I pedalled frantically, alone in a city of millions.

Two days took me through the wealthy middle-class suburban communities of Newport Beach, Oceanside, and Encinitas. Everyone I saw looked healthy and tanned, and as I cycled past they beamed at me with their gleamingly white smiles and pressed polo shirts. The appeal to live here was obvious – fine weather all year round, the beach on your doorstep and a nice, hard-working set of neighbours to watch your back and come over for barbeques. Yet I could imagine better living in Missoula at the foot of the Rockies, or even Salinas with the rugged coast and Sierra Nevadas at my beck and call. Coastal 'SoCal' was comfortable and perfect in a conventional sense, but held little appeal for me.

I was slightly disappointed to skip through LA so quickly. Bemoaning my bad luck I wondered, if I'd arrived on a different day, who I might have met, and what weird and wonderful sights I might have seen on Muscle Beach? I knew by now, though, that these variables were, more than almost anything else, the key aspects that defined my journey in time and space. I could've chosen a thousand different routes across the country, and had as many separate experiences. No single traverse could ever capture the essence of a country, and certainly not my traverse. On my first day I'd sat beside a homeless man near the George Washington Bridge and listened to him tell me: 'You can cross this here country 'hundred times, and see it different every time,' he had started. 'Just take my advice: don't get yourself caught up with guns, girls or government. That's the unholy trinity. Avoid them, you'll do just fine.'

He was right, on all counts. On the coast too, then, I was destined to only ever see a slice of life. Passing through a certain town in morning is very different to seeing that same place by evening, or on market day. Five minutes before or after my passing another traveller may have found a different world. The real beauty of travel lies within this fact that it is an ever-changing, wild and erratic beast, forever impossible to predict.

Through this cross-section of life that I saw, I had come to know America infinitely better than I had when I left New York. A country, we learn, is defined in global and economic terms by history, government and culture. But on the ground level it is characterised by people. I had found, despite huge diversity, that the Americans I met across the country were connected (with just a couple of dramatic exceptions) by an innate sense of hospitality and curiosity. Within this beautiful and varied country there is a pleasant openness, both in the land and peoples. For somewhere with so much space, the inhabitants certainly know how to make a stranger feel at ease.

* * *

San Diego grew as LA did, in a haze of smog and buildings that gradually obscured the natural landscape. Soon I was downtown, amongst the trams, leaning on railings by the harbour. The southern boundary of the United States of America was just a couple of miles further along. A few hundred more pedal strokes after a journey of millions. My odometer read just over six thousand miles travelled; six thousand separate and unique stretches of road that connected a country and a people.

A man in a smart suit with a smile to win an election and a chin that could've cut diamonds came striding over.

'Where have you ridden from?' he asked.

'New York,' I answered, aware that now sounded quite far away.

'Good for you, sir!' He clapped me on the shoulder. 'Listen, that's just one hell of an achievement. You should be extremely proud. I can't imagine the fortitude it takes to do that.' He shook my hand firmly. 'So where next, or is this the end?'

'I don't know, really, but I think I'll keep going.' A vague statement delivered with conviction.

'Keep going long enough, and you'll make it home, I guess!' He flashed me that winning smile once more. 'Well, good luck. I wish I could do what you've done. You take it easy out there.'

Sometime and somehow I would make it home. When I did it would be wonderful, I was confident of that now – but that time was not yet. I would keep riding out the recession; keep living the life I had come to love. I would pedal until my money ran out, and only then would I re-evaluate. This was the time to live life in the moment.

The ribbon of tarmac stretching out before me held myriad possibilities. I pedalled onwards to the international border, the point at which the USA ceases to be and Mexico takes over. I knew now, though, that this wasn't the end, only the end of the beginning.

EPILOGUE

The end of all our exploring,
Will be to arrive where we started
And know the place for the first time.
T. S. Eliot

After a little while in Mexico I rode back north to LA on a whim, and eventually made my way to New Zealand. Passage came courtesy of a free air ticket that was bestowed upon me by a large Kiwi corporation after I sent them an email telling them I would like to visit their country and ride my bicycle and keep a blog about my travels.

After a month on each of the North and South islands of New Zealand, I flew to Australia and pedalled along the East Coast. Subsequently I went to Thailand and rode from there through Cambodia, Laos, Vietnam and China, eventually finishing my journey of just over fourteen thousand miles by the harbour front in Hong Kong.

Perhaps some day I will write a book of those cycling days, for there are certainly good stories to be told – both of the pleasant (being taken under the wing of the New Zealand Tourism Board, swimming amongst the limestone karsts at

Ha Long Bay) and the unpleasant variety (malaria, tarantulas down my trousers).

To some readers, these latter destinations may seem more exotic or challenging than America. For me they were the easy part. My ride across America was a rite of passage; a journey of discovery in every sense. By the time I reached San Diego, many insecurities and uncertainties I had had were either gone or I had learned how to manage them. I had seen America in a way that relatively few people do. Successfully reaching the Mexican border bred confidence in myself and, even more crucially, confidence in the world around me.

***

Since returning from Hong Kong after my fourteen months of cycling, I have continued to seek out new adventures. In 2011–2012 I walked three thousand miles across Mongolia and China, from the Gobi Desert to the South China Sea, filming the experience for a National Geographic TV show. At the end of 2012 I trudged a thousand miles through the Empty Quarter desert in Oman and the United Arab Emirates, following in the footsteps of the great British explorer Wilfred Thesiger and making a film about the journey. In 2013 I rode a folding bicycle around the British Isles and climbed the highest peak in each of our six major regions, and most recently I followed the Karun, the longest river in Iran, from source to sea by a variety of human-powered methods.

I am now based in the UK and am fortunate that, through filming my expeditions, writing articles and giving talks, I can make a living from these journeys. I try and balance this unpredictable but hugely rewarding career with another novel adventure – being married.

On New Year's Day 2013 I proposed and in August of the same year Clare and I got married. She was waiting for me when I returned from my cycling days, just as she was when I came home sore and nauseous after my Chinese journey, or sunburned and exhausted from the Middle East. Clare has carved out a successful career for herself as a teacher and is not afraid to lead her own independent life, as I have led mine. Our paths alone were enjoyable but we have learned from time apart that they are infinitely better when entwined. I hope that someday soon we will take to wandering the world together.

I would not necessarily recommend for couples to spend fourteen months apart, nor for one of the pair to choose a career that requires months away in remote parts of the world. Clare and I struggle with the time apart and the distance it puts between us in every sense, but subsequently the time we have together is so much more precious because we know what it is like to be denied it. I am the person I am, for better or worse, because of the decisions I made and make and the things I do. My time on bicycle or foot is at the core of that.

**

I have written this book largely for selfish reasons. There is much catharsis and evaluation to be found in the process. As someone who enjoys a healthy dose of self-analysis, this appealed. I also wrote the book, however, because I believe strongly in the need for us to engage with our passions in life; to do what we love as often as we can, and to acknowledge that need. Not everyone will dream of setting off into the unknown on a bicycle as I did, but taking a step into the unknown in a different way, one that fans the flame of your own personal passion – that is a leap worth making.

I've come to believe that all of us crave challenge and unpredictability and adventure to a greater or lesser degree, but we are also wired to feel a natural fear of these things because they can represent great change and instability. Fear should never be a barrier to us doing things that we otherwise yearn to do. The greatest decision I ever made was to cycle across America, and the bravest thing I ever did was to keep going through the first week when it all seemed difficult and scary and miserable. Only by facing the fear can we conquer it.

If I were to distil what I learned from cycling across America it would come out something like this: embrace fear, embrace change, grasp opportunity. Commit, go… and don't stop.

CYCLE TOURING:
A HOW-TO OF BICYCLE TRAVEL

In my opinion, cycle touring is one of the simplest and most effective ways to travel. As long as you have a bicycle and a desire to go slow, you'll be fine. Ask almost anyone who has been on a bike adventure and they will inevitably tell you that it was so much easier than they had thought before leaving. Get a bike (new, old, scrapyard-rebuild, it doesn't matter) and some sort of receptacle to carry your gear in. Pack a peanut butter and jam sandwich (optional) and off you go!

If this sounds all too simplistic to be true, then that's the point I am trying to make, I suppose. It could barely be simpler. However, I know from experience that many people desire more information and reassurance before committing to riding off into the sunset – I certainly did. Below I've briefly highlighted some of the major issues and discussions in cycle touring, in the hope that you may find them of use.

Supported vs Self-supported vs Credit Card Touring
Cycling terminology can be confusing for the uninformed. I'm not a big fan of these labels, but they get used a lot so it's worth unpacking them.

Do you want someone else to carry all of your kit and plan your route, or do you want to do it yourself? The latter is *self-supported* (occasionally also called *unsupported*) and gives you the freedom to go wherever you want, whenever and however. This is what I did. This generally means you're responsible for everything from route planning and daily budgeting to finding campsites and bike repairs. The world lies beyond your front wheel – choose a direction, crank the pedals and set forth.

If that sounds like too much work (it's not!) then perhaps consider a *supported* tour. Many organisers exist to ensure that all you'll need to do is keep spinning and have fun. Each day you will receive a map with directions, distance and elevations. A SAG (support and gear) vehicle will transport your belongings, fix your bike and keep you well fed and hydrated.

If it's freedom you're after but without the commitment to self-sufficiency, then pack a few essentials into a seat pack (raincoat, puncture repair kit, camera) and plan a route that will take you from one hotel to the next. This is commonly called *credit card touring*. You'll speed along unburdened by gear, and any problems that occur can be solved by the piece of plastic in your wallet.

All three methods have their place, but I have only ever experienced being self-supported. It is not very difficult, and provides the most reward, and therefore the majority of my advice below will assume that you are self-supported.

How far should I ride each day, and for how long?
Ride as far as you want for as long as you can. Begin with forty miles a day (no problem for anyone who cycles regularly) and

gradually increase to seventy or eighty. Judge your own fitness honestly, and work from there. A century is a good target to hit at least once – you'll be amazed at how feasible it is. Most supported tours will range from twenty to a hundred miles per day.

At the extreme end of the scale, there have recently been a number of attempts to break the world record for fastest global circumnavigation by bicycle. These cyclists ride minimalist, lightweight set-ups, and are often able to sustain anything up to two hundred miles a day for months on end.

What bike should I bring?

There are three basic options – mountain, touring or road bike.

Mountain bikes are normally the cheapest of the three, and my personal choice. They balance a rugged build with an affordable price tag, and you can switch the wide, knobbly MTB tyres (designed for off-road) to skinnier road tyres if you desire a little less rolling resistance on tarmac.

Touring bikes are glorified mountain bikes, modified slightly to facilitate long-distance travel (longer wheelbase, flexible materials, multiple mounting points for racks, etc.). You certainly can't go wrong with one of these, but I would hesitate to recommend them to everyone, as the price tag can be off-putting. For the most part, a mountain bike will do the same job.

Road bikes are lighter, sleeker, faster. They are also much less robust, and unable to carry as much equipment easily. Take one of these if you want to travel fast, light and almost entirely on good-quality road surfaces. If you're even considering heading onto gravel or trails, stay clear of road bikes.

How should I carry my gear?

The two standard options are: to use pannier bags (saddlebags) that clip on to either side of the back and front wheel; or to pull everything behind your bike in a trailer.

Panniers are generally a less expensive and more readily available option, but can leave your bike feeling heavier and cumbersome. Trailers take some getting used to, but allow more control on the bike (as the frame is almost completely unloaded). Just don't do what I did, which was to take both – that should never be considered!

For panniers, choose Ortlieb or Arkel. If you can't afford them, then buy some cheap versions on eBay and line them with bin bags for waterproofing. Decide if you need four bags (two on each wheel) or just the rear bags. For trailers, the single-wheeled BOB and double-wheeled Wandertec Bongo come highly recommended. A handlebar bag (to hold things you want to be able to grab quickly and regularly during the day) is a nice addition to whatever method you choose.

What should I pack?

You can probably guess what I'm going to say here – you don't *need* very much at all! I learned that the hard way. Below is a basic template for a very comfortable cycling kit. At the risk of repeating myself, none of the specifics here are really important, and you certainly shouldn't feel the need to follow them directly. It makes sense to buy the best kit you can afford, but don't be put off if you have to gather everything together from eBay for a few quid. If you're trying to decide between buying a fancy £100 raincoat or a budget jacket online for £10, then make sure you think about how many days on the road that extra £90 could help facilitate…

- Clothes – two sets is usually fine for most trips (one for on the bike, one for off)
- Waterproofs
- Helmet
- Sunglasses
- Tent (or bivvy bag if not travelling in extreme cold)
- Sleeping bag
- Sleeping mat
- Camping stove and utensils. Don't forget a spoon!
- Head torch
- Bike tool and repair kit
- Bike lights
- Basic medical kit
- Toothbrush
- Camera, journal, phone, passport and documents
- Books (this is optional, but adventures are better with some Steinbeck)
- Hip flask of whiskey (this is not optional)

What bike tools do I need?

Not many, and you definitely don't need to be an expert. I carried two spare inner tubes, a puncture repair kit, tyre levers and a Leatherman multi-tool. Zip-ties, gaffer tape and WD-40 are very useful indeed – I have yet to find an emergency that can't be fixed by one of these! Every so often you will need to replace brake pads and brake cables and readjust your derailleur.

Learn as much as you can about how your bike works if you have the time (try a few repairs at home, book yourself on a course if you're really keen), but don't stress too much about this aspect – you will inevitably learn as you go. Remember this: when your bike breaks, either you will fix it or someone else will. Either way, it will all be fine.

What should I wear?

To Lycra, or not to Lycra? I started out just wearing ordinary clothes (cotton T-shirt and surf shorts), which was fine. Cycling-specific clothes are designed to make you more comfortable when riding but, if you're like me, you may feel uncomfortable in skintight gear when you are not on the bike. Touring is much more about the places you see and the people you meet than it is about cycling (as far as I'm concerned anyway). Therefore, there's a balance to be trod between comfort and practicality.

My personal preference is for Lycra cycling shorts with a padded chamois, with regular surfboard shorts over the top. A lightweight synthetic T-shirt or cotton collared shirt is ideal for riding.

Bring additional clothes as appropriate for the climate you are going to be in. Merino wool is a great base layer, and down jackets are superb for warming you up quickly (and taking up almost zero space and weight in your bags). Being too cold is *very* miserable on a bicycle.

Should I bring a friend?

Travelling alone and travelling with company are very different experiences. I know many friends and couples that have set off on long journeys together only to discover they find each other very annoying. Equally, companionship is a wonderful thing on the road, and can make memorable experiences all the more special. It's also very comforting to have another person there when times are tough.

I think solo travel offers the greatest rewards in terms of personal development. As you will have noticed from my story, however, I often sought out company for sections of the journey. Choose wisely!

Where should I go?

Wherever you want! Hopefully no one is really asking this question. Much of the world is accessible by bicycle (much more so than by bus or car). You can be certain that wherever you want to travel to, an intrepid cyclist will have been there already. Check online for information on your desired country/ region – www.crazyguyonabike.com is a good resource for mad trips – and see if it sounds feasible for your level of adventurousness. My only other advice here would be: don't be put off by naysayers. Of course, avoid war zones and very sensitive areas, and be careful, but don't let the fears of others put you off unnecessarily.

Take into consideration visas and inoculations that you may need. Research online, ask in online forums (The Thorn Tree on the Lonely Planet website is great – www.lonelyplanet.com/thorntree) or use an agent such as The Visa Machine for trickier entries to countries (www.thevisamachine.com).

Many cyclists I know have started with shorter, more localised journeys, or long-distance cycling within their own country, before they set off into deserts, across continents or around the world. John O'Groats to Land's End is a perennially popular UK route.

ADDITIONAL RESOURCES

Adventure Cycle-Touring Handbook, by Stephen Lord

Tom Allen's website is full of gems, especially regarding travelling on a budget (*www.tomsbiketrip.com*)

Alastair Humphreys is a modern-day cycling legend (*www. alastairhumphreys.com*)

Rob Lilwall's book *Cycling Home From Siberia* is a great example of the rewards that bicycle travel can bring (*www. roblilwall.com*)

'Explore' is an annual expedition-planning event held at the Royal Geographical Society (*www.rgs.org/explore*)

Adventure Cycling Association is a US-based non-profit organisation dedicated to two-wheeled adventures (*www. adventurecycling.org*)

Sustrans is the sustainable transport network in the UK, with some superb routes and resources throughout the country (*www.sustrans.org.uk*)

Cycling adventure travel writing: there is a huge amount of books written about cycling trips. Some are great, many aren't. Nevertheless, almost all share the message that cycling is a great way to travel and see the world. As well as my recommendations above, check out Dervla Murphy and Nicholas Crane for the cream of the crop.

Finally, do feel free to contact me via my website – www.leonmccarron.com – if you have any other questions or queries, or would just like an additional bit of encouragement to convince you that bicycle touring is the future. I am always happy to help.

MY KIT LIST

Camping:
The North Face Cat's Meow sleeping bag
Marmot Limelight two-person tent
Thermarest Prolite Plus sleeping mat
Leatherman multi-tool
Head lamp
Compass

Clothing:
Untouched World cycling jersey
Untouched World bib shorts
Assorted Buff headwear
1 pair surf shorts
1 cotton T-shirt
(Fake) North Face Summit Series jacket and fleece
1 pair trousers
1 pair waterproof trousers
1 flannel shirt
Sunglasses

Bicycle:
Santos Travelmaster 2.6 aluminium bicycle
2 Schwalbe Marathon XR tyres
Tubus front and rear racks
Pedalite lights
Green Oil chain lube
Ortlieb Back Roller Classic panniers
Ortlieb Front Roller Classic panniers
Wandertec Bongo trailer
Topeak handlebar bag
Cateye Enduro cycle computer
Spare cables and inner tubes

Other:
Sony HVR-A1E HDV camcorder
Kata R-104 camera rucksack
Kata CRC-13 rain cover
iPod Touch and headphones
Books
Local maps
Journal
Cellphone
Hip flask
Medical kit

ACKNOWLEDGEMENTS

There are many people that I would like to thank in regard to both the journey across America and this resulting book. In the interests of (at least relative) brevity, however, I will not be able to mention everyone. So my first 'thank you' is to all the people that I have left out of these acknowledgements: please be assured that I am extremely grateful for all of your assistance, help and support – whatever it might have been. A special thank you to everyone who brightened my days on the road – the countless gifts of conversation, food, drink and places to stay were an enormous help, and made this trip such a special and memorable experience.

The journey:
Firstly, to Mum – your support never wavered even when you were all but convinced that I was going to die! Thank you for encouraging my adventures, past, present and future, and always trusting in my choices and decisions in life.

To the rest of my family who've put up with this for the longest – Grandma, Diana, Chris, Paul, Oisin, Dad, Alison, Calum, Hannah, Lys and Jimmy. To Mark, Anne, Katie, Becca and Jessica. To the Heaneys, Wynesses and Symonses (plus Hardings, Fidlers and Croslands!).

To everyone who came to see me off from England, especially Declan, Tom, Will, Gazz, Chazz and Davey Crooks. The folks at the Gulbenkian, and to Pip, for giving me a place to live while I sorted out my life! Sheila, for your advice and kind gifts.

To Michael at Santos for all your advice and for the discount on the bike, and to Alasdair and Shelagh at MSG for the thorough bike-fitting. Thanks also to Bike Shop Hub, Mountain Man Outdoors, Kata, Buff and the Adventure Cycling Association for your help.

Everyone in New York, especially those at DCTV and Arts Engine – I will never love a city more than NYC, that's for sure. Rob and Christine Lilwall, for the advice and seemingly harmless coffee meeting that sunny morning in Barnes and Noble – look where that got us! Michael Apichella and Lizzie Hoeppner for the encouragement. Blake, for the whiskey times.

The DeMaggio family, Heather Piper, Jack and Milly, the Hart family, the Armstrong family, the Waterman family, Leslie and Joe Buckalew, Ross and Yvonne Jannesen, Dustin Tatroe – many folk took me in on this journey, but you all went even further above and beyond, and I am deeply grateful.

Susie, Matt, Alex, Bryan and Sean – you were all responsible for keeping me encouraged and inspired on the road. The greatest debt of all during the ride is to you, and I am delighted that we are still in touch. Matt – I look forward to our future adventures with the YP! (www.theyp.org)

There is a more substantial, yet still by no means comprehensive, list of friends from the journey at www. leonmccarron.com/thanks

The book:
Thanks to all of those people who took time to read through early, muddled drafts – Will van Wyngaarden, Tom Floyd, Lizzie and Zach Hoeppner, Declan Wiffen, Rupert Clague and Dave Cornthwaite. To Lily Barlow, Matt Friedlund and Mike Gallagher for useful corrections and guidance. To Alastair Humphreys and Rob Lilwall for your honest and insightful feedback, as well as for all the other book-writing knowledge that I have plundered over the last few years from your combined wealth of experience.

Diana, for, as well as being my aunt, your wonderful illustrations that bring the book to life so well.

To Jennifer Barclay for first showing an interest in my writing. To Debbie Chapman, my fantastic editor – it has been such a pleasure working with you! And, of course, to all at Summersdale for showing faith in this book.

Finally, the biggest thanks of all, through the journey, the book and life, must go to Clare – thank you for understanding everything, for being patient and for agreeing to share adventures together for many years to come.

ABOUT THE AUTHOR

Leon is a highly-regarded public speaker. He has lectured throughout the UK and further afield in schools, universities and societies, and at motivational corporate events and after-dinner speeches.

The hub for all of Leon's adventures, filmmaking and writing is his website, www.leonmccarron.com

You can also:

'Like' his page on Facebook at
www.facebook.com/leonmccarron
Tweet him @leonmccarron
(www.twitter.com/leonmccarron)
Follow his Instagram pictures at
www.instagram.com/leonmccarron

For more information, references and contact details, please visit www.leonmccarron.com/speaking